WildFly 8 Administration guide

Francesco Marchioni

WildFly 8 Administration guide

ISBN 978-88-940389-3-4

Foreword

WildFly 8 is the latest version of the popular open source JBoss application server. It is exceptionally lightweight, featuring unparalleled speed and supporting the latest standards, including Java EE 7. I'm Brian Stansberry, the technical lead for WildFly's Operations, Administration and Management (OA&M) functionality, a role I've been in since the start of the JBoss AS 7 project. So as you can imagine this book's topic is near and dear to my heart. One of the biggest priorities of AS 7, WildFly and JBoss Enterprise Application Platform 6 has been to improve the application server's manageability, and after a lot of dedication, sleepless nights and coffee I feel we've come a long way. I hope after reading this book you'll agree. The biggest improvement in WildFly 8 over AS 7 besides the new Java EE 7 API compatibility is in the OA&M area with the addition of fine-grained role based administrative access control, a feature that is a focus of the Security chapter of this book.

I first heard about the author when he authored "*JBoss AS 5 Development*" in 2010 and was a *JBoss Community Recognition Award* Winner for his application server documentation. For many years now he has been an active and important part of the JBoss Application Server and WildFly community, consistently producing high quality documentation covering the application server and middleware in general.

I was very pleased to hear that Francesco was planning to write a book on WildFly 8. High quality books like this one are critical to the success of open source software, and Francesco has the expertise to cover the topic well and a great reputation for doing an excellent job.

I hope you'll find this WildFly 8 Administration Guide as thorough and well written as I did. WildFly's web console and its command line interface (CLI) administration tool are well covered, as are all of the key areas of application server administration. This book definitely belongs on the bookshelf of anyone administering WildFly 8 or developing application for it.

Brian Stansberry

Preface

WildFly 8 is the continuation of the release cycle of the application server community edition, which was previously known as JBoss AS 7. The last official release of JBoss AS 7 was the 7.1.1.Final, although a more recent 7.2 version is available as source to be built on Github (https://github.com/jbossas/jboss-as/archive/7.2.0.Final.tar.gz) source code repository

You might wonder why the application server changed its popular name. Actually, there's more than one reason for this change, the first one being to avoid confusion between the commonly referred community version (JBoss AS) and the Enterprise version supported by Redhat. Besides this, in the last years lots of new projects grew up in the *JBoss.org* site which included the "JBoss" brand in it (e.g. JBoss ESB). For this reason, the term "JBoss" was often misused sometimes to mean the application server sometimes else to mean a brand of products.

The rename applies, however, only for the JBoss Application Server community edition. The licensed version is still named JBoss Enterprise Application Platform (JBoss EAP). So from now on, when someone refers to WildFly, we clearly know they are talking about the Community project and specifically the application server project.

Besides the new brand name, the WildFly application server follows the same path traced by JBoss AS 7: this means a truly modular and lightweight kernel with advanced management capabilities. In addition to this, the new application version supports the latest changes in terms of Java EE technology, offering richer management capabilities, a more advanced security control and some important updates as well in the Web server tier.

The Author of the Book

Francesco Marchioni is a freelance consultant and trainer for RedHat middleware products. He has joined the JBoss community in early 2000 when the application server was a mere EJB container, running release 2.x.

He has worked on all the earlier versions of the JBoss application server envisioning many successful software migrations and integrations from vendor platforms to open source products and vice versa. 5 years ago he has started an IT portal focused on JBoss products (http://www.mastertheboss.com) which is pleased to serve an average of 8000 daily visits.

He has authored the following titles:

- JBoss AS 5 Development, Packt Publishing (December 2009)
- JBoss AS 5 Performance Tuning, Packt Publishing (December 2010)
- JBoss AS 7 Configuration, Deployment, and Administration, Packt Publishing (December 2011)
- Infinispan Data Grid Platform, Packt Publishing (June 2012) co-authored with Manik Surtani (Infinispan Project lead)
- JBoss AS 7 Development, Packt Publishing (June 2013)
- Enterprise Application Server CookBook, ItBuzzPress (September 2013)

The reviewers

Jaikiran Pai works at Red Hat and is part of the JBoss AS and EJB3 development team. In his role as a software developer, Jaikiran has been mainly involved in Java language and Java EE technologies. Since 2004 he started working in a software company in Pune, India where he developed an interest in JBoss Application Server and has been active in the JBoss community ever since. Subsequently, he joined Red Hat to be part of the JBoss EJB3 team. Jaikiran is one of the co-authors of JBoss AS Getting Started DZone RefCard http://refcardz.dzone.com/refcardz/getting-started-jboss. When he's not doing anything JBoss related, you'll find him at his other favorite and friendly place - JavaRanch (http://www.javaranch.com), where he has been a moderator since 2007.

Mylos Kathos is a senior developer for a French based company leading the development of Utility Smart Metering Systems for the global market.

He has been involved in Enterprise Java technologies since he was introduced to Java in 2003, using tools and technologies encompassing both the standard Java EE stack and non-standard ones such as Hibernate and Spring.

What this book covers

Chapter 1, Installing WildFly covers the installation of the server platform and introduces the reader to the most significant changes brought by release 8 of the application server components

Chapter 2, Basic server configuration discusses the core configuration of the application server both in standalone mode and in domain mode, including detailed steps to setup a suggested domain configuration topology.

Chapter 3, Deploying applications covers in detail all available options to deploy Java Enterprise applications on the application server.

Chapter 4, Database connectivity, is about configuring connections to relational databases by installing JDBC Drivers and Datasources.

Chapter 5, EJB and Web server configuration discusses about the two core subsystems used as container for your applications: the new fast and furious Web server implementation named Undertow and the EJB container which is now compliant with EJB 3.2 specifications.

Chapter 6, Configuring Logging covers the configuration of log subsystem, including all available log handlers, and best practices to log to your own requirements

Chapter 7, JMS Configuration is about the nuts and bolts of WildFly's JMS provider which continues to be HornetQ messaging system, now including new clustering options.

Chapter 8, Application Server classloading is a deep dive into the application server's modular kernel and how to configure it to load libraries needed by your applications.

Chapter 9, Clustering covers the application server clustering capabilities that serve as an essential component to provide scalability and high availability to your applications.

Chapter 10, Load Balancing Web Applications discusses the other key concern of clustering, that is the ability to make several servers participate in the same service and do the same work.

Chapter 11, Server Management with the CLI discusses in depth about the Command Line Interface which is the recommended management tool.

Chapter 12, Securing WildFly covers the foundation of the application server Security framework with special focus on the new Role Based Access Control.

Who this book is for

This book is especially suited for Java system administrators that are going to manage the new release of the application server. Developers, and application testers will be as well more productive after learning this book. Prior knowledge of the earlier version of the application server is not required, although that could make easier to understand some core concepts contained in this book.

How to Contact Us

Please address comments and questions concerning this book to the publisher: info@itbuzzpress.com . We have created a web page for this book, where we list errata, examples, and any other information. You can access this page at:

http://www.itbuzzpress.com/news/wildflyadmin-errata.html

For more information about our books, and future projects see our website at:

http://www.itbuzzpress.com

Piracy

The uploading/downloading of copyrighted material without the express written consent of the content copyright holder is strictly forbidden. Piracy is an illegal act that you may aspire to reconsider. Besides this, piracy is not a victimless crime! It is financially damaging and personally hurtful to company employees and their families. Legitimate users suffer as well. We appreciate your help in protecting the valuable content of this book.

This book is dedicated is lovingly dedicated to all people that helped me to find my verse in the powerful play that's life.

Table of Contents

Chapter 1: Installation

In this chapter, we will move our first steps with the new release of the application server by learning the following topics:

- A brief introduction to the changes and enhancements introduced in WildFly 8
- How to install and verify the installation of the application server
- How to create a management user which will be in charge to handle server administration
- Installing the application server as a service using Windows or Linux environment

What is new in WildFly 8?

The new release of the application server contains several enhancements over the AS7/EAP6 baseline both in terms of Administration and in terms of development API. Let's see a drill down of the changes you are going to experience:

Java SE 7 baseline

The first upgrade we will mention is the new Java SE baseline: actually, the new release of the application server has been built using a Java SE 7 and thus requires that you have a matching Java 7 or higher installation on your machine.

> WildFly 8 runs just fine also with **Java SE 8** but you have to replace the deprecated JVM parameter named **-XX:MaxPermSize** with the new **-XX:MaxMetaspaceSize**. See section *"Application server JVM settings and bootstrap configuration"* to learn more about it.

Administration changes

The new application server greatly improves the administration areas by providing the following features:

- **Fine Grained Administration Control**: before WildFly 8, administrative users were not associated with a particular role, in other words, once created a Management user then you are entitled to perform any change to the server configuration like a classic super user. Now you can associate each Management user with one role and even configure constraints, which allow you to tweak the behavior of roles.
- **New Web Server**: WildFly 8 has switched to a different Web Server implementation named **Undertow**, which is an embeddable Web server providing both blocking and non-blocking

API based on NIO. Besides the API enhancements, the Undertow Web server can provide better flexibility thanks to its composition based architecture that allows you to build a Web server by combining small single purpose handlers. More details about the Undertow Web server are contained in chapter 5 of this book.

- **Richer Management Interfaces**: WildFly 8 can use a richer set of management commands, which have been added to the Command Line Interface such as the ability to **patch** the module baseline, thus avoiding costly server installations in order to solve some issues. Also the Web Administration Console has been greatly improved allowing a complete management of the application server subsystem along with a comprehensive set of performance indicators.
- **Simplified socket management**: The new release of the application server uses a reduced number of ports, multiplexing invocations over the HTTP channel; therefore, administrators and your security staff will spend less time in setting up firewall policies.

Besides this, take in consideration that in the Final release of WildFly 8 the new public API classes will have the **org.wildfly** package whereas existing ones will continue to have what they had (like **org.jboss.***).

New Java EE 7 API

The last area of improvement is in the Java Enterprise API, which now fully supports Java EE 7. Some of the major enhancements included in the application server include:

- **WebSocket 1.0**: Before the advent of HTML 5, the traditional request-response model used in HTTP meant that the client requested resources and the server provided responses. Therefore, unless you are continuously polling the server, there is no way to way to provide dynamic changes to your Web pages. The WebSocket protocol addresses these limitations by providing a full-duplex communication channel between the client and the server without any latency problem. Combined with other client technologies, such as JavaScript and HTML5, WebSocket enables web applications to deliver a richer user experience.
- **Java API for JSON Processing 1.0 (JSON-P):** This API elevates the capabilities of JSON based applications by defining a new API to parse, generate, transform and query JSON documents. Therefore, you will be able to build a JSON object model (just like you did with DOM for XML based applications) and consume them in a streaming fashion (as you did with XML using StAX).
- **Batch Application API 1.0:** this API has been designed to standardize batch processing for Java applications. You can think of it as a replacement for your older, bulk, long running procedures that were managed by shell scripting or dated languages such as COBOL. The

new Batch API provides a rich programming model oriented to batch scripting which allows defining, partition and forking the execution of jobs.

- **Concurrency Utilities for Java EE 1.0:** this API is an extension to the Java SE Concurrency Utility (JSR-166) which aims to provide a simple and standard API for using Concurrency from Java Enterprise components preserving the container integrity. This API can be used along with asynchronous processing APIs in Servlets or for creating custom executors in advanced use cases.
- Other API enhancements: besides the additions mentioned so far, there are further enhancements in existing areas such the **JAX-RS 2.0**, which now includes a Client API for async processing, a matching Server side asynchronous HTTP response and the addition of Filter and Interceptors for proxying REST communications. Another area of improvement is the **JMS 2.0** API, which now delivers a JMSContext resource as a wrapper for JMS Connection, Session and Message Producer objects, and several enhancements such as the simplified ConnectionFactory injection (which has finally a platform default) or the inclusion of delayed delivery and async send. Other minor improvements are spread across the entire API (e.g. EJB 3.2, Servlet 3.1, EL 3.0, CDI 1.2 etc.). If you want to learn more details about it please consult the official Java EE 7 tutorial at:
http://docs.oracle.com/javaee/7/tutorial/doc/

Installing WildFly 8

The pre-requisite to the Application Server installation is that you have available a JDK 1.7 or higher on your machine. Once installed the JDK, you have to set the JAVA_HOME environment variable accordingly. See the following frame if you don't know how to do it:

Windows users: Right click on the My Computer icon on your desktop and select properties. Then select the Advanced Tab contained in the **Environment Variables** button.

Under System Variable, click New. Enter the variable name as JAVA_HOME and value the Java install path. Click OK and Click Apply Changes.

Linux users: Enter in your *.profile* / *.bash_profile* script the following (substitute with the actual JDK installation path):

```
export JAVA_HOME=/usr/java/jdk1.7.0_45
```

Done with JDK installation, let's move to the application server. WildFly 8 can be downloaded from http://www.wildfly.org by following the Downloads link in the home page which will take you to the following screen:

Version	Date	Description	License	Size	Format
8.2.0.Final	2014-11-20	Java EE7 Full & Web Distribution	LGPL	126 MB	⬇ ZIP
				113 MB	⬇ TGZ
		Update Existing 8.1.0.Final Install	LGPL	62 MB	⬇ ZIP
		Minimalistic Core Distribution	LGPL	15 MB	⬇ ZIP

Once downloaded, extract the archive to a folder and you are done with the installation.

```
unzip wildfly-8.2.0.Final.zip
```

 Linux users should be aware that running WildFly as the root user could lead to security breaches; therefore if you installed the application server in a folder owned by root (e.g. /usr/share), change its ownership so that it can be executed by another user without super-user privileges.

You can optionally set the *JBOSS_HOME* environment variable to the location where WildFly is installed. This will enable starting the application server, which is located on a different path of your file system. For example Linux users:

```
export JBOSS_HOME=/usr/share/wildfly-8.2.0.Final.zip
```

A look into the application server file system

Once unzipped, the application server will create the following file structure on your file system:

As you can see, the WildFly file system is divided into two main parts: the first one, which is pertinent to a **standalone** server mode and the other that is dedicated to **domain** server mode. Common to both server modes is the **modules** directory, which is the heart of the application server.

Following here are some details about the application server folders:

- **appclient**: contains configuration files, deployment content, and writable areas used by the application client container run from this installation.
- **bin**: contains start up scripts, startup configuration files and various command line utilities like vault.sh, add-user.sh. Inside the client subfolder, you can find a client jar for use by non-maven based clients. The other folders (service, init.d) are used respectively to install WildFly as a Service on Windows and Linux machines.
- **docs/schema:** contains the XML schema definition files

- **docs/examples/config:** contains some sample standalone configurations (such as standalone-minimalistic.xml).
- **domain:** contains domain configuration files, server data and writable areas used by the domain mode processes.
- **modules:** contains all the modules installed on the application server.
- **standalone:** contains configuration files, deployment content, and writable areas used by the single standalone server run from this installation.
- **welcome-content:** contains content related to the default (ROOT) web application.

Starting WildFly 8

The application server ships with two server modes: **standalone** and **domain** mode. The difference between the two modes is not about the functionalities available but is related to the management of the application server: in particular, domain is used when you run several instances of WildFly and you want a single point where you can manage servers and their configuration (see chapter 2 for more information about the different server modes).

In order to start WildFly using the default configuration in "standalone" mode, change directory to *$JBOSS_HOME/bin* and issue:

```
./standalone.sh
```

To start the application server using the default configuration in "domain" mode, change directory to *$JBOSS_HOME /bin*.

```
./domain.sh
```

In the server console, you should find something like this, at the end of startup process:

```
09:29:40,852 INFO  [org.jboss.as] (Controller Boot Thread) JBAS015961: Http mana
gement interface listening on http://127.0.0.1:9990/management
09:29:40,852 INFO  [org.jboss.as] (Controller Boot Thread) JBAS015951: Admin con
sole listening on http://127.0.0.1:9990
09:29:40,852 INFO  [org.jboss.as] (Controller Boot Thread) JBAS015874: WildFly 8
.2.0.Final "Tweek" started in 3869ms - Started 184 of 234 services (82 services
are lazy, passive or on-demand)
```

You can verify that the server is reachable from the network by simply pointing your browser to the application server's welcome page, which is reachable by default at the following address:
http://localhost:8080

Welcome to WildFly 8

Your WildFly 8 is running.

Documentation | Quickstarts | Administration Console

WildFly Project | User Forum | Report an issue

Application server JVM settings and bootstrap configuration

If you had a quick look in the *bin* folder of your server installation, you should have discovered a large amount of shell scripts, which serve to different purposes. In particular, a couple of them named *standalone.conf* and *domain.conf* (*standalone.conf.bat* and *domain.conf.bat* for Windows users) are executed on server boot in standalone mode and domain mode. These script files can be used for a variety of purposes such as setting **JVM settings** when the server is running in **standalone mode**.

Here is for example how to change the JVM settings on a Windows machine to use the J2SE 8 **MaxMetaspace** parameter:

```
set "JAVA_OPTS=-Xms64M -Xmx512M -XX:MaxMetaspaceSize=256M"
```

Another possible use of this file is setting the application server's home directory, which is done through the **JBOSS_HOME** environment variable. Setting the **JBOSS_HOME** configuration variable is not a mandatory step. By defining it in your bootstrap file (or in your user's profile), you are specifying the folder where WildFly distribution is located. The impact on your administration is that you can use the standalone/domain startup script from a different location than the server distribution. The reverse side of the coin is that this can lead to confusion your server administrator especially if you have this variable buried in one of the many Linux configuration files. For this reason we would rather discourage the usage of this environment variable.

Your first task: create an user to manage WildFly

If you want to manage the application server configuration using its management instruments, you need to create a management user.

In order to create a new user, just execute the ***add-user.sh/add-user.bat***, which is located in the bin folder of the application server's home. Here's a transcript of the creation of a management user:

```
What type of user do you wish to add?
 a) Management User (mgmt-users.properties)
 b) Application User (application-users.properties)
(a): a


Enter the details of the new user to add.
Using realm 'ManagementRealm' as discovered from the existing property files.
Username : wildflyadmin
Password requirements are listed below. To modify these restrictions edit the add-
user.properties configuration file.
. . . .
Password :
Re-enter Password :
What groups do you want this user to belong to? (Please enter a comma separated
list, or leave blank for none)[ ]:
About to add user 'wildflyadmin' for realm 'ManagementRealm'
Is this correct yes/no? yes
Added user 'wildflyadmin' to file
'C:\jboss\wildfly-8.2.0.Final\standalone\configuration\mgmt-users.properties'
. . . .
Is this new user going to be used for one AS process to connect to another AS process?
e.g. for a slave host controller connecting to the master or for a Remoting connection
for server to server EJB calls.
yes/no? yes
To represent the user add the following to the server-identities definition <secret
value="RXJpY3Nzb24xIQ==" />
```

In the above example, we have created a management user named "**wildflyadmin**" which belongs to the **ManagementRealm** and is not part of any group of users (See Chapter 12 which is about Security for more information about it). Also, mind to answer the last question with yes or y to indicate that the user will be used to connect to the domain controller from the host controller. The generated secret value is the Base64-encoded password of the new created user and we will use it when setting up a Domain of application servers.

> Since WildFly 8 there is a stricter control over your passwords. If you want to loosen or strengthen the password checks, you can edit the *add-user.properties* file, which is contained in the *bin* folder of your server distribution.

Creating an user in non-interactive mode

You can also create users using non-interactive mode. In the following example, we are adding a **management** (-m flag) user by issuing:

```
add-user.bat -m -u administrator1 -p password1!
```

If you need adding an **application** user, you need to include as well the -a flag as in the following example, where we are setting as well a group to which the user belongs (See the Chapter 12 for more information about User groups):

```
add-user.bat -a -u applicationuser1 -p password1! -g guest
```

Bear in mind that as side effect the user credentials will be visible in the OS process table, if you are using a Linux/Unix machine.

Stopping WildFly

The simplest way to stop the application server is by sending an interrupt signal with Ctrl+C to the server console. Linux/Unix users might as well have a look at the process table with the "ps" command and issue a "kill" to stop the application server.

On the other hand, the recommended approach is to use the **Command Line Interface (CLI)** interface to issue an immediate shutdown command. The CLI interface can be started from the *$JBOSS_HOME/bin* folder of your installation:

```
./jboss-cli.sh
```

Windows user will start the CLI using the equivalent batch file:

```
jboss-cli.bat
```

Once there, issue the **connect** command:

```
[disconnected /] connect
Connected to localhost:9990
```

Now issue the **shutdown** command that will stop the application server:

```
[localhost:9990 /] shutdown
```

You can optionally include the **--restart=true** parameter to trigger a server restart:

```
[standalone@localhost:9990 /] shutdown --restart=true
```

Additionally, we will learn a first CLI trick that is executing a command in *no-interactive mode*. So here is how to shut down the application server with a single command line:

```
jboss-cli.bat -c --command=shutdown
```

 As we said for the add-user script using the non-interactive mode is discouraged for application servers running in production as it could reveal the user credentials in the process table. Consider using it for learning/development purposes.

Stopping WildFly running on a remote host

If you are connecting to a remote WildFly instance, then a password will be requested when you issue the CLI command:

```
[disconnected /] connect 192.168.10.1
Username: wildflyadmin
Password:
Connected to 192.168.10.1:9990
```

Once connected, we will issue the shutdown command just like we did from the local host:

```
[192.168.10.1:9990 /] shutdown
```

Installing WildFly as Service

WildFly can be as well installed as a service and allowed to be started at boot time. In order to do that, you need to use some script files, which are contained within the server. The next two sections (one for Linux users and one for Windows users) discuss about it:

Linux users

In order to start the application server as service using a Linux distribution you can use the scripts which are located under the *JBOSS_HOME/bin/init.d* folder. If you look into this folder, you will find the following files:

- **wildfly-init-redhat.sh** : this file needs to be used for Red Hat Enterprise-like Linux distributions (e.g. RHEL, Centos)
- **wildfly-init-debian.sh**: this file needs to be used for Debian-like Linux distributions (e.g. Debian, Ubuntu)
- **wildfly.conf**: this file contains the configuration used by the above init files

As first step, copy the shell script, which is required by your Linux distribution into the */etc/init.d* folder. For example, if we were to install WildFly as a service on RHEL:

```
[root@dev2 init.d]# cp wildfly-init-redhat.sh /etc/init.d/wildfly
```

Now we will copy as well the *wildfly.conf* configuration file in the location where the startup script expects it:

```
[root@dev2 init.d]# mkdir -p /etc/default
[root@dev2 init.d]# cp wildfly.conf /etc/default
```

Within the *wildfly.conf* file adjust the settings in order to fit your installation:

```
JAVA_HOME=/usr/java/jdk1.7.0_21


# Location of WildFly
JBOSS_HOME=/usr/share/wildfly-8.2.0.Final


# The username who should own the process.
JBOSS_USER=wildfly


# The mode WildFly should start, standalone or domain
JBOSS_MODE=standalone


# Configuration for standalone mode
JBOSS_CONFIG=standalone.xml
```

Next, we will use the **chkconfig** command to install WildFly as a service: the first command will add the wildfly shell script to the chkconfig list:

```
[root@dev2 init.d]# chkconfig --add wildfly
```

The second one, sets the boot levels where the service will be started:

```
[root@dev2 init.d]# chkconfig --level 2345 wildfly  on
```

In order to test that the service starts correctly issue:

```
service wildfly  start
```

And here's the corresponding service stopping:

```
service wildfly  stop
```

Windows users

Installing WildFly 8 as a service on Windows is much simpler than the older AS7/EAP6 counterpart. As a matter of fact it's not necessary to install any third party native library because WildFly 8 already ships with all you need. So move to the *JBOSS_HOME/bin/service* folder.
If you want to install WildFly 8 as a service in standalone mode simple issue:

```
service install
```

Now you can use the Windows Services tab in order to manage the service start/stop
As an alternative you can use the service command to perform basic service management (start/stop/restart). Example:

```
service restart
```

Installing WildFly 8 in domain mode requires that you specify some additional settings such as the Domain controller (default 127.0.0.1 on port 9990) and the host name we are going to start (default "master").

```
service install /controller localhost:9990 /host master
```

The concept of Domain controller deserves some additional explanations; luckily, you don't need to wait so long for it, as next chapter discusses in detail about the server configuration (standalone mode and domain mode).

Chapter 2: Core Server configuration

This chapter provides a detailed description of the application server configuration. Since JBoss AS 7, the application server configuration is centralized in a single XML file with a variable set of services configured in it depending on your server mode. Therefore, in order to grasp the basics of server configuration we will start learning the following topics:

- At first, we will introduce the two available server modes: **standalone** mode and **domain** mode.
- Next, we will have an overview of the server configuration file and its main components.
- Then, our focus will move to the standalone server configuration file
- Finally, we will enter into the details of domain configuration.

The two available server modes

As we have already announced, the application server can be run in two different server modes; if you are arriving from an AS7 background, you will find the two concepts unchanged for you, whilst for older JBoss AS users it's a brand new thing to learn. The difference between the two server modes can be summarized in the following bullets:

- In "**standalone**" mode each application server instance is an independent process (similar to earlier JBoss AS versions; e.g., 4, 5, or 6). The standalone configuration files can be located under the *JBOSS_HOME/standalone/configuration* folder of the application server.
- In "**domain**" mode, you can run multiple application servers and manage them from a central point. A domain can span multiple physical (or virtual) machines. Each machine can host several instances of the application server, which are under the control of a Host Controller process. The configuration files, in domain mode, can be located under the *JBOSS_HOME/domain/configuration* folder.

In the following sections, we will learn how the application server configuration file is structured and how it can be customized. In order to do that, we will be using the following management instruments:

- The **Administration Console**: this is an intuitive Web application, which is part of the WildFly distribution and allows managing the core components of your server configuration, deploying new applications and querying for runtime statistics as well. This management instrument is suited for beginners to intermediate users that want to get quickly into the heart of the application server. If you are arriving from an older JBoss server distribution, this is the core and only Web Administrative channel since the older *jmx-console* is no more part of the application server distribution.

- The **Command Line Interface**: this is a terminal-based instrument that allows a more advanced management of the application server, allowing to access a wider range of options and properties and inspecting as well all the available runtime statistics. In this chapter, we will provide a first taste of its power, while we will go more in deep in Chapter 11, which is fully dedicated to this management interface.

 Actually one more option exist for changing the configuration file, which is manually editing the XML configuration file. This is however discouraged as it can lead to a failure in the server boot if you insert inconsistent data in it. We will resort to this option in just a few exceptional circumstances.

Understanding the server configuration file

All the above-mentioned Management interfaces operate on the application server configuration file. Although the application server ships with several built-in configurations (both for the standalone mode and for the domain mode) only one is used at server startup. Configuration files are based on a tree-like structure that contains, at the root element, the **server** definition and a set of elements, which are displayed in the following picture.

extensions

paths

management

profiles

interfaces

socket-
binding-
group

system-
properties

server

1..*

profile

subsystem

logging

datasources

ejb3

infinispan

jaxrs

Wild**Fly**

Configuration File
structure

. . . .

In the following sections, we will have an initial look at the individual elements that are contained within the server definition that, taken as a whole, make up the server configuration. Next, we will also learn how to configure them using the Administration Console.

Extensions

Most of the application server functionalities are provided by means of **extensions**. As a matter of fact, most of the modules in the WildFly codebase are extension implementations, with each extension providing support for some aspects of the Java EE specifications or for core server functionalities.

Extensions need to implement an interface (*org.jboss.as.controller.Extension*) that allows integration with the core AS management layer. Via that mechanism, extensions are able to be part of the application server core configuration, to register resources, install services into the AS's service container and register deployment units.

If you are on the hook to create your how server extensions you can have a look at the AS7 server wiki at: https://docs.jboss.org/author/display/AS71/Extending+JBoss+AS+7 .

For all the other humans, it is enough to know that if you want a particular extension to be available, you have to include an <extension/> element -which states its module- in the *domain.xml* or *standalone.xml* file.

```
<extensions>
        <extension module="org.jboss.as.clustering.infinispan"/>
        <extension module="org.jboss.as.connector"/>
        <extension module="org.jboss.as.deployment-scanner"/>
        <extension module="org.jboss.as.ee"/>
        <extension module="org.jboss.as.ejb3"/>
        . . . . . . .
    </extensions>
```

Paths

A path is a logical name for a file system path, which can be included as a section in the server configuration file. Other sections of the configuration can then reference those paths by their logical name, rather than having to include the full details of the path (which may vary on different machines). For example, you can declare the following path in your configuration, which points to the folder */home/wildfly/logs*:

```
<path name="log.dir" path="/home/wildfly/logs" />
```

You can then reference your path in other part of the configuration file, such as in the logging subsystem:

```
<file relative-to="log.dir" path="server.log"/>
```

In the above example, the file logger will trace output in the folder */home/wildfly/logs/server.log*

A path can be as well *relative* to an existing path definition such as in the following example that references the server's *data* directory:

```
<path name="logdata.dir" path="example" relative-to="jboss.server.data.dir"/>
```

When a **relative-to** parameter is provided, the final path will be made up of the **relative-to** folder, combined with the **path** element. (For example, if the application server is installed in */usr/share* folder then the above path could translate to */usr/share/wildfly-8.2.0.Final/standalone/data/example* for a standalone configuration)

Interfaces

The **interfaces** section contains the network interfaces/IP addresses or host names where the application server can be bound. By default, the standalone application server defines three available network interfaces: the **management**, the **public** and the **unsecure** interface. The management interfaces are used to provide management connectivity to the application server (for example via the CLI shell). The public interface is used to provide access to the application server services. The unsecure interface is used for IIOP sockets in the standard configuration

```
<interfaces>
  <interface name="management">
    <inet-address value="${jboss.bind.address.management:127.0.0.1}"/>
  </interface>

  <interface name="public">
    <inet-address value="${jboss.bind.address:127.0.0.1}"/>
  </interface>
  <interface name="unsecure">
    <inet-address value="${jboss.bind.address.unsecure:127.0.0.1}"/>
  </interface>
</interfaces>
```

In the above snippet, the management and public interfaces are bound to the application server system properties **jboss.bind.address.management** and **jboss.bind.address** respectively. These properties can be overridden on the startup script of the application server as in the following example:

```
standalone.bat -Djboss.bind.address=141.137.17.62
```

 Please note that the **jboss.bind.address** property can be substituted with the -b parameter, which has been added for compatibility with earlier releases.

Socket binding groups

A **socket binding** makes up a named configuration of a socket. Within this section, you are able to configure the network ports, which will be open and listening for incoming connections. As we have just seen, every socket binding group references a network interface through the default-interface attribute:

```
<socket-binding-group name="standard-sockets" default-interface="public"
                       port-offset="${jboss.socket.binding.port-offset:0}">
    <socket-binding name="management-http"
                    interface="management" port="${jboss.management.http.port:9990}"/>
    <socket-binding name="management-https"
                    interface="management" port="${jboss.management.https.port:9993}"/>
    <socket-binding name="ajp" port="${jboss.ajp.port:8009}"/>
    <socket-binding name="http" port="8080"/>
    <socket-binding name="https" port="${jboss.https.port:8443}"/>
. . . .
</socket-binding-group>
```

The **port-offset** attribute can be used to shift all port definitions of a fixed number, in case you want to run multiple application servers on the same machine, although the suggested approach to shift ports is to pass the **jboss.socket.binding.port-offset** as argument at server startup.

 Please notice that WildFly 8 uses the port 9990 for *all* management interfaces (Web interface and CLI). The native port 9999 has been deprecated so update your scripts accordingly.

System-Properties

System properties can be either set as part of the application server startup script or included in the application server configuration file, like in the following example, which sets the property "myproperty" to "false":

```
<system-properties>
    <property name="myproperty" value="false"/>
</system-properties>
```

Other ways to set a system property

System properties can be also set by means of the management instruments (See "General configuration management") or by passing arguments to your server startup scripts. For example, in order to set the property "key" at server startup, you can use the –D option as follows:

```
standalone.sh -Dkey=value
```

If your list of property is quite large, then you can use as well the –P flag which points to a file based list of system properties:

```
standalone.sh -P /tmp/file.properties
```

Profile

As you can see from the tree of elements contained in the server configuration, the **profile** element holds a collection of subsystems: each subsystem in turn contains a subset of functionalities used by the application server.

```
<profile>
        <subsystem xmlns="urn:jboss:domain:logging:2.0">

        . . . ..
</profile>
```

For example, the web subsystem contains the definition of a set of connectors used by the container, the messaging subsystem defines the JMS configuration and modules used by the AS's messaging provider, and so on.

> The content of an individual profile configuration looks largely the same in *domain.xml* and *standalone.xml.* The only difference is that a standalone configuration is only allowed to have a *single* profile element (the profile the server will run), while a domain can have *multiple* profiles.

The content of individual subsystem configurations are the same between standalone and domain configuration files.

Configuring WildFly in standalone mode

The standalone configuration is contained into the *JBOSS_HOME/standalone/configuration* folder. The server configuration in standalone mode is based on a single "profile" which includes the detailed configuration of the various subsystems and definition of the network interfaces and sockets that those subsystems may open. Out of the box, the following built-in server configurations are available:

- *standalone.xml* - This is the default standalone configuration file used by the application server. It does not include the messaging subsystem and is not able to run in a cluster.
- *standalone-full.xml* - This configuration adds to the default configuration the Jacorb libraries and the messaging provider (HornetQ)
- *standalone-ha.xml* - This configuration enhances the default configuration with clustering support (JGroups / mod_cluster).
- *standalone-full-ha.xml* - This configuration adds both clustering capabilities and messaging / Jacorb libraries.

If you want to start the application server with a non-default configuration, you can use the **-c** parameter. Here's for example how to start WildFly using the "full" server configuration:

```
standalone.bat -c standalone-full.xml
```

Once started the application server, launch from your browser the **Administration Console**, which can be reached at the following default address: http://localhost:9990

Enter the credentials of the management user we have formerly created. Once logged, an introduction screen will guide you to a quick tour of the most interesting settings:

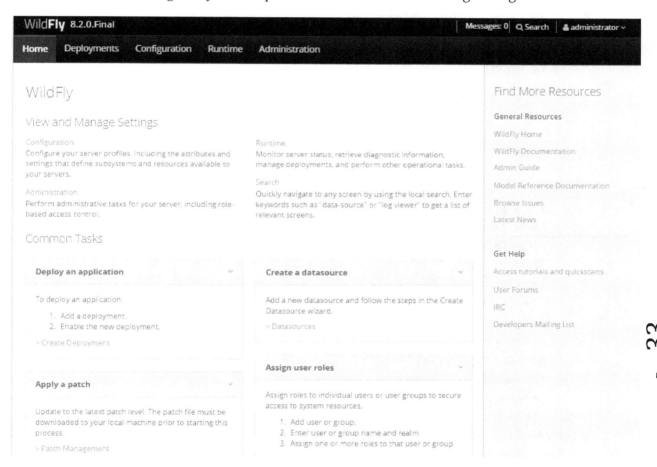

Although this welcome page can help you to reach a mix of handy features like application deployment, datasource creation or handy links to docs and forums, we need to follow a well-organized educational approach, so just enter in your Configuration by clicking on the upper Tab named "**Configuration**" to have a look on the Administration Console structure. As you can see from the following snapshot, the Admin Console is composed of the following main panels:

- The **Upper Tab (1)** lets you choose your management working area by selecting **Deployments** (applications deployment), **Configuration** (Server Configuration), **Runtime** Mode (Server metrics) and **Administration** mode (Server Access Control).
- The **Left panel (2),** reflects your upper tab selection. Hence, if you selected the Deployments upper tab it will allow contains pointers for deploying applications. In case you selected the Configuration upper tab, it allows configuring the available subsystems, arranged as a tree of resources. Then if you clicked on the Runtime upper tab, this panel can trigger runtime information for a chosen area. Finally, when Administration mode is selected allows configuring server Administration users and roles.
- The **Mid panel (3)** can be used to execute the tasks or configure the items, which are selected in the left panel.

In the next section, we will learn how to configure some general elements of your configuration, which are located in the **General Configuration** panel of the Left tree menu. Then, in the following chapters of this book, we will complete our administration skills by learning the individual subsystems that are part of the server configuration.

General Server configuration

The **General Configuration** left panel contains four core elements (Network interfaces, Socket Bindings, Paths, System properties) which we already had a look at in the server configuration file. The recommended best practice is not to alter the configuration file manually therefore we will learn now how to configure them using the Admin Console.

Configuring Network Interfaces:

In order to configure Network interfaces select from the **General Configuration** panel the option "**Interfaces**" which will show the following screen:

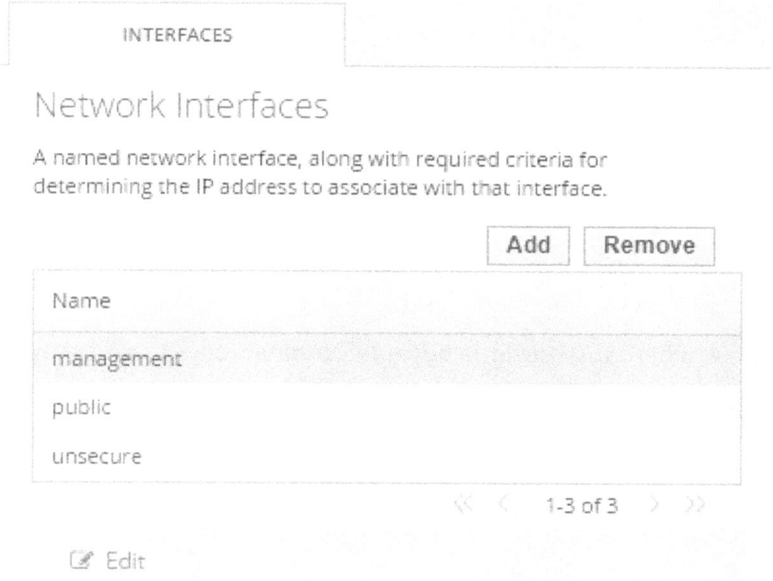

INTERFACES

Network Interfaces

A named network interface, along with required criteria for determining the IP address to associate with that interface.

	Add	Remove
Name		
management		
public		
unsecure		

« ‹   1-3 of 3   › »

✎ Edit

In the Network Interfaces window, you can either add/remove interface definitions by clicking on the **Add** and **Remove** button or you can edit the existing interfaces by clicking on the lower "**Edit**" link. Let's see as an example, how to change IP Address where the application server is bound. For this purpose, select the **public** interface and click on "**Edit**":

☑ Edit

Name:	public
Inet Address:	${jboss.bind.address:127.0.0.1}
Address Wildcard:	
Nic:	
Nic Match:	
Loopback:	☐
Loopback Address:	

In order to configure the IP Address where the server is bound you have to enter an appropriate value in the **Inet Address** textbox. Please note that, since the Inet Address accepts Beanshell expression resolution, by clicking on the right paperclip link, you can experiment the **Resolved value** for your expression as shown by the following popup window:

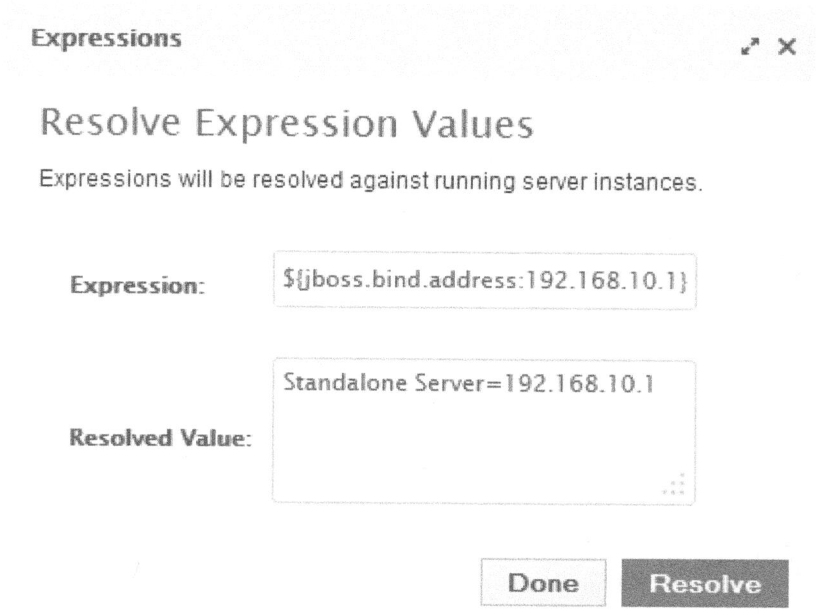

Expressions ↗ ✕

Resolve Expression Values

Expressions will be resolved against running server instances.

Expression: ${jboss.bind.address:192.168.10.1}

Resolved Value: Standalone Server=192.168.10.1

[Done] [Resolve]

The above Beanshell expression means that if the *jboss.bind.address* is not provided as system property, the resolved value for this interface will be the IP 192.168.10.1. Another viable option is using the **Address Wildcard** option, which lets you, for example, to bind the interface to any available IP4 or IP6 address:

Name: public

Inet Address:

Address Wildcard: Any IP4   ▼

Nic:

Nic Match:

Loopback: ☐

Loopback Address:

In the above example, we have bound the public interface to any available IP4 address, which also includes the loopback address. If on the other hand you are binding your server against a fixed IP address, you need to explicitly flag the "**Loopback**" option if you want to be able to respond on the loopback interface as well.

For the sake of completeness we will mention that it's possible to bind an interface against a Network card interface name such as "eth0" (Nic option), a Network interface name defined using a regular expression (Nic Match option) or even define the Loopback address to be used (Loopback Address option).

Advanced Interfaces configuration

The Interfaces configuration contains at the bottom an **Advanced** configuration panel, which can be expanded by clicking on its arrow. The following menu will be revealed:

▼ Advanced

Up: ☐

Virtual: ☐

Public Address: ☐

Site Local Address: ☐

Link Local Address: ☐

Multicast: ☐

Point to Point: ☐

Cancel   Save

The purpose of this menu is to provide to the application server some selection criteria for choosing the IP addresses to be assigned to the application server. This is typically used in conjunction with a "Any-Address" binding which gather all available addresses found on the machine. More in detail:

Up: the selection criteria for choosing an IP address for this interface should be whether its network interface is currently up.

Virtual: the selection criteria for choosing an IP address for this interface should be whether its network interface is a virtual interface.

Public Address: the selection criteria for choosing an IP address for this interface should be whether it is a publicly routable address.

Site Local Address: the selection criteria for choosing an IP address for this interface should be whether or it is a site-local address

Link Local Address: the selection criteria for choosing an IP address for this interface should be whether a link-local address (i.e. a network address that is valid only for communications within the network segment or the broadcast domain that the host is connected to).

Multicast: the selection criteria for choosing an IP address for this interface should be whether its network interface supports multicast.

Point to Point: the selection criteria for choosing an IP address for this interface should be whether or not its network interface is a point-to-point interface.

Configuring Socket Bindings

Socket bindings allow you to set the ports that will be used by your interfaces. If you have started a standalone server, you will see just one option, the standard-sockets. Click on **View** to enter the settings of your sockets.

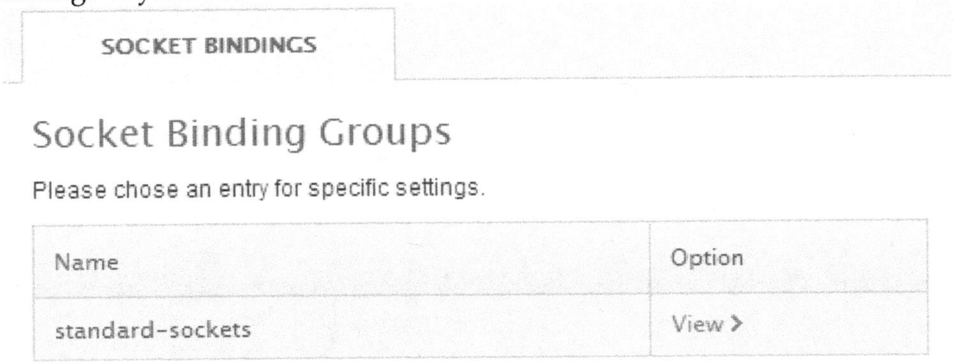

SOCKET BINDINGS

Socket Binding Groups

Please chose an entry for specific settings.

Name	Option
standard-sockets	View >

Once in the Socket Bindings view, you can choose between **Inbound** and **Outbound** (Remote and Local) Socket Bindings. Inbound socket bindings control the list of socket connections that are *accepted* by the application server. Almost all bindings fall in this group. On the other hand, Outbound sockets control *outgoing* connections such as mail connections. The following picture shows how to configure some Inbound Socket Bindings:

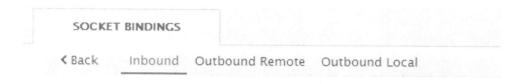

SOCKET BINDINGS

< Back   Inbound   Outbound Remote   Outbound Local

Socket Bindings: Group standard-sockets

A list of socket configurations. These configurations are referenced throughout
the overall server/domain configuration.

Available Socket Bindings   [Add]   [Remove]

▲ Name	Port	MCast Port
ajp	${jboss.ajp.port:8009}	
http	${jboss.http.port:8080}	
https	${jboss.https.port:8443}	

Click on **Add** to add new Bindings or **Remove** to delete them. Most often you will need to modify a
single port binding, so select it from the available list, for example, the http socket binding, and
click on the lower "**Edit**" link:

☑ Edit

Name: http

Interface:

Port: ${jboss.http.port:8080}

Fixed Port?:   false

▶ Multicast   [Cancel]   [Save]

As you can see from the above picture, you can set the Socket Binding in the **Port** field, which contains as well a paperclip icon that lets you validate a variable expression. The option "**Fixed Port?**" can be used to determine whether the port value should remain fixed even if numeric offsets are applied to the other sockets in the socket group.

Configure Path references

The last block contained in the General Configuration deals with **Path references** that can be added by clicking on the Add button of their panel and removed by clicking on the corresponding button.

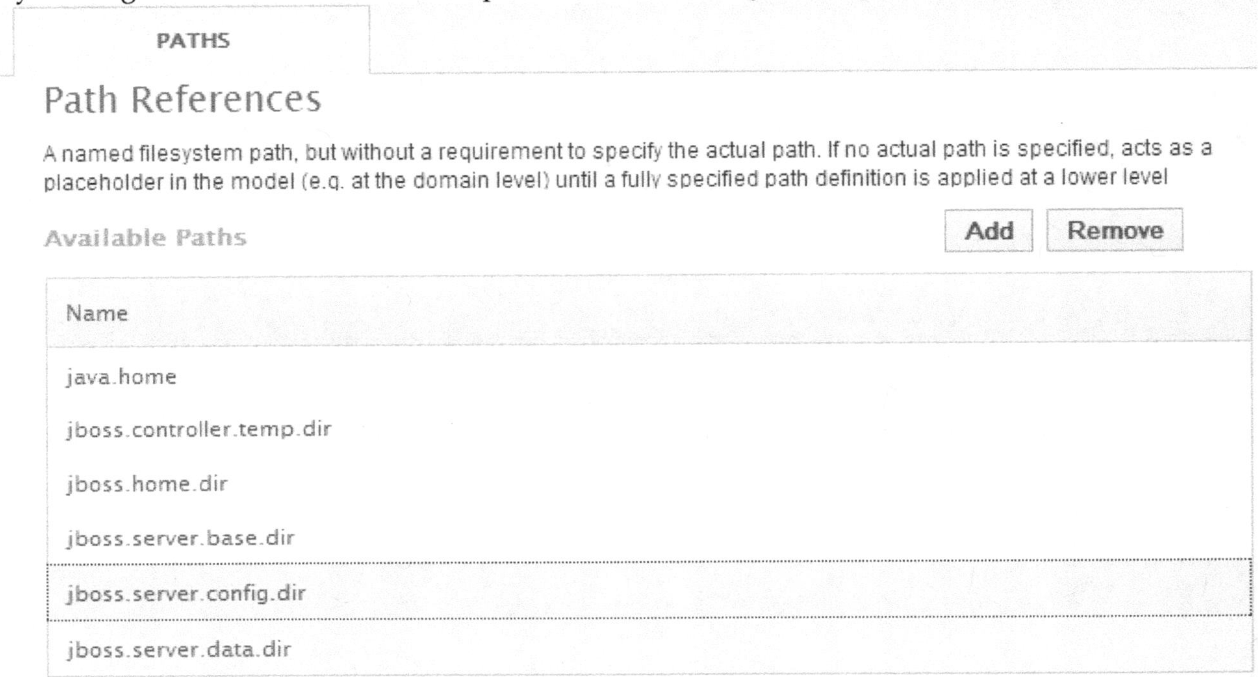

PATHS

Path References

A named filesystem path, but without a requirement to specify the actual path. If no actual path is specified, acts as a placeholder in the model (e.g. at the domain level) until a fully specified path definition is applied at a lower level

Available Paths   Add   Remove

Name
java.home
jboss.controller.temp.dir
jboss.home.dir
jboss.server.base.dir
jboss.server.config.dir
jboss.server.data.dir

By clicking on the **Add** button, you can add a new Path reference which will trigger the following popup window:

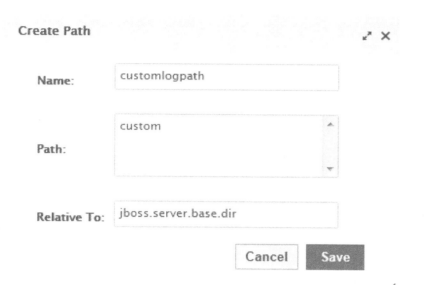

Here we have defined a Path variable named "customlogpath" which points to the folder customlogpath that is relative to the "*jboss.server.base.dir*". If you don't include the *Relative To* text item, the Path is intended to be an absolute path.

Configuring System Properties

The last block contained in the General Configuration deals with **System Properties**, which can be added by clicking on the Add button of their panel, and removed by clicking on the corresponding **Remove** button.

SYSTEM PROPERTIES

System Properties

These properties are available throughout the configuration. The Boot-Time flag specifies if a property should be passed into the JVM start (-Dproperty=value)

| Add | Remove |

▲ Key	Value

By clicking on the **Add** button, you can specify your System property name and value as shown by the following window:

Create System Property

Name: `myproperty`

Value: `value`

Cancel   Save

Configuring WildFly in Domain mode

In order to understand the domain configuration, we need at first to understand which are the key components of a domain. A domain is a collection of **server groups**; a server group is in turn a collection of **servers**.

> The concept of server groups can be seen as a set of servers managed as a single unit by the domain. You can actually use server groups for fine-grained configuration of nodes; for example, each server group is able to define its own settings such as customized JVM settings, socket bindings interfaces, or deployed applications.

From the process point of view, a domain is made up of the following elements:

1. **Domain Controller**: The domain controller is the management control point of your domain. An AS instance running in domain mode will have *at most* one process instance acting as a Domain Controller. The Domain Controller holds a centralized configuration, which is shared by the node instances belonging to the domain.

2. **Host controller**: It's a process that is responsible for coordinating with a Domain Controller the lifecycle of server processes and the distribution of deployments, from the Domain Controller to the server instances.

3. **Application server nodes**: These are regular Java processes that map to instances of the application server. Each server node, in turn, belongs to a Server group.

Additionally, when starting a domain, you will see another JVM process running on your machine: this is the **Process controller**. It's a very lightweight process whose primary function is to spawn server processes and host controller processes, and manage their input/output streams. Since it's not configurable, we will not further discuss about it.

The following picture summarizes the concepts exposed so far:

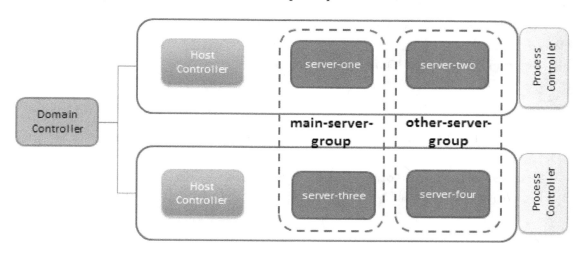

In the above picture, we have designed a domain made up of a **Domain Controller**, running on a dedicated server instance and two **Host Controllers**. The Domain defines two **Server Groups** (main-server-group and other-server-group which are the default WildFly server group names); each Server Group in turn contains two **Servers**, making up a total of 4 WildFly servers.

 Pay attention on the Server Group distribution, which spans across the two different Hosts. Since each Server Group is able to provide distinct applications (e.g. a production stable application version on main-server-group and a test application version on the other-server-group) with this Domain topology you are able to run both applications **without a single point of failure**.

In the following section we will show how to create in practice this Domain configuration by configuring at first configure the Domain Controller and its *domain.xml* configuration file. Next we will configure the single host where the application server will run.

Domain Controller set up (domain.xml)

The server configuration of the domain is centralized in the *domain.xml* file of the Domain Controller. The *domain.xml* is located in the domain/configuration folder and it contains the main configuration that will be used for all server instances. This file is only required for the Domain Controller. In the *domain.xml* file we will define the **server group** configuration (which can be anyway changed at runtime, as we will see in a minute).

```
<server-groups>
        <server-group name="main-server-group" profile="full">
            <jvm name="default">
                <heap size="64m" max-size="512m"/>
            </jvm>
            <socket-binding-group ref="full-sockets"/>
        </server-group>
        <server-group name="other-server-group" profile="full">
            <jvm name="default">
                <heap size="64m" max-size="512m"/>
            </jvm>
            <socket-binding-group ref="full-sockets"/>
        </server-group>
</server-groups>
```

As you can see, we have defined two server groups: **main-server-group** and **other-server-group**. Each server group is in turn associated with a **server profile** and a **socket-binding-group**. The default configuration includes four preconfigured profiles:

- **default**: Supports the Java EE Web-Profile plus some extensions like REST Web Services or support for EJB3 remote invocations. You should associate this profile with the "standard-sockets" socket-binding-group.
- **full**: supports of Java EE Full-Profile and all server capabilities without clustering. You should associate this profile with the "full-sockets" socket-binding-group.
- **ha**: the default profile with clustering capabilities. You should associate this profile with the "ha-sockets" socket-binding-group.
- **full-ha**: the full profile with clustering capabilities. You should associate this profile with the "full-ha-sockets" socket-binding-group.

Quick Recap! When running in **domain mode** you can choose the server groups configuration among the preconfigured profiles. When running in **standalone mode** you can choose the server configuration by selecting (-c) among the available configuration files.

Configuring the host.xml of the Domain Controller

The other key domain configuration file is *host.xml* which defines:

- The application servers which are part of a domain server distribution and the server group to which they belong.
- The network interfaces and security settings for these application servers
- The location of the Domain Controller

In our example Domain configuration, there are no application servers running on this host; this means that we have an host which is dedicated to the Domain Controller. This is stated by the following empty **servers** element:

```
<servers />
```

Next, we need to specify the location of the **Domain Controller**. Since the Domain Controller will be running on the same Host, we will include a "local" element into the domain-controller stanza:

```
<domain-controller>
    <local/>
</domain-controller>
```

Now we can start the Domain Controller so that will be bound to the IP Address 192.168.0.1:

```
domain.sh -b 192.168.0.1 -Djboss.bind.address.management=192.168.0.1
```

You can choose to start the domain using a non-standard configuration file by passing the **--domain-config** parameter. Example ./domain.sh --domain-config=domain-alternate.xml.

Configuring the host.xml of the slave hosts

After the Domain Controller is configured and started, the next step is to setup the two hosts where the application server is installed. The host configuration is done on the *host.xml* file, which is contained in the domain distribution.

As an alternative you can name the host file as you like and start the domain with the the **--host-config** parameter. Example ./domain.sh --host-config=host-slave.xml.

The first thing is to choose a **unique** name for each host in our domain to avoid name conflicts. So we will choose for the first host name:

```
<host name="server1" xmlns="urn:jboss:domain:2.2">
   ...
</host>
```

And for the other host:

```
<host name="server2" xmlns="urn:jboss:domain:2.2">
   ...
</host>
```

Next, we need to specify that the host controller will connect to a remote Domain Controller. We will not specify the actual IP and port of the Domain Controller but leave them as a property named **jboss.domain.master.address** and **jboss.domain.master.port**.

Additionally, we need to specify the username, which will be used to connect to the Domain Controller. So let's add to the Domain Controller the user **wildflyadmin** which we have formerly created:

```
<domain-controller>
    <remote host="${jboss.domain.master.address}" port="${jboss.domain.master.port:9990}"
username="wildflyadmin" security-realm="ManagementRealm"/>
</domain-controller>
```

Finally, we need to specify the Base64 password for the server identity we have included in the remote element:

```
<management>
   <security-realms>
      <security-realm name="ManagementRealm">
         <server-identities>
            <secret value="RXJpY3Nzb24xIQ" />
         </server-identities>
         . . . . . .
      </security-realm>
   </security-realms>
   <management-interfaces>
         . . . . . .
   </management-interfaces>
</management>
```

The secret Base64 password is produced as output by the *add-user.sh* script, if you care to answer "yes" to the last question, as shown in the first chapter.

The last step is to configure the **server** nodes inside the *host.xml* file on both hosts.
So we will configure on the first host (server1):

```
<servers>
        <server name="server-one" group="main-server-group"/>
        <server name="server-two" group="other-server-group" auto-start="false">
            <socket-bindings port-offset="150"/>
        </server>
</servers>
```

And on the second host (server2)

```
<servers>
        <server name="server-three" group="other-server-group"/>
        <server name="server-four" group="main-server-group" auto-start="false">
            <socket-bindings port-offset="150"/>
        </server>
</servers>
```

 Please notice the **auto-start** flag indicates that the server instances will not be started automatically if the host controller is started. If the auto-start is omitted, by default the server will start.

For the second server a port-offset of 150 is configured to avoid port conflicts. With the port offset, we can reuse the socket-binding group of the domain configuration for multiple server instances on one host. Ok, now we are done with our configuration and we can start the first host with:

```
domain.sh \
  -b 192.168.0.2
  -Djboss.domain.master.address=192.168.0.1
  -Djboss.bind.address.management=192.168.0.2
```

And the second one with:

```
domain.sh \
  -b 192.168.0.3
  -Djboss.domain.master.address=192.168.0.1
  -Djboss.bind.address.management=192.168.0.3
```

If you look at the Domain Controller console, you should notice the following output, which shows that the Domain Controller has started and the other slave hosts have successfully connected:

```
[Host Controller] 16:05:46,111 INFO  [org.jboss.as] (Controller Boot Thread) JBAS015874:
WildFly 8.2.0.Final (Host Controller) started in 4493ms - Started 11 of 11 services (0
services are passive or on-demand)

[Host Controller] 16:06:01,750 INFO  [org.jboss.as.domain] (slave-request-threads - 1)
JBAS010918: Registered remote slave host "server1", WildFly 8.2.0.Final

[Host Controller] 16:06:02,330 INFO  [org.jboss.as.domain] (slave-request-threads - 1)
JBAS010918: Registered remote slave host "server2", WildFly 8.2.0.Final
```

Domain breakdown

The above configuration has produced a domain configuration made up of a dedicated Domain Controller and a set of four server nodes split into two Server Groups and two different Hosts as shown by the following picture:

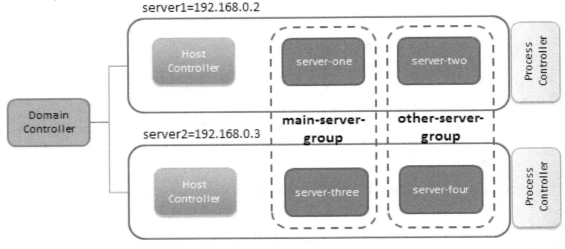

With the above architecture, the hosts where applications are deployed are completely independent from administrative tasks. On the other hand, the Domain Controller is solely responsible for the management of the domain. As per definition, there can be at most one Domain Controller in a Domain, this means that you should care for Domain Controller restart in case of failure. Although this might appear a limitation, it is not so critical as it might seems: at first the Domain Controller is not at all necessary to keep running your applications on server nodes. Let's repeat it again, the Domain Controller is *solely* responsible for managing your Domain (e.g server start/stop, application deployment etc.).

Next, you can get notified of a Domain Controller failure with very simple network instruments such as any port monitoring script or, if you are looking for more advanced options, have a look at Nagios which has a dedicated **JBoss monitoring plugin** (http://www.nagios.com/solutions/jboss-monitoring).

Actually, it is possible to start slave Host Controllers using two additional parameters which are **--backup** and **--cached-dc**. The first one (**--backup**) can be used to keep a copy of the domain configuration even if this host is not the Domain Controller. The other one (**--cached-dc**) can be used to boot the host using the copy of its locally cached copy of the Domain configuration, in case the host cannot contact the Domain Controller.

If you use them together, you can enable an Host Controller to be elected as Domain Controller, if the latter one fails yet there's an open issue about this point at https://issues.jboss.org/browse/WFLY-773 so you are encouraged to track this issue if you are on the hook for Domain Controller HA.

Choosing between standalone mode and domain mode

The choice of domain mode versus standalone mode comes down to whether the user wants to use the centralized management capability domain mode provides. Some enterprises have developed their own sophisticated multi-server management capabilities and are comfortable coordinating changes across a number of independent WildFly instances. If this is your case, a multi-server architecture comprised of individual standalone mode AS instances is a good option.

Standalone mode is better suited for most development scenarios. You should definitely use if you are running a single server installation; also you should consider using it when the "domain mode" is not a feasible choice, such as if you are running a WildFly instance in an Arquillian-based test suite. Generally speaking, any individual server configuration that can be achieved in domain mode can also be achieved in standalone mode, so even if the application being developed will eventually run in production on a domain mode installation, much (probably most) development can be done using standalone mode.

Domain mode can be helpful in some advanced development scenarios; i.e. those involving interaction between multiple AS instances. Developers may find that setting up various servers as members of a domain is an efficient way to launch a multi-server cluster.

Managing the WildFly Domain

The application server domain can be managed from the Web admin console or as well using the Command Line Interface. The CLI is discussed in chapter 11 of this book so we will now show how to perform basic domain management using the Web admin console.
You can reach it the console by pointing at the **jboss.bind.address.management** (if not set defaults to 127.0.0.1) and to the port **jboss.management.http.port** (if not set defaults to 9990). In our example it would be: http://192.168.0.1:9990
If you want to have a look where these parameters are configured, here's the core section of the Domain controller's *host.xml* where you define the two parameters.

```
<management-interfaces>

    . . . . .

    <http-interface security-realm="ManagementRealm">
        <socket interface="management" port="${jboss.management.http.port:9990}"/>
    </http-interface>
</management-interfaces>

    . . . . .

<interfaces>
    <interface name="management">
        <inet-address value="${jboss.bind.address.management:127.0.0.1}"/>
    </interface>
</interfaces>
```

Once you open your browser, a login prompt will require entering the password which is the same we have already configured. After successful logging, you will see that the Web admin console of the server domain is composed of four main areas:

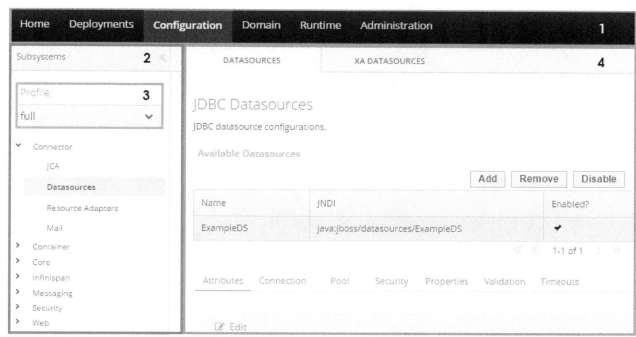

- The **Upper Tab (1)** allows switching between **Deployments** (applications deployment), **Configuration** mode (Server Configuration), **Domain** (Server Groups and Servers control) **Runtime** (Server Statistics) and **Administration** mode (Server Access Control).
- **The Left Tree Panel** (2): when the **Configuration** option is selected, allows configuring the available subsystems, which are arranged as a tree of resources. When the **Domain** option is selected allows managing Server Groups and control the single Servers. When the **Deployments** is active it lets you deploy application. Next, when the **Runtime** option is selected, allows displaying runtime statistics for the server modules. Finally, when the **Administration** option is selected allows managing Administrative functions.
- **The ComboBox Panel** (3): this combo box is used to define the target of your operations. So for example, if you have selected the **Configuration** option it allows selecting the Profile on which we will operate.
- The **Mid panel** (4): once that you have selected a resource on the left panel, you will manage it from this panel.

In the next sections, we will show how to operate on these tabs to perform basic management operations.

How to start / stop server nodes

In order to start a server node of your domain, you have to select the upper **Domain** tab.

From there, move the Domain left panel and click on **"Overview"**. Now select from the mid-screen table cell the server you are interested to start and click on the **Start Server** link:

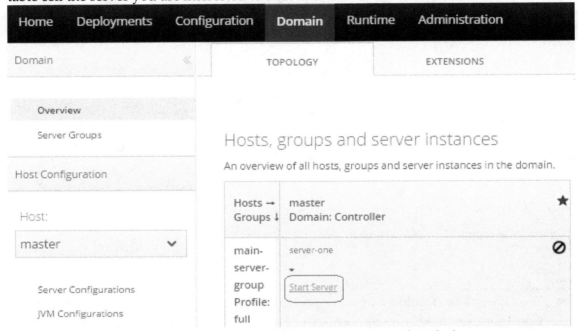

A confirm dialog will ask you to confirm if you want to proceed with the server startup.

Much the same way, you can stop a server by selecting an active instance and clicking on the Stop link:

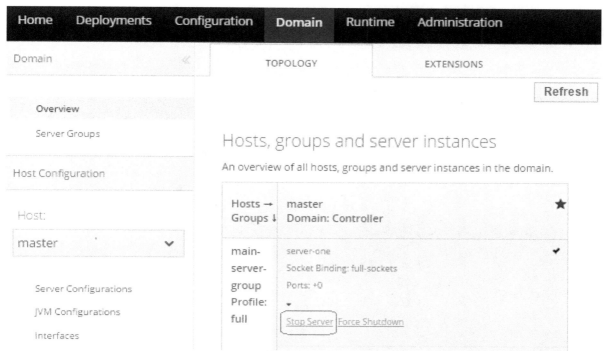

As a side note, since WildFly 8 it is possible to use **Force Shutdown** option, which will abruptly stop the server without waiting for termination of running jobs.

Additionally the start and stop options can be issued also against a **Server Group** by selecting the left table cell where servers are displayed and clicking on the desired option, as shown by the following picture:

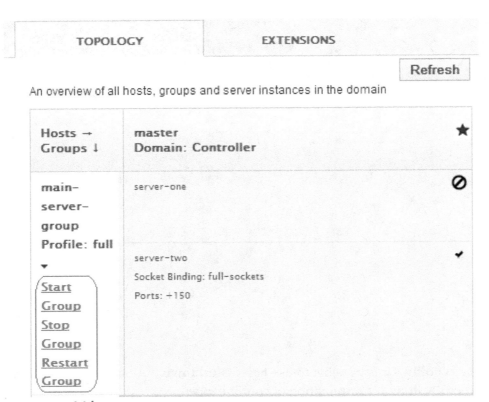

How to add/remove server groups

In order to add a new server group, select the **Domain** upper tab and, from the left menu choose "**Server Groups**". That will bring a view of the available Server Groups.

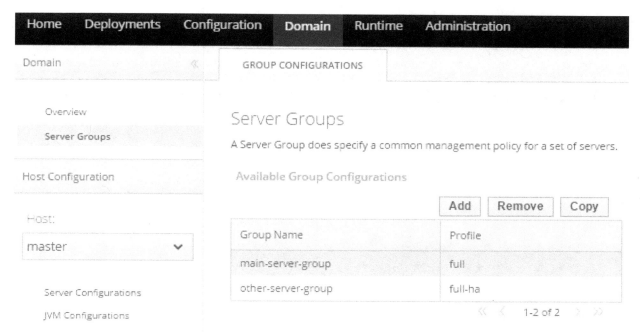

From there, you can choose the **Add** or **Remove** button to add or remove Server Groups through a simple dialog window (The Remove button will conversely remove a selected group). If you were to add a new Group, click on the **Add** button. That will trigger the following screen:

Create Server Group

Name: test-group

Profile: full

Socket Binding: full-sockets

Cancel   Save

Fill up the GUI with the group **Name**, the appropriate server **Profile** and **Socket Binding** associated.

How to add/remove servers

In order to add or remove a new server, you have to pick up the **Domain** upper tab, select on the left panel the **Host** where you are going to operate, then click on the left **"Server Configurations"** option. From there, you can choose the **Add** or **Remove** button to add or remove server instances.

Home	Deployments	Configuration	Domain	Runtime	Administration

Domain «	GROUP CONFIGURATIONS

Overview

Server Groups

Host Configuration

Host:

master ∨

Server Configurations

JVM Configurations

Server Configurations: Host 'master'

A server configuration does specify the overall configuration of a server. A server configuration can be started work. Server configurations belong to server groups.

Available Server Configurations

Add | Remove | Copy

Configuration Name	Server Group	Start Mode	Running?
server-one	main-server-group	auto	✔
server-three	other-server-group	on-demand	
server-two	main-server-group	auto	✔

Assuming you want to add a new Server, click on the **Add** button. In the following window, we are going to add a new server named **"server-test"** which belongs to the **"test-group"** we have just created and uses a Port Offset of 250, in order to avoid conflicts. The server is not configured to start automatically. That would result in the following new server definition:

Create Server Configuration

Name: server-four

Server Group: test-group

Port Offset: 250

Auto Start?: ☐

Cancel Save

 Additionally note the **Copy** button, which has been included to allow copying a server definition into a new server, specifying a Port offset in order to avoid conflicts.

Configuring Domain JVM Settings

The JVM settings of a domain of servers can be done at three different levels:

- **Host** level: the configuration will apply to all servers that are defined in *host.xml*
- **Server group** level: the configuration applies to all servers that are part of the group.
- **Server** level: the configuration is used just for the single host.

The general rule (that is applied to all elements configurable at multiple levels including also System properties, Paths and Interfaces) is that the most *specific* configuration overrides the most general one. So for example, the JVM Server Group configuration will override the JVM Host configuration, while the Server configuration will override all others available configurations.

Configuring Host JVM Settings

The JVM Settings of an host can be configured through the **Domain** upper tab menu, and selecting the **Host** where the server is located expanding **Host settings** from the left menu and from there click on **JVM configurations**:

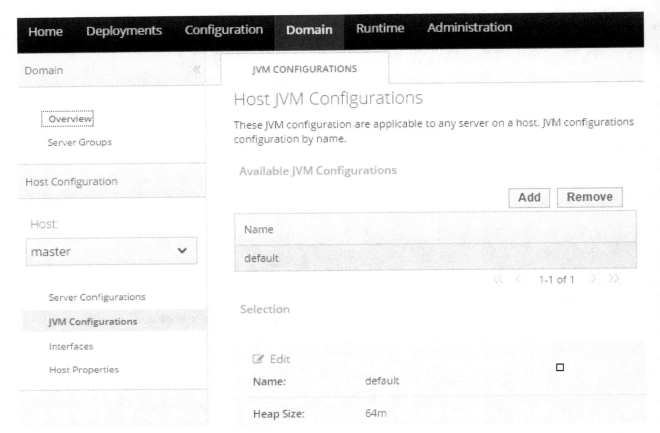

Here you can either edit the default JVM configuration -assisted by a nice autocompleting feature- or Add/Remove new JVM configurations.

Configuring Server Groups JVM Settings

The Server Group JVM Settings are valid across all members of a group, unless redefined at server level. In order to configure the Server Group JVM Settings, select the **Domain** upper tab menu and then the **Server Groups** option contained in the left panel, as shown by the following picture:

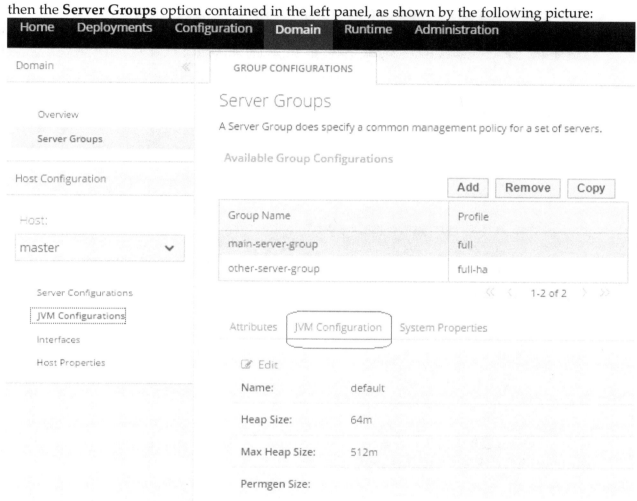

You can edit JVM Server Groups settings by selecting the **JVM Configuration** lower tab and clicking on the **Edit** link.

Configuring Server JVM Settings

The single server JVM settings can be changed by selecting the **Domain** upper tab menu then selecting the appropriate **Host** where the server is contained. From there, click on **Server**

Configurations as displayed by the following picture:

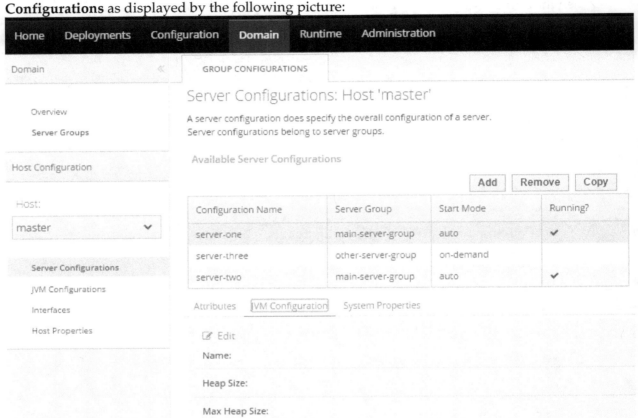

There you can edit JVM Server settings by selecting the Server name in the central panel and then clicking on the **JVM Configuration** lower tab.

Finding elements using Admin console

So far, we have seen how to pin-point a resource of the application server by digging into the tree of resources contained in the left panel of the Admin console. Since WildFly 8.2 it is available an useful shortcut which allows searching through the set of resources with a powerful ajax search. The search is located in the top right section of the Admin console:

Once clicked, you will be able to use the timesaver search which returns all the matches for the keywords entered:

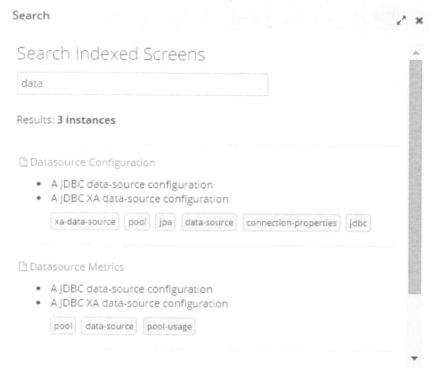

On the other hand, if you want a complete description over the attributes configurable through the Management interface, you can enter the Management Model which is a view availably by clicking on the **Management Model** option contained in the bottom right corner:

This option has been enriched so that now you can actually use it to *modify* your server configuration in a Visual CLI style like. The first image shows how to use it to go through the Management Model **Description**:

By clicking on the **Data** tab, you can actually change the Model parameters. Here is for example how to set the public interfaces address:

Management Model View

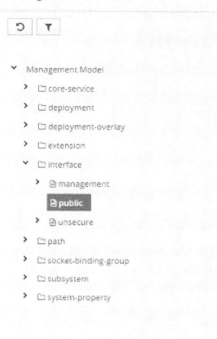

/interface=public

Interface definition

Description   Data

✎ Edit

Any address: ☐

Any ipv4 address: ☐

Any ipv6 address: ☐

Inet address: ${jboss.bind.address:127.0.0.1}   ⚲

Link local address: ☐

Loopback: ☐

Loopback address:

Chapter 3: Deploying applications

This chapter discusses about deploying applications on WildFly application server. As we will see in a minute, deploying applications with the new release of the application server is still an immediate task, which can be accomplished using a different number of instruments such as:

- File system copy of files (standalone mode only)
- Using the management interfaces (Admin Console or CLI)
- Using Maven to deploy WildFly applications

File system deployment

File system is the old school approach to deploy applications that is well known to the majority of developers. This kind of deployment is available on **standalone mode only** therefore, if you are about to deploy applications on a WildFly domain, you have to use the standard management instruments (CLI or Admin Console).

File system deployment just requires that you copy an **archived** application into the deployments folder, and it will be automatically deployed. Example:

```
$ cp example.war /usr/wildfly-8.2.0/standalone/deployments
```

You should then expect to find in your server's log some evidence of your deployment along with the dependencies activated by your deployment (See chapter 8 "Classloading and modules" to learn more about it).

In our case, since we deployed a web application, we will find the following info on the Console

```
12:35:13,724 INFO  [org.wildfly.extension.undertow] (MSC service thread 1-7) JBAS018210:
Register web context: /example

12:35:13,872 INFO  [org.jboss.as.server] (Controller Boot Thread) JBAS018559: Deployed
"example.war" (runtime-name : "example.war")
```

What just happened is that a process named the **Deployment scanner** picked up your application and prepared it for deployment. The scanner can operate in one of two different modes:

Mode 1: Auto-deploy mode:

When running in auto-deploy mode, the scanner will directly monitor the deployment content, automatically deploying new content and redeploying content whose timestamp has changed. This is similar to the behavior of previous AS releases, except that the deployment scanner will not monitor any more changes in deployment descriptors, since Java EE 6/7 applications do not require deployment descriptors.

Mode 2: Manual deploy mode:

When running the manual deploy mode, the scanner will not attempt to deploy the application. Instead, the scanner relies on a system of marker files, with the user's addition or removal of a marker file serving as a sort of command telling the scanner to deploy, undeploy or redeploy content.

 The default rule is that *archived* applications use the **auto-deploy mode** while *exploded* archives require **manual** deploy mode.

In order to perform manual deploy mode, you have to add a marker file named ***application.dodeploy*** to the deployment folder. For example supposing you want to deploy the Example.ear folder to the deployments folder, using a Linux machine:

```
$ cp -r Example.ear $JBOSS_HOME/standalone/deployments
$ touch $JBOSS_HOME/standalone/deployments/Example.ear.dodeploy
```

 In case a deployment fails, the deployment scanner places a marker file *application.failed* (ex. *Example.ear.failed*) in the deployment directory to indicate that the given content failed to deploy into the runtime. The content of the file will include some information about the cause of the failure. Note that with auto-deploy mode, removing this file will make the deployment eligible for deployment again.

Configuring the Deployment scanner attributes

The deployment scanner attributes are part of the deployment-scanner subsystem and can be easily reached from the Administration console by expanding the **Core** left side menu and clicking on the **Deployments Scanners** option as shown by the following picture:

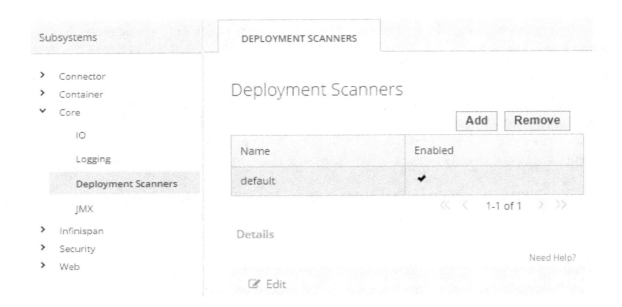

By clicking on the **Edit** attribute, you can set the following parameters, which can be used to vary the default configuration:

Name:	default
Path:	deployments
Path Relative To:	jboss.server.base.dir
Enabled:	true
Scan Interval (ms):	5000
Auto-deploy Zipped:	true
Auto-deploy Exploded:	false
Deployment Timeout (sec):	600

And here's an explanation to the above parameters:

Path	This is the folder inspected by the deployment scanner. If "Path Relative To" is configured, this will be the Path relative to that variable, otherwise it is intended to be an absolute path.
Enabled	If true (default) the Deployment scanner will be enabled.
Path relative to:	If configured, this is the file system path will be appended to the Path variable (default jboss.server.base.dir).
Scan interval	This is the amount of time between each directory scan.
Auto-deploy Exploded	When set to true, automatically deploys exploded archives. (default false)
Auto-deploy Zipped	When set to true automatically deploys zipped archives (default true).
Deployment timeout	Sets the time limit to complete an application deployment (default 600 seconds).

Deploying using the Web interface

Deploying an application using the management instruments (such as the Web console and the CLI) is the recommended choice for production environments. This is also the only choice available if you are running the AS in **domain mode** or if you don't have remote access to the deployments folder of a standalone distribution. Let's see at first how to perform a standalone deployment:

Standalone Deployment

Deployments can be managed by selecting the **Deployments** upper tab of the Administration console as shown in the following picture:

Home	**Deployments**	Configuration	Runtime	Administration

DEPLOYMENTS

Deployments

Currently deployed application components.

Available Deployments

Filter: [   ]   [Add] [Remove] [En/Disable] [Replace]

From the mid panel you can manage your deployment by clicking on the **Add**, **Remove**, **En/Disable**, and **Replace** button. In order to deploy a new application, click on the **Add** button. In the next screen, select the application you want to deploy:

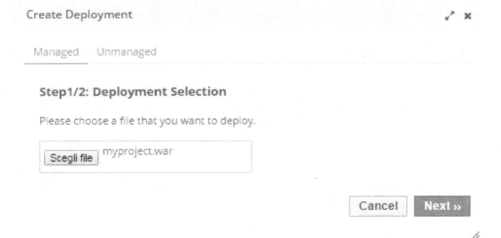

Create Deployment   ↗ ✕

Managed   Unmanaged

Step1/2: Deployment Selection

Please choose a file that you want to deploy.

[Scegli file] myproject.war

[Cancel] [Next »]

Browse to your application and click **Next** to continue.

  If you need to deploy an exploded archive, you can select the **Unmanaged** upper option in the Step 1 window.

In the following screen you will verify the deployment unit name as shown by the following picture:

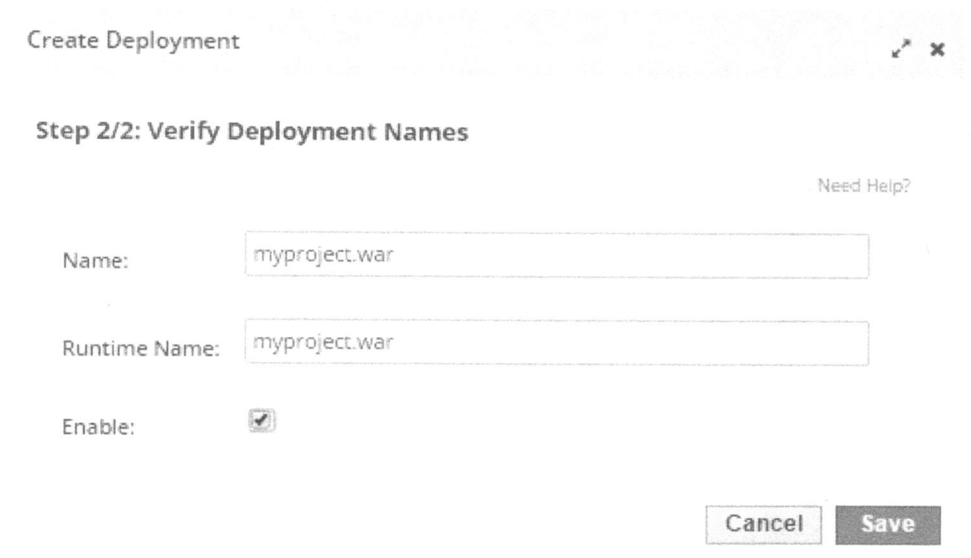

Create Deployment

Step 2/2: Verify Deployment Names

Need Help?

Name: myproject.war

Runtime Name: myproject.war

Enable: ☑

Cancel   **Save**

By selecting the **Enable** checkbox, you will make your application ready to be used by clients. Click **Save** to complete. Verify from the deployments panel that the application has been deployed correctly:

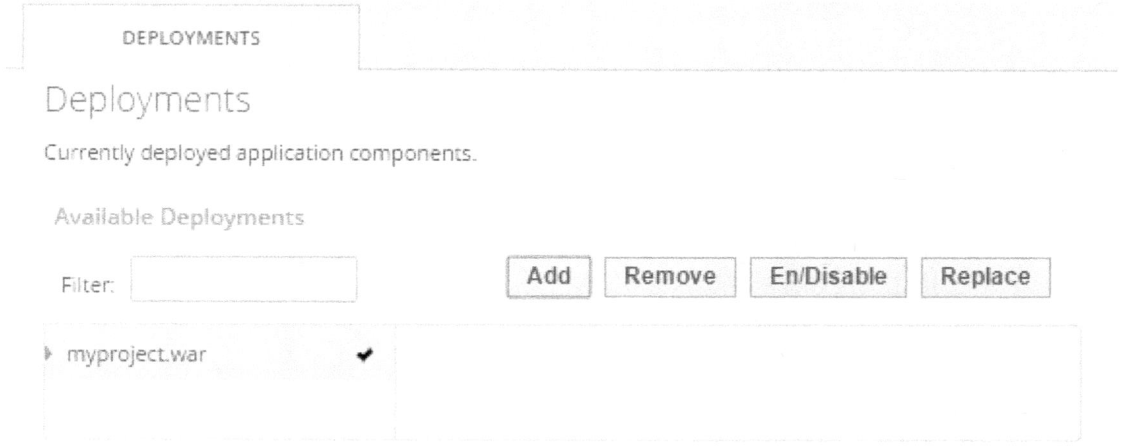

DEPLOYMENTS

Deployments

Currently deployed application components.

Available Deployments

Filter: Add   Remove   En/Disable   Replace

▸ myproject.war   ✔

Domain Deployment

Domain deployment is similar to standalone deployment but with an important difference: domain deployments are targeted against a server group instead of deploying to a single node.

The first steps are similar to the standalone deployment, that is, select the upper **Runtime** tab and from there select the **Manage deployments** option contained in the **Domain** left side menu. From there, click on **Add** in order to deploy a new application.

Once that the application has been uploaded, check that it is enlisted in the **Content Repository** as shown by the following picture:

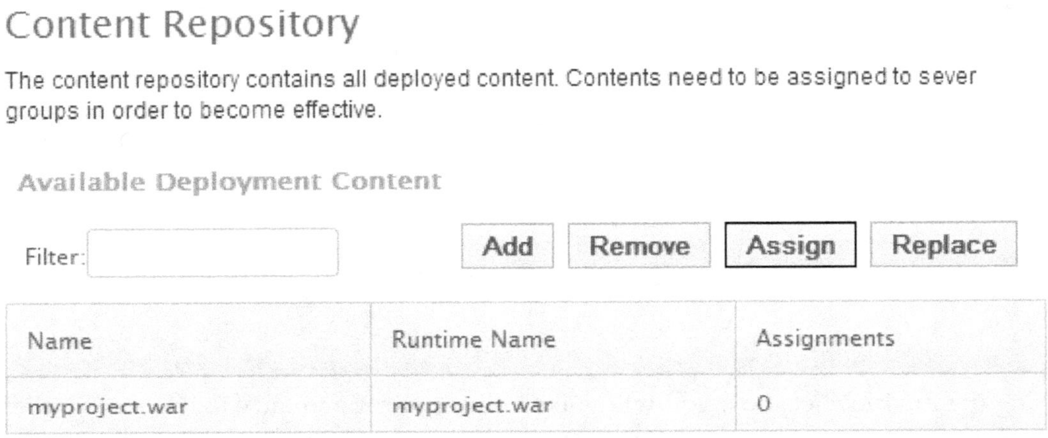

Content Repository

The content repository contains all deployed content. Contents need to be assigned to sever groups in order to become effective.

Available Deployment Content

Filter:		Add	Remove	Assign	Replace

Name	Runtime Name	Assignments
myproject.war	myproject.war	0

Now click on the **Assign** button in order to assign your application to one **Server Group**. In the following example, we are assigning it to the **main-server-group** and enabling it as well:

Select server groups   ↗ ✕

Select server groups for myproject.war

Assign	Server Group	Profile
☑	main-server-group	full
☐	other-server-group	full-ha

《 ‹   1-2 of 2   › 》

☑ Enable myproject.war

Cancel   **Save**

Click on Save in order to persist changes. If you have checked as well the "**Enable**" checkbox, the application will be immediately available.

Deploying the application using the CLI

Finally yet importantly, we will mention another valuable option for deploying your applications: the **Command Line Interface**. Although you might think that using a terminal to deploy an application is more tedious, I can promise you that at the end of this chapter it will take less time than a 100 meters Olympic final!

Let's provide some proof of concept. The first thing we will learn is how to use the **deploy** command to deploy an application to a standalone server:

```
| deploy /home/user1/myproject.war
```

Quite simple isn't it? The great thing is that the file system paths are expandable (using the Tab key) therefore you can deploy an application just like if you are using your friendly bash shell!

The corresponding command to undeploy the application is obviously **undeploy**:

```
| undeploy myproject.war
```

Again, you don't need even to remember the application name you are going to undeploy. Just hit tab after typing "undeploy" as shown here:

```
undeploy
--headers=        --help         --path=          myproject.war
```

Re-deploying an application requires an additional flag (**-f**) in order to **force** application redeployment:

```
deploy -f myproject.war
```

The above deployment commands are meant to be executed on a packaged application. What about **exploded** archives? Never mind! WildFly CLI is extremely powerful and can let you deploy as well exploded archives using the **--unmanaged** flag:

```
deploy --unmanaged c:\myapps\my-exploded-app.war
```

 Here's a small trick! Thanks to the CLI conditional operators you can also issue a conditional deployment- e.g. if the application is not already deployed:
```
if (outcome != success) of /deployment=myproject.war:read-resource
    deploy myproject.war
end-if
```

CLI Domain deployment

As we already learnt, when running in domain mode deployments are bound to one or more server groups. In order to deploy an application to all server groups in a domain you have to issue the following command:

```
deploy application.war --all-server-groups
```

On the other hand, if you want to deploy your application to one or more (comma separated) sever groups, use the **--server-groups** flag instead:

```
deploy application.war --server-groups=main-server-group
```

Un-deploying an application can be done as well on all server groups as follows:

```
undeploy application.war --all-relevant-server-groups
```

On the other hand, undeploying one application from a single (or a set) of server groups is a bit more troublesome. If the application is not available on the other server groups you can simply issue:

```
undeploy application.war --server-groups=main-server-group
```

On the other hand, if the application to be undeployed is available on other server groups, you need to force the deployer to perform a safe undeploy (i.e. without deleting the content) by issuing the following command:

```
undeploy application.war --server-groups=main-server-group --keep-content
```

Deploying applications using Maven

Today Maven is the most popular tool for assisting the developer in structuring the project, compiling, packaging and deploying it as an application. Maven is essentially based on a set of plugins which can be used to enhance its capabilities and a plugin does exist to manage and deploy applications on WildFly. You are therefore encouraged to upgrade your Maven's **pom.xml** to use the **wildfly-maven-plugin** plugin:

```
<plugin>
    <groupId>org.wildfly.plugins</groupId>
        <artifactId>wildfly-maven-plugin</artifactId>
        <version>1.0.2.Final</version>
</plugin>
```

With the WildFly plugin configured, you should at first check that the application server is up and running, then you can issue the command to deploy your Maven project:

```
mvn wildfly:deploy
```

Once you are done with your application, you can undeploy it using the corresponding goal:

```
mvn wildfly:undeploy
```

In order to redeploy your application, issue the following command:

```
mvn wildfly:redeploy
```

Domain Deployment

The above settings can be used for deploying your applications to standalone servers. If you are planning to deploy your application to a domain of servers, then you can specify the domain settings through the **configuration** stanza of your plugin. In this case, we are deploying our application to the other-server-group:

```
<plugin>
    <configuration>
        <domain>
            <server-groups>
                <server-group>main-server-group</server-group>
            </server-groups>
        </domain>
    </configuration>
</plugin>
```

Chapter 4: Configuring Database connectivity

In this chapter, we will learn how to configure connections to Databases using WildFly 8. Database connectivity is part of every –even trivial- application; therefore, we have included it at the top of the list. If you are arriving from a JBoss AS 7 background this chapter should be rather smooth for you, on the other hand if you are migrating from an older JBoss AS 4/5/6 version there will be more miles to go for you. These are the topics we are going to cover in this chapter:

- Manual Datasource configuration
- Datasource configuration using the Command Line Interface
- Configuring a Datasource as a deployable resource (packaged along with your applications)

As any of these options will take you to the same result so you can choose to start from the section you prefer; however if your JBoss skill are a bit outdated, we suggest to follow closely our outline. Before diving into the Datasource configuration you should anyway have available the JDBC library of the database we are connecting to. In our examples, we are using the MySQL database JDBC Drivers that can be downloaded from: http://dev.mysql.com/downloads/connector/j/

Manual Datasource configuration

Actually, this is not the quickest way to configure a Datasource but we decided to include it as first option as it is a good learning exercise that includes manual module creation and understanding of where changes are applied in the server configuration. It can be broken down in the following steps:

- JDBC Module creation
- Datasource and Driver definition in the server configuration file

Let's see each step in detail:

JDBC Module creation

As we have learnt, the application server modules are installed in the application server's *modules* folder. In order to install the JDBC Driver as module you need to perform the following steps:

1. Create a file path structure under the *JBOSS_HOME/modules* directory. For example, in order to install a MySQL JDBC driver, create a directory structure as follows: *JBOSS_HOME/modules/com/mysql/main*.
2. Copy the JDBC driver JAR into the **main** subdirectory.
3. In the **main** subdirectory, create a *module.xml* file containing the following definitions (just adapt the JDBC driver name to your case):

```xml
<?xml version="1.0" encoding="UTF-8"?>
<module xmlns="urn:jboss:module:1.0" name="com.mysql">
  <resources>
    <resource-root path="mysql-connector-java-5.1.24-bin.jar"/>
  </resources>
  <dependencies>
    <module name="javax.api"/>
    <module name="javax.transaction.api"/>
  </dependencies>
</module>
```

Done with the JDBC module installation, check that you have the following file system structure under your modules tree:

```
C:\wildfly-8.2.0.Final\modules\
└──com
    └──mysql
        └──main
                module.xml
                mysql-connector-java-5.1.24.jar
```

Now restart the application server and move to the next section, where we will be configuring the data source into the application server.

Configuring the Datasource and JDBC Driver

As it is, we have just a module named "com.mysql" installed on our application server, which barely loads a library named *mysql-connector-java-5.1.24.jar*. In order to configure a Datasource we will add a definition of the Datasource and of the JDBC driver into your server configuration file. Therefore, open the *standalone.xml* file (or whatever configuration you want to install it to) and include the following elements:

```xml
<datasources>
        . . . .
    <datasource jndi-name="java:/jboss/datasources/MySQLDS"
                pool-name="MySQLPool" enabled="true">
        <connection-url>jdbc:mysql://localhost:3306/mysqlschema</connection-url>
        <driver>mysql</driver>
        <security>
                <user-name>jboss</user-name>
                <password>jboss</password>
        </security>
    </datasource>
    <drivers>

        . . . .
        <driver name="mysql" module="com.mysql"/>
    </drivers>
</datasources>
```

As you can see we have nested into the datasources element a definition for the Datasource that is bound under the JNDI name "**java:/jboss/datasources/MySQLDS**". Next, we have included the **connection-url**, which points to a MySQL server on localhost running a "mysqlschema". Next element is the **driver** name that references the "mysql" driver defined into the "drivers" section. Last mandatory element that we have included is the **user-name** and **password** information that is nested within the security section. Reload your server configuration or restart the server in order to apply the changes.

Testing the Datasource

Done with the configuration it is time to test your Database connection. In order to do that, select the Datasource "**Connection**" panel, which contains a "**Test Connection**" button.

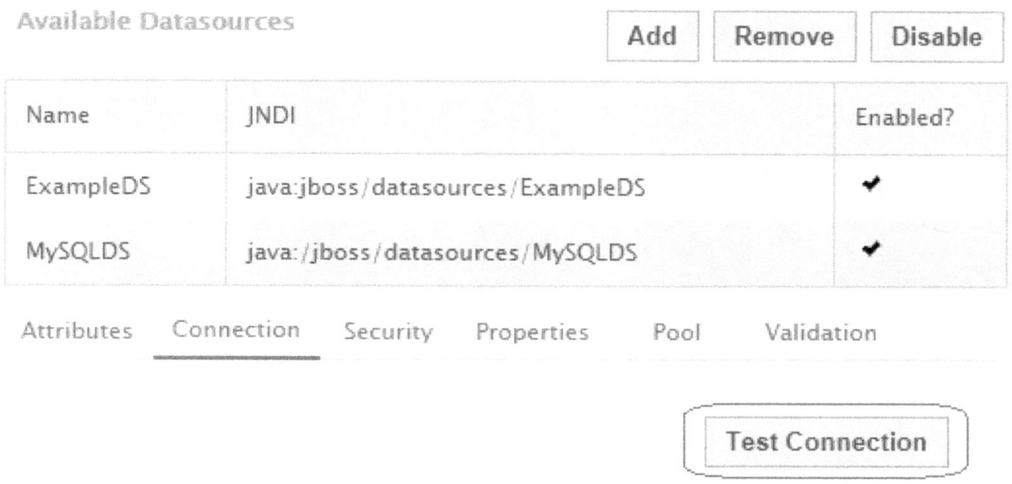

Available Datasources

| | Add | Remove | Disable |

Name	JNDI	Enabled?
ExampleDS	java:jboss/datasources/ExampleDS	✔
MySQLDS	java:/jboss/datasources/MySQLDS	✔

Attributes   Connection   Security   Properties   Pool   Validation

Test Connection

If the test succeeds you should see a message like "*Successfully created JDBC connection*" in a pop-up window.

Configuring the Datasource pool attributes

As it is, the data source is created using some default settings that might be good for an initial shot; however, you should consider varying them according to your application requirements. In order to do that, select your Datasource and then the **Pool** tab, just below the data source table. Inside the **Pool** panel, you can modify the pool attributes by clicking on **Edit**, as shown by the following picture:

Attributes   Connection   Security   Properties | Pool | Validation

☑ Edit   **Flush**

Min Pool Size: 0

Max Pool Size: 0

Strict Minimum: false

Prefill enabled: false

Flush Strategy:

Idle Timeout: 0

Track Statements:

Here's an explanation to the attributes included in the pool configuration:

Min Pool Size	The minimum number of connections in the pool (default 0)
Max Pool Size	The maximum number of connections in the pool (default 20)
Strict Minimum	Whether idle connections below the min-pool-size should be closed
Prefill Enabled	Attempt to pre-fill the connection pool to the minimum number of connections. This will check your connections as soon as the Datasource is installed.
Flush Strategy	Specifies how the pool should be flushed in case of an error. The default one (*FailingConnectionOnly*) forces destroying only connections with error. Possible values include also InvalidIdleConnections, IdleConnections, Gracefully, EntirePool, AllInvalidIdleConnections, AllIdleConnections, AllGracefully, AllConnections. Flush Strategies with the "All" prefix will be valid across all user's credentials in the DB, while the "Gracefully" suffix will wait for the connection to return to the pool before flushing. More info about it on IronJacamar docs:

	http://www.ironjacamar.org/doc/userguide/1.1/en-US/html/ch05.html
Idle Timeout	Specifies the maximum time, in minutes, a connection may be idle before being closed. The actual maximum time depends also on the IdleRemover scan time, which is half of the smallest idle-timeout-minutes value of any pool.
Track Statements	Whether to check for unclosed statements when a connection is returned to the pool, result sets are closed, a statement is closed or return to the prepared statement cache. Valid values are: "false" - do not track statements, "true" - track statements and result sets and warn when they are not closed, "nowarn" - track statements but do not warn about them being unclosed

 Please note that the Datasource needs to be **disabled** in order to change the pool attributes.

Configuring an XA Datasource

The above configuration can be used to install a Datasource which does not need a two-phase commit support; if, on the other hand, you need that your transactions span across multiple databases, then you need to install an **XA Datasource**.

In order to install the XA Datasource, check at first that you have created the module named "com.mysql" as described at the beginning of this chapter (See section "JDBC Module creation" for more information).

Next, you will need to include the Datasource and JDBC Driver definition within your server configuration. As you can see from the following snipped, the XA Datasource configuration is slightly different from the non-xa counterpart as it references the JDBC Connection parameters through a set of **xa-datasource-property**. In addition, the Driver class name needs to be updated accordingly to use the **com.mysql.jdbc.jdbc2.optional.MysqlXADataSource** class:

```
<datasources>
    . . . .
    <xa-datasource jndi-name="java:jboss/MysqlXADS" pool-name="MysqlXADS">
        <driver>mysql</driver>
        <xa-datasource-property name="ServerName">localhost</xa-datasource-property>
        <xa-datasource-property name="DatabaseName">mysqlschema</xa-datasource-property>

        <security>
            <user-name>jboss</user-name>
            <password>jboss</password>
        </security>

    </xa-datasource>
    <drivers>
        . . . .
        <driver name="mysql" module="com.mysql">
            <xa-datasource-class>com.mysql.jdbc.jdbc2.optional.MysqlXADataSource</xa-
datasource-class>
        </driver>
    </drivers>
</datasources>
```

Restart your server and from the Administration Console "**Connection**" sub panel you can check the Database connection via the "**Test Connection**" button.

Creating a Datasource using the Command Line Interface

Installing the data source using the Command Line Interface is the faster and recommended option as it can also be included in your scripts so that you can replicate it across your installations. Launch the *jboss-cli.sh/ jboss-cli.bat* and connect as usual.

The following command will install the **com.mysql** module creating for you the module directory structure just as we did at the beginning of this chapter:

```
module add --name=com.mysql --resources=c:\mysql\mysql-connector-java-5.1.24-bin.jar --
dependencies=javax.api,javax.transaction.api
```

Next, we need to install the JDBC driver using the above module:

```
/subsystem=datasources/jdbc-driver=mysql:add(driver-name=mysql,driver-module-
name=com.mysql)
```

At this point, although not mandatory, you can check that your MySQL driver is enlisted through the available JDBC Drivers:

```
[standalone@localhost:9990 /] /subsystem=datasources:installed-drivers-list
{
        . . . .
            "driver-name" => "mysql",
            "driver-module-name" => "com.mysql",
            "module-slot" => "main",
            "driver-xa-datasource-class-name" => "",
            "driver-class-name" => "com.mysql.jdbc.Driver",
            "jdbc-compliant" => false
        }
    ]
}
```

Finally, install the data source by using the **data-source** shortcut command, which requires as input the Pool name, the JNDI bindings, the JDBC Connection parameters and finally the security settings:

```
data-source add --jndi-name=java:/MySQLDS --name=MySQLPool --connection-
url=jdbc:mysql://localhost:3306/mysqlschema --driver-name=mysql --user-name=jboss --
password=jboss
```

Installing an XA Datasource using the Command Line Interface

If you are going to use an XA Datasource in your applications there are some changes that you need to apply to your CLI scripts. Start as usual by creating the module at first:

```
module add --name=com.mysql --resources=c:\mysql\mysql-connector-java-5.1.24-bin.jar --
dependencies=javax.api,javax.transaction.api
```

Next, install the JDBC driver using the above module:

```
/subsystem=datasources/jdbc-driver=mysql:add(driver-name=mysql,driver-module-
name=com.mysql)
```

Now we will use the **xa-data-source** shortcut command in order to create the XA Datasource. This command requires that you specify the Datasource name, its JNDI Bindings, the Datasource class (in our case *com.mysql.jdbc.jdbc2.optional.MysqlXADataSource*), the Security settings and, finally, at least one property must be specified (in our case we have specified the Server host name and the Database name):

```
xa-data-source add --name=MySqlDSXA --jndi-name=java:/MySqlDSXA --driver-name=mysql --xa-
datasource-class=com.mysql.jdbc.jdbc2.optional.MysqlXADataSource --user-name=jboss --
password=jboss --xa-datasource-
properties=[{ServerName=localhost},{DatabaseName=mysqlschema}]
```

Configuring a Datasource as a deployable resource

If you don't have access rights to the application server module folder, an alternative approach consists in distributing the JDBC driver into the deployments folder (which elects it to be a module as well) and then providing a –*ds.xml* file in the deployments folder of your standalone server. Let's see each step in detail:

Step 1: copy the JDBC driver into the deployments folder:

```
cp mysql-connector-java-5.1.24-bin.jar /usr/share/wildfly-
8.2.0.Final/standalone/deployments
```

Once copied the file, you should be able to see on your server logs that the driver has been deployed successfully:

```
09:32:10,400 INFO  [org.jboss.as.server] (DeploymentScanner-threads - 2) JBAS018559:
Deployed "mysql-connector-java-5.1.24-bin.jar"
```

Step 2: Deploy the data source file:

Now we will just fill in an xml file, which ends with -*ds.xml*; the syntax for this file is not different from the Datasource definition contained in your server configuration file. For example, this is a *mysql-ds.xml*, which is suitable for MySQL database:

```
<datasources xmlns="http://www.jboss.org/ironjacamar/schema">
  <datasource jndi-name="java:jboss/datasources/MySQLDS" pool-name="MySQLPool">
  <connection-url>jdbc:mysql://localhost:3306/mysqlschema</connection-url>
  <driver>mysql-connector-java-5.1.24-bin.jar</driver>
  <pool>
    <max-pool-size>30</max-pool-size>
  </pool>
  <security>
    <user-name>jboss</user-name>
    <password>jboss</password>
  </security>
  </datasource>
</datasources>
```

Once created the *-ds.xml* copy it in your **deployments** folder (or package it along with your applications). The application server should log your successful data source deployment:

```
09:37:45,949 INFO  [org.jboss.as.server.deployment] (MSC service thread 1-2) JBAS015876:
Starting deployment of "mysql-ds.xml"

09:37:46,001 INFO  [org.jboss.as.connector.subsystems.datasources] (MSC service thread 1-
8) JBAS010400: Bound data source [jboss/datasources/mysqlchema]

09:37:46,042 INFO  [org.jboss.as.server] (DeploymentScanner-threads - 2) JBAS018559:
Deployed "mysql-ds.xml"
```

Drawbacks?

You might wonder if there is any pitfall when using the older *-ds.xml* approach. Well actually if you "bypass" the management interface and deploy the Datasource by copying it in the *deployments* folder, you will not be able to manage it through the CLI or Web admin interface.

Hence, you should consider using deployable data source for development/testing purpose and rather switch to the module installation in a production environment.

Packaging Datasources in your applications

Data source definitions can be also packed in your application so that you don't have to modify at all the server configuration. The format of the deployable data source is the same described in the earlier section, where the data source was dropped in the deployments folder of the application server. When deploying data source as part of your application you have to add them in a specific folder, which varies depending on the application package format:

Application	Location
Web application (.war)	WEB-INF
EJB application (.jar)	META-INF
Enterprise application (.ear)	META-INF (of top level archive)

As an example, the following snapshot shows a Web application that ships with a data source definition named *example-ds.xml*:

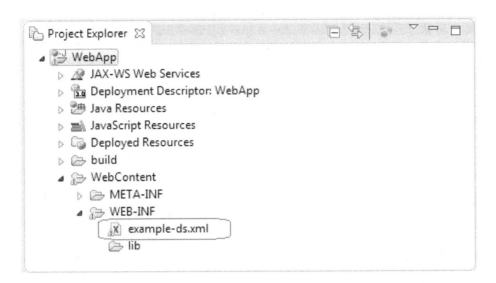

 Warning! As for deployable resources, you cannot manage these resources through the application server management interfaces; therefore should be used just for development or testing purposes.

In the above example we have just included the –ds.xml file in your application, therefore we suppose that you have separately deployed the mysql-connector-java-5.1.24-bin.jar into the deployments folder. As an alternative, you can pack the JDBC driver along with your application (in our example in the WEB-INF/lib folder) so that you create a self-consistent application.

Advanced Datasource configuration

In the last part of this chapter, we will discuss about some advanced configuration hints that can be applied to your Datasources. In particular we will learn how to avoid using clear text user name and password in your data source configuration and next how to use System Properties in your deployable Datasources.

Protecting a Datasource username and password

Until now, we have specified the username and password of your Datasource connection using clear text format; this can lead to a potential security hole in case a malicious user is able to intercept your datasource configuration. Luckily, it is possible to protect against these issues by specifying in your security area a **Security Domain** instead of clear text credentials:

```
<datasource jndi-name="java:jboss/datasources/MySQLDS" pool-name="MySQLPool">
  <connection-url>jdbc:mysql://localhost:3306/mysqlschema</connection-url>
  <driver>mysql</driver>
     <security>
        <security-domain>ds-encrypted</security-domain>
     </security>
</datasource>
```

Security domains are explained in detail in chapter 12 (see section "WildFly Security Domains"), however right now you can think of them as a database of user credentials which are used to access and use a sensitive resource.

Done with the Datasource, we will now specify the database password (which is "jboss") using an encrypted format. In order to do that, we can use a class named *SecureIdentityLoginModule* which is part of the PickteBox libraries. Launch the class name passing as parameter the text to encrypt as shown in the following example:

```
cd C:\wildfly-8.2.0.Final\modules\system\layers\base\org\picketbox\main>
java -classpath picketbox-4.0.21.Final.jar
org.picketbox.datasource.security.SecureIdentityLoginModule jboss
Encoded password: -e898e7e4930a22
```

Now create a **security domain** in your security subsystem and name it "**ds-encrypted**". This security domain will be based on the **SecureIdentityLoginModule** which takes as input the username, the encrypted password and some options such as the Database pool name (as part of the managedConnectionFactoryName):

```
<security-domain name="ds-encrypted" cache-type="default">
    <authentication>
        <login-module code="org.picketbox.datasource.security.SecureIdentityLoginModule"
flag="required">
            <module-option name="username" value="jboss"/>
            <module-option name="password" value="-e898e7e4930a22"/>
            <module-option name="managedConnectionFactoryName"
                      value="jboss.jca:service=LocalTxCM,name=MySQLDS"/>
        </login-module>
    </authentication>
</security-domain>
```

You should reload your configuration in order to see the above changes reflected. Next, you can verify from the Administration Console or the CLI if your connection pool is able to connect to the database. Example:

```
[standalone@localhost:9990 /] /subsystem=datasources/data-source=MySQLDS:test-connection-in-pool
{
    "outcome" => "success",
    "result" => [true]
}
```

Using System Properties in your deployable data sources

Sometimes it can be useful not to hardcode properties contained in your –ds.xml files. For example, in the following data source file we are defining the connection-url as a System Property:

```
<datasources xmlns="http://www.jboss.org/ironjacamar/schema">
  <datasource jndi-name="java:jboss/datasources/MySqlDS" pool-name="MySQLPool">
  <connection-url>${connection.url}</connection-url>
  <driver>mysql-connector-java-5.1.24-bin.jar</driver>
   . . . .
  </datasource>
</datasources>
```

In order to activate the replacement of the reference with the actual property, you have to check that the **jboss-descriptor-property-replacement** (part of the "ee" domain) is set to true.

```
<subsystem xmlns="urn:jboss:domain:ee:2.0">
  <jboss-descriptor-property-replacement>true</jboss-descriptor-property-replacement>
</subsystem>
```

Now you can either pass the System Property using the standard Java way (-D in the application server startup script) or adding a System Property element at the top of the configuration:

```
<system-properties>
   <property name="connection.url" value="jdbc:mysql://localhost:3306/mysqlschema"/>
</system-properties>
```

Configuring Multi Datasources

When configuring the connection-url parameter of the data source, it's possible to specify a set of JDBC URLs which is somewhat similar to Oracle WLS multi data source feature. You need to specify the list of connection urls and a **delimiter** to separate them:

```
<connection-url>jdbc:sqlserver://SERVER_ONE:1433;databaseName=MyDB|
               jdbc:sqlserver://SERVER_TWO:1433;databaseName=MyDB
</connection-url>
<url-delimiter>|</url-delimiter>
```

For a production environment, it's however recommended to use a more robust approach such as **Oracle Real Application Cluster (RAC)**, which allows data high availability. In the following example, we are using a connection-url, which features an Oracle RAC made up of two nodes (host1 and host2):

```
<connection-
url>jdbc:oracle:thin:@(description=(address_list=(load_balance=on)(failover=on)(address=(
protocol=tcp)(host=host1)(port=1521))(address=(protocol=tcp)(host=host2)(port=1521)))(con
nect_data=(service_name=sid)(failover_mode=(type=select)(method=basic))))</connection-
url>
```

Chapter 5: Configuring Webserver & EJB Container

This chapter introduces you to the new Web container, named **Undertow** that can be used to execute your Java EE 7 compliant Web applications. Since the Web server uses the Java NIO (New Input Output) API to construct its responses, we will also learn how to configure the **io** subsystem that is part of all server configurations. Finally, in the latter part of this chapter, we will learn how to configure as well the EJB container that now uses the Web server as a façade to remote clients. Summing up, here are the topics that we are going to discuss in this chapter:

- Undertow Web server architecture and configuration
- Input-Output Core subsystem configuration
- EJB Container configuration

Entering Undertow Web server

With the arrival of Java EE 7 and the requirement to handle advanced features such as the Web Sockets API and HTTP upgrades (e.g. EJB over HTTP), an important decision has been made by the WildFly development team. After a long commitment to JBoss Web Server (a fork of Apache Tomcat), the new release of the application server is now based on a new Web server named **Undertow**.

 Undertow makes a large use of XNIO (http://www.jboss.org/xnio) which is a low-level I/O layer which can be used anywhere to simplify the usage of NIO API. It solves out some of the complexities of using Selectors and the lack of NIO support for multicast sockets and non-socket I/O such as serial ports, while still maintaining all the capabilities available in NIO.

In terms of architecture, Undertow is designed around a composition-based architecture that allows you to build a fully functional Web server by combining small single components called **handlers**. These handlers are chained together to form either a fully functional Java EE servlet 3.1 container or a simpler HTTP Process handler embedded in your code.

As you can see from the following picture, an handler chain is composed of several individual handlers which eventually produce either a Servlet response or an error, for example in case that the requested Path is not found:

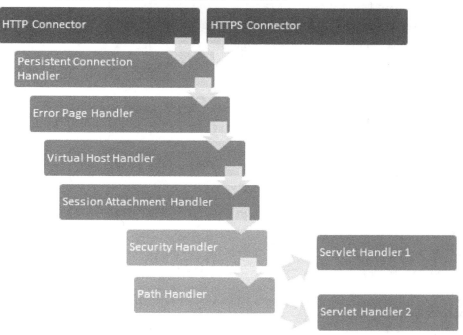

Undertow Web server also the flexibility to choose between the non-blocking asynchronous handlers to handle tasks, or delegate requests to a blocking handler, backed by a Thread Pool.

Undertow configuration under the hoods

The configuration of the Undertow web server is a combination of two core subsystems:

1) The **IO** subsystem where you can configure the Worker threads and Buffer pools used by the Web server. Here is the io subsystem contained in the server configuration, which merely contains the default worker name and buffer pool name:

```
<subsystem xmlns="urn:jboss:domain:io:1.1">
        <worker name="default"/>
        <buffer-pool name="default"/>
</subsystem>
```

2) The **Undertow** subsystem, which contains the core configuration of the Web server. Here is the default configuration of the Undertow Web server:

```xml
<subsystem xmlns="urn:jboss:domain:undertow:1.2">
    <buffer-cache name="default"/>
    <server name="default-server">
        <http-listener name="default" socket-binding="http"/>
        <host name="default-host" alias="localhost">
            <location name="/" handler="welcome-content"/>
            <filter-ref name="server-header"/>
            <filter-ref name="x-powered-by-header"/>
        </host>
    </server>
    <servlet-container name="default">
        <jsp-config/>
        <websockets/>
    </servlet-container>
    <handlers>
        <file name="welcome-content" path="${jboss.home.dir}/welcome-content"/>
    </handlers>
    <filters>
        <response-header name="server-header" header-name="Server" header-
value="WildFly/8"/>
        <response-header name="x-powered-by-header" header-name="X-Powered-By"
header-value="Undertow/1"/>
    </filters>
</subsystem>
```

As you can see, also the Undertow configuration relies largely on defaults and is not self-explanatory. We will therefore use the easy-to-go Administration console to dissect the Undertow listeners, the Servlet container and Worker threads configuration. Next, we will learn how to configure filters and reverse proxy attributes by means of the Command Line Interface.

Configuring the Undertow Listeners

The heart of Undertow configuration is contained in the **HTTP** option, which is available by expanding the **Web** left panel option.

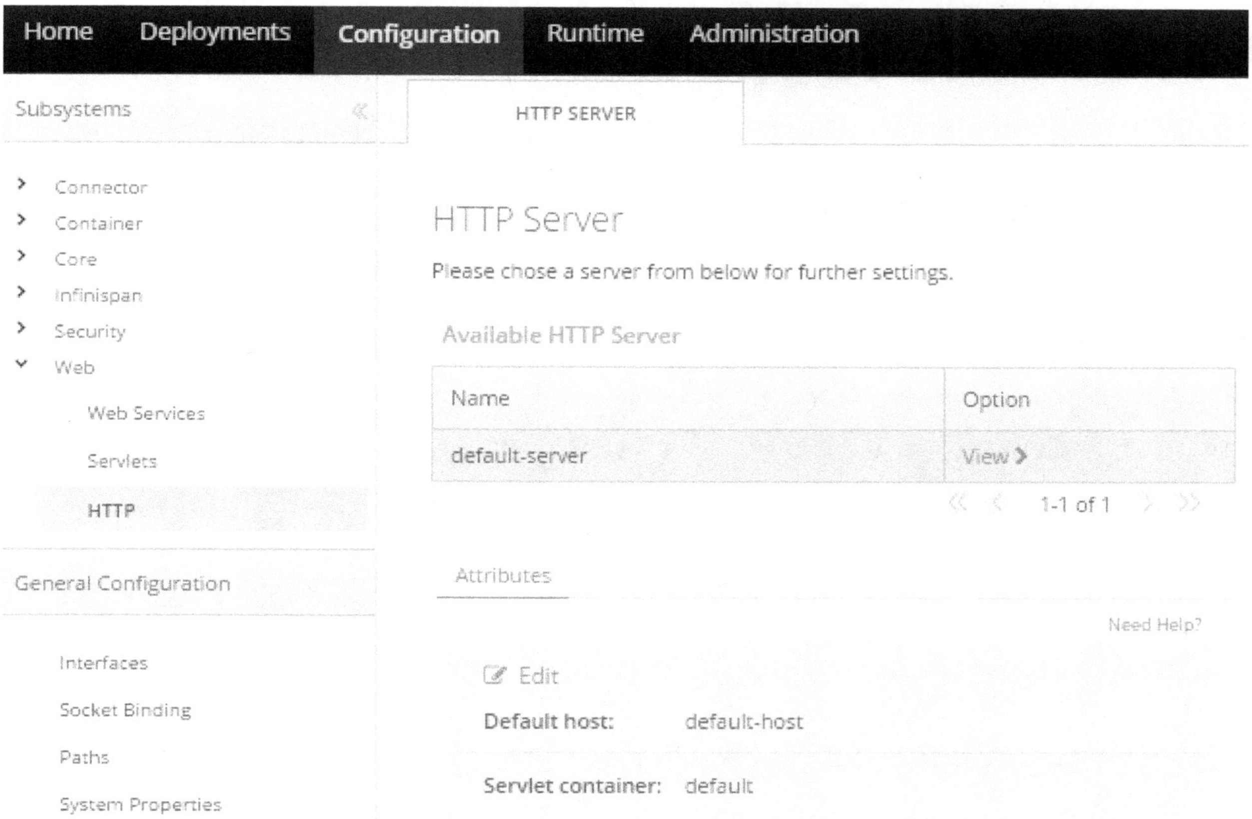

| Home | Deployments | Configuration | Runtime | Administration |

Subsystems «

HTTP SERVER

> Connector
> Container
> Core
> Infinispan
> Security
˅ Web

  Web Services

  Servlets

HTTP

General Configuration

Interfaces

Socket Binding

Paths

System Properties

HTTP Server

Please chose a server from below for further settings.

Available HTTP Server

Name	Option
default-server	View ›

《 ‹ 1-1 of 1 › 》

Attributes

Need Help?

✐ Edit

Default host: default-host

Servlet container: default

The server named "**default-server**" maps the corresponding attribute contained in the "server" subsystem configuration. In order to configure the Undertow listeners, click on the **View** link, next to the default-server. You will be taken to the following screen, where you will be able to configure the available Server listeners:

< Back | HTTP Listener | HTTPS Listener | AJP Listener | Hosts

HTTP Listener

	Add	Remove

Name	Is Enabled?
default	true

‹ ‹ 1-1 of 1 › ››

Attributes

Need Help?

☑ Edit

Allow encoded slash:	false
Allow equals in cookie value:	false
Always set keep alive:	true
Buffer pipelined data:	true
Buffer pool:	default

From the Mid-panel screen, you will have the following set of options available:

- **HTTP Listener**: used to configure the Web server listener in the default (clear text) mode
- **HTTPs Listener**: used to configure the Web server listener when using a secure protocol for communication
- **AJP Listener**: used for configuring the connectivity using the AJP Protocol (used to receive requests from an Apache Web server front-end)
- **Hosts**: used to configure the host settings such as the virtual host settings and the default root Web application

The list of configurable attributes for the listeners is pretty lengthy; for a quick reference, we suggest having a look at the **Management Model** option and look into the listeners description available under "*/subsystem=undertow/server=default-server*"

As far as it concerns the HTTP listener attributes, the following table, however, summarizes them with a short description of each property:

Property	Description
Allow encoded slash	If true, enables encoding characters (i.e. %2F).
Allow equals in cookie value	If this is true then Undertow will allow non-escaped equals characters in unquoted cookie values. Unquoted cookie values may not contain equals characters. If present the value ends before the equals sign. The remainder of the cookie value will be dropped.
Always set keep alive	If this is true then a Connection: keep-alive header will be added to responses, even when it is not strictly required by the specification.
Buffer pipelined data	If set to true, pipelined requests are buffered.
Buffer pool:	The buffer pool to be used by the listener (See *"Configuring Undertow buffer pool"*).
Certificate forwarding	If certificate forwarding should be enabled. If this is enabled then the listener will take the certificate from the SSL_CLIENT_CERT attribute. This should only be enabled if behind a proxy, and the proxy is configured to always set these headers.
Decode url	If this is true then the parser will decode the URL and query parameters using the selected character encoding (UTF-8 by default). If this is false they will not be decoded.
Enabled	If true, enables the listener.
Max buffered request size	Maximum size of a buffered request, in bytes.
Max cookies	The maximum number of cookies that will be parsed.
Max header size	The maximum size in bytes of a http request header.
Max headers	The maximum number of headers that will be parsed. This is used to protect against hash vulnerabilities.
Max parameters	The maximum number of parameters that will be parsed. This is used to protect against hash vulnerabilities.This applies to both query parameters, and to POST data, but is not cumulative

Max post size	The maximum size of a post that will be accepted
No request timeout	How long a connection can sit idle with no requests before being closed
Proxy address forwarding	Enables x-forwarded-host and similar headers and set a remote ip address and hostname
Read timeout	Configure a read timeout for a socket, in milliseconds. If the given amount of time elapses without a successful read taking place, the socket's next read will throw a ReadTimeoutException.
Receive buffer	Configures the receive buffer size.
Record request start time	If this is true then Undertow will record the request start time, to allow for request time to be logged. This has a small performance impact.
Redirect socket	If this listener is supporting non-SSL requests, and a request is received for which a matching requires SSL transport, undertow will automatically redirect the request to the socket binding port specified here.
Request parse timeout	The maximum amount of time that can be spent parsing a request.
Resolve peer address	If true enables host dns lookup. It has a negative impact on performance.
Send buffer	The send buffer size in bytes.
Socket binding	The socket binding to be used by the listener.
Tcp backlog:	Configure a server with the specified backlog.
Tcp keep alive	Configure a channel to send TCP keep-alive messages in an implementation-dependent manner.
Url charset	The URL charset used.
Worker	The XNIO worker to be used by the listener. To be used for configuring the Web server pool.
Write timeout	Configure a write timeout for a socket, in milliseconds. If the given amount of time elapses without a successful write taking place, the socket's next write will throw a WriteTimeoutException.

Configuring the Web server Pool

XNIO workers are the central point of coordination of undertow network activity. There are two types of XNIO workers, which are used by Undertow:

- **I/O threads**, which perform non-blocking tasks and are used to handle callback events for read/write operations.
- **Worker threads**, which are from a fully configurable standard Executor-based thread pool. When performing blocking operations such as Servlet requests, the **Worker** threads will come into play.

 Worker are easy to detect on log files and stack traces as they are tagged with the **Worker name**, to make them easier to identify in thread dumps and log files.

The default configuration of the Worker threads used by Undertow uses a **bounded-queue-thread-pool** configuration. The bounded-queue-thread-pool thread pool executor has a **core**, a **maximum size**, and a specified **queue** length. The following picture depicts a workflow of a bounded-queue thread pool:

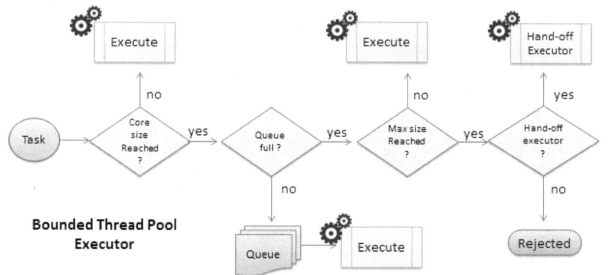

As you can see, if the number of running threads is less than the core size when a task is submitted, a new thread will be created; otherwise, it will be put in the queue. If there is no room in the queue but the maximum number of threads hasn't been reached, a new thread is also created. If max-threads is hit, the call will be sent to the handoff-executor. Finally, if no handoff-executor is configured, the call will be discarded.

Getting into the Web server Pool configuration

Now that we aware of the inner details of Undertow executors let's see how to configure them. From the Administration console, expand the **Core** option from the left tree menu and select "**IO**" as shown by this picture:

The "**Worker**" tab needs to be selected from the main panel. As you can see a "default" worker already exists. You can at any time Create or Remove new ones by clicking on the corresponding buttons. However right now we will click on the "**Edit**" link so that we customize the number of Threads to be used in our default Worker. Once clicked on the link, we will edit the following attributes:

Subsystems	WORKER	BUFFER POOL

Attributes

✎ Edit

- Connector
- Container
- Core
  - IO
  - Logging
  - Deployment Scanners
  - JMX
- Infinispan
- Security
- Web

Io threads: `25`

Stack size: `0`

Task core threads: `2`

Task keepalive: `60`

Task max threads: ` `

General Configuration

Interfaces

Cancel   **Save**

The number of **Io threads** corresponds to the number of Web server Threads available. This is an important tuning parameter, which needs to be increased for Web applications, which experience a high traffic.

The **Stack size** corresponds to the Web server Thread stack size. With a larger Thread stack size, the Web server will consume more resources, and thus fewer users can be supported.

The **Task core threads** and **Task max threads** correspond to the max-threads and max-threads of the XNIO pool discussed before.

The **Task keepalive** (default 60) controls the number of seconds to wait for the next request from the same client on the same connection. With Keep-Alives the browser gets to eliminate a full round trip for every request after the first, usually cutting full page load times in half.

Click **Save** when you are fine with your IO Worker configuration.

 Provided that there are enough **io-threads** to serve your http request, the **core-max-threads** (first) and the **task-max-threads** (after) are used to determine in the request is served or if it is going to be discarded.

Now that we have refined our IO Worker configuration, we will learn how the Undertow subsystem can reference it. In order to do that, from the left tree menu expand the **Web** subsystem and select the **HTTP** option. From there, select the Listener you want to associate with the Executor. In our case, we will reference the **HTTP Listener**:

Subsystems «		HTTP SERVER			
		‹ Back HTTP Listener HTTPS Listener AJP Listener Hosts			
> Connector					
> Container		Tcp keep alive:	☐		
> Core					
> Infinispan		Url charset:	UTF-8		
> Security					
∨ Web		Worker:	default		
Web Services					
Servlets		Write timeout:			
HTTP			Cancel	Save	

The worker needs to be **enabled** in order to be usable. Next, we need to associate the HTTP listener with a **Socket binding** (see from the General Configuration left menu the option Socket Binding to check the available socket bindings for your configuration). Finally, an HTTP server is also bound to a Java NIO **Buffer Pool** implementation, which is discussed in the next section.

Once you have completed your HTTP's worker configuration, the Web server will use its worker Threads which are named using the following criteria: **[worker name]-[worker id].** The Thread pool can then be monitored using any tool like the JConsole utility (included as part of the JDK standard edition) that allows printing a dump of the Threads stack traces running in a JVM:

```
Threads
xmu-me-watcher [watcher for D. (wild
RMI TCP Accept-0                        Name: default task-1
RMI TCP Connection(1)-192.168.1.65      State: WAITING on java.util.concurrent.locks.AbstractQueuedSynchronizer$Conditic
RMI Scheduler(0)                        Total blocked: 0  Total waited: 1
JMX server connection timeout 106
RMI TCP Connection(2)-192.168.1.65      Stack trace:
RMI TCP Connection(3)-192.168.1.65      sun.misc.Unsafe.park(Native Method)
RMI TCP Connection(4)-192.168.1.65      java.util.concurrent.locks.LockSupport.park(LockSupport.java:186)
default task-1                          java.util.concurrent.locks.AbstractQueuedSynchronizer$ConditionObject.await(Abst
default task-2                          java.util.concurrent.LinkedBlockingQueue.take(LinkedBlockingQueue.java:442)
default task-3                          java.util.concurrent.ThreadPoolExecutor.getTask(ThreadPoolExecutor.java:1068)
default task-4                          java.util.concurrent.ThreadPoolExecutor.runWorker(ThreadPoolExecutor.java:1130)
default task-5                          java.util.concurrent.ThreadPoolExecutor$Worker.run(ThreadPoolExecutor.java:615)
default task-6                          java.lang.Thread.run(Thread.java:745)
default task-7
```

Please note that if you don't provide a Worker thread configuration to Undertow, the application server will **automatically configure the Web server thread pool** by looking at the number of processors available on the machine and sizing the pool appropriately.

Configuring Undertow Buffer Pool

As we said, Undertow is based on the Java NIO API and makes use of a pool of J2SE's *java.nio.ByteBuffer* whenever buffering is needed.

 A **Buffer** is an object, which holds some data, that is to be written to or that has just been read from. The addition of the Buffer object in NIO marks one of the most significant differences between the new library and original I/O. In stream-oriented I/O you used to write data directly to, and read data directly from, *Stream objects*. In the NIO library, all data is handled with *Buffers*. When data is read, it is read directly into a buffer. When data is written, it is written into a buffer. Anytime you access data in NIO, you are pulling it out of the Buffer.

Undertow IO Buffer Pool configuration is contained in the **Core | IO** left menu, within the **Buffer Pools** option as shown by the following picture:

WORKER   BUFFER POOL

> Connector
> Container
∨ Core

   IO

   Logging

   Deployment Scanners

   JMX

> Infinispan
> Security
> Web

General Configuration

   Interfaces

   Socket Binding

   Paths

   System Properties

Buffer Pools

Please chose a buffer pool from below for specific settings.

Available Buffer Pool

| | Add | Remove |

Name
default

Attributes

Need Help?

✎ Edit

Buffer size:

Buffers per slice:

Direct buffers:

A short description, along with the default values for the Buffer Pools is contained in the following table:

Buffers per slice	This parameter defines how many buffers per slice are assigned. Slices are used for manipulating sub-portions of large buffers, avoiding the overhead of processing the entire buffer. Default value:128
Direct buffers	A Direct buffer is a kind of buffer that is allocated outside the Java heap; hence, their memory address is fixed for the lifetime of the buffer. This in turn causes that the kernel can safely access them directly and, hence, direct buffers can be used more efficiently in I/O operations. Default value: true
Buffer size	This option let you define the *java.nio.ByteBuffer* size. Provided that *direct* buffers are being used, the default 16kb buffers are optimal if maximum performance is required (as this corresponds to the default socket buffer size on Linux). Default value: 16384

Configuring the Servlet Container and JSP Settings

If you are interested in configuring the settings of your **Servlet Container**, then expand the **Web** left side option and choose **Servlets**. Within this option panel, you will be able to configure the Servlet Container settings which are contained in the lower part of the Mid Panel, as shown by the following picture:

The most important setting is the Default **HTTP Session timeout**, which governs the length (in minutes) of the HTTP Session. By default, this attribute is set to 30 minutes. The following table details all the available attributes:

Attribute	Description
Allow non-standard wrappers	If true then request and response wrappers that do not extend the standard wrapper classes can be used
Default buffer cache	The buffer cache to use for caching static resources
Default encoding	Default encoding to use for all deployed applications
Default session timeout	The default session timeout (in minutes) for all applications deployed in the container.
Disable caching for secured pages	If Undertow should set headers to disable caching for secured paged. Disabling this can cause security problems, as sensitive pages may be cached by an intermediary.
Eager filter initialization	If true undertow calls filter init() on deployment start rather than when first requested.
Ignore flush	Ignore flushes on the servlet output stream. In most cases these just hurt performance for no good reason.
Stack trace on error	If an error page with the stack trace should be generated on error. Values are all, none and local-only
Use listener encoding	Use encoding defined on listener

By clicking on the available Servlet container (default) and clicking on the **View** link, you will be able to configure the JSP Settings for the Servlet container.

The number of JSP Settings, which are configurable, is quite large and the following picture depicts a part of them:

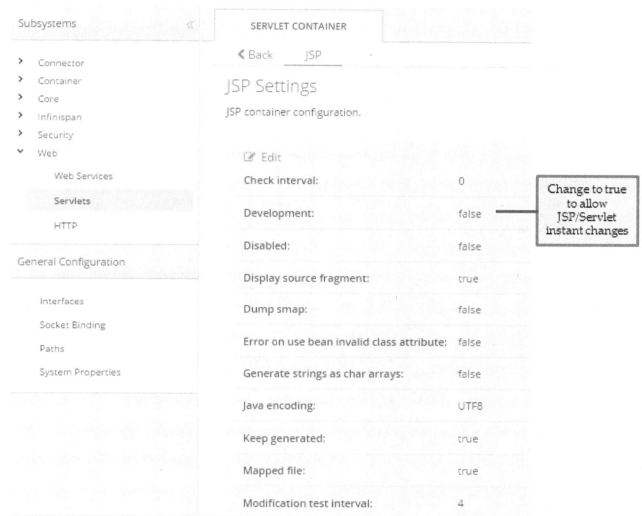

Subsystems

> Connector
> Container
> Core
> Infinispan
> Security
∨ Web
    Web Services
    Servlets
    HTTP

General Configuration

    Interfaces
    Socket Binding
    Paths
    System Properties

SERVLET CONTAINER

‹ Back   JSP

JSP Settings

JSP container configuration.

✎ Edit

Check interval:	0
Development:	false
Disabled:	false
Display source fragment:	true
Dump smap:	false
Error on use bean invalid class attribute:	false
Generate strings as char arrays:	false
Java encoding:	UTF8
Keep generated:	true
Mapped file:	true
Modification test interval:	4

Change to true to allow JSP/Servlet instant changes

The most important setting is the **Development** mode that affects the way your changes are reflected in your deployed applications (when set to true enables on-the-fly reload of JSP pages). Of set to true, a check is done based on the Check Interval to control if the JSP pages have been changed.

For your reference, we have included a short description for all the properties that you can set in the following table:

Check interval:	Check interval for JSP updates using a background thread.
Development:	Enable Development mode which enables reloading JSP on-the-fly
Disabled:	Enable the JSP container.
Display source fragment:	When a runtime error occurs, attempts to display corresponding JSP source fragment
Dump smap:	If set to true, dumps the SMAP info for JSR 045 debugging to a file.
Error on use bean invalid class attribute:	If set to true, causes a compilation error when the bean can't be instantiated. The default value is false.
Generate strings as char arrays:	Generate String constants as char arrays.
Java encoding:	Specify the encoding used for Java sources. Default value is UTF8.
Keep generated:	Keep the generated Servlets.
Mapped file:	Map to the JSP source.
Modification test interval:	Minimum amount of time between two tests for updates, in seconds. Default is 4 seconds.
Recompile on fail:	Retry failed JSP compilations on each request.
Scratch dir:	Specify a different work directory.
Smap:	If true, generates some debugging support for other languages (JSR 045). The default value is true.
Source vm:	Source VM level for compilation.
Tag pooling:	If set to true, tag handler instances are pooled and reused.
Target vm:	Target VM level for compilation.
Trim spaces:	Allows some optimization by trimming some spaces from the generated Servlet.
X powered by:	Enable advertising the JSP engine in x-powered-by.

Configuring Undertow filters

One peculiar feature of the Undertow Web server is the ability to include **custom filters** to the underlying HTTP Connection. This can result in adding custom header elements to the HTTP response. For example, here is how to set the "**No Cache**" header to the response:

```
/subsystem=undertow/configuration=filter/response-header=Cache-Control/:add(header-
value=no-cache,header-name=Cache-Control)
```

Another kind of filter, which is available out of the box, is the **gzip** filter, which instructs Undertow to return, zipped content if the browser can handle it, saving bandwidth and time:

```
/subsystem=undertow/configuration=filter/gzip=gzipfilter/:add
```

Configuring Undertow as reverse proxy

A **Reverse Proxy** is a common component used in network architecture to proxy data on behalf of backend HTTP servers. It works as a gateway to an HTTP server or HTTP server farm by acting as the final IP address for requests from the outside.

> A reverse proxy differs from the forward proxy, which is used to proxy data on behalf the client's request.

Undertow can act as reverse proxy in order to proxy a mix of protocols such as HTTP and AJP. It currently supports proxy load balancing using a round-robin algorithm and in the future will be able to support as well load balancing using mod_cluster. (See chapter 9 for more information about mod_cluster).

Configuring reverse proxy support can be done either via the Admin console or via the CLI. We will show here how to do it via the CLI. Start by creating a new reverse proxy element:

```
/subsystem=undertow/configuration=handler/reverse-proxy=demo-proxy:add
```

Now in order to proxy the app named "myapp" to the HTTP endpoint 192.168.10.1

```
/subsystem=undertow/configuration=handler/reverse-proxy=demo-
proxy/host=http\:\/\/192.168.10.1\/my-app:add
```

Now, as final step bind your reverse proxy to your host configuration as follows:

```
/subsystem=undertow/server=default-server/host=default-host/location=\/my-
app:add(handler=demo-proxy)
```

Much the same way, you can add other protocol endpoint configurations to your proxy, such as AJP proxying:

```
/subsystem=undertow/configuration=handler/reverse-proxy=demo-
proxy/host=ajp\:\/\/192.168.10.1\/my-app:add
```

Configuring the EJB container

Next section of this chapter discusses about the EJB container configuration, which contains many settings that affect the performance of your Java EE applications. In particular, we will learn how to configure the EJB container through the following units:

- **Stateless and Message Driven Bean pool** configuration: this section discusses about defining the number of EJB used in a pool
- **Stateful bean cache** configuration: this part of the chapter will illustrate how to configure your Stateful session beans (SFSBs) cache used to store conversational state.
- **EJB thread pool** configuration: since the EJB container uses a Thread pool to serve the different type of beans, we will complete the chapter by showing how to configure its pool of threads.

As with other areas, we will use the Web Administration Console or the Command Line Interface to track the configuration profile and update it accordingly.

Configuring the Stateless and Message Driven Bean Pool

Java EE containers typically allow storing stateless beans (SLSBs) and message driven beans (MDBs) in a pool. A bean in the pool represents the pooled state in the EJB lifecycle. A pooled EJB does not have an identity. The advantage of having beans in the pool is that the time to create a bean can be saved for a request.

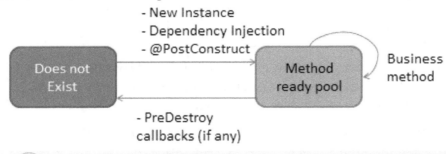

 Pooling is not a mandatory requirement of EJB specifications. The EJB container can either pool the instances or create a new one for each request. Since WildFly 8, EJB pooling is *not* enabled by default. See section "Enabling EJB pooling".

The pool for stateless session beans needs to be sized, based on the number of stateless session beans in the application, and the concurrency rate in which those beans are invoked. The key parameter used by is named **max-pool-size**.

You can change this parameter through the Web console: select the **Configuration** tab, expand **Container** and then select **EJB 3**. Click on the Bean Pools tab as shown in the following picture:

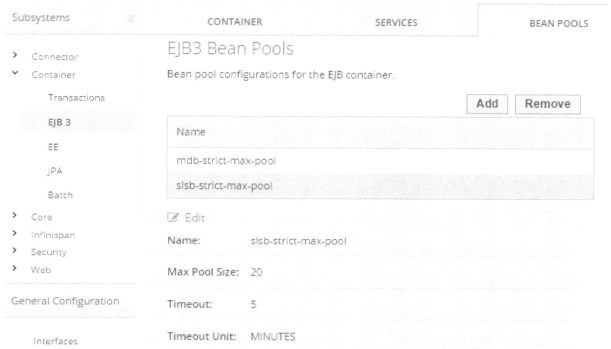

From the above picture, you can see the EJB pools configurations available. By default, two configurations are included:

- **mdb-strict-max-pool**: default pool used by Message driven beans
- **slsb-strict-max-pool**: default pool used by Stateless session beans

By clicking on the **Add** and **Remove** buttons, you can create/delete pool definitions. On the other hand, if you want to edit an EJB 3 pool, select the pool from the list and click **Edit**.

The parameters, which you can set, are the following:

Max Pool Size	The maximum number of beans allowed in the pool
Timeout	The maximum time the container waits to acquire an instance from the pool before raising an exception.
Timeout Unit	Specifies the time unit (Nanoseconds up to Days) used in Timeout parameter.

The actual pool used by the EJB container is defined into the **Container** Tab of the EJB 3 configuration screen. The next picture shows the Container view:

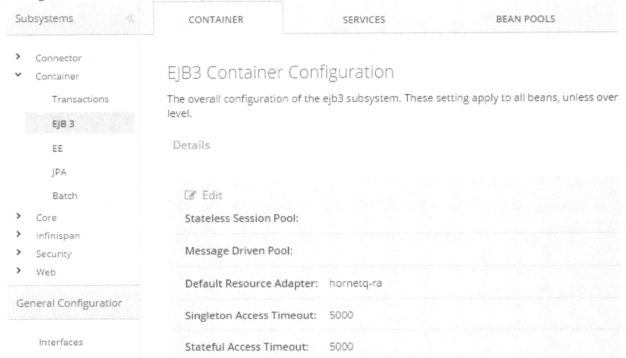

The EJB3 Container Configuration is a key point of your WildFly configuration as it lets you define the following parameters:

- The **Stateless Session Pool**: this is the pool to be associated with Stateless Session Beans.

- The **Message Driven pool**: this is the pool to be associated with Message Driven Beans.

- The **Default resource adapter:** which defaults to hornetq resource adapter (See next section named *"Using a different resource adapter for your MDBs"* for more information about it)

- The **EJB Singleton** Access Timeout.

- The **Stateful Access Timeout**. Access Timeout.

Enabling the Stateless Session Bean Pool

The configuration that we have seen so far lets you define the pool to be used by the EJB Container (e.g. slsb-strict-max-pool) and its key parameters. However, as we have anticipated, **EJB pooling is**

not enabled by default on WildFly 8. The rationale behind this decision is that an accurate pool size is tightly dependent on your application and cannot be easily guessed. Therefore, a poorly configured pool of EJBs could be even detrimental in terms of performance, causing excessive cycles of garbage collections. For this reasons, it's up to you to turn on this feature and set a correct configuration for its parameters.

This requires however just as little as a combo box selection from the **EJB3 Container** tab:

✐ Edit

Stateless Session Pool:	slsb-strict-max-pool ▼
Message Driven Pool:	▼
Default Resource Adapter:	hornetq-ra
Singleton Access Timeout:	5000
Stateful Access Timeout:	5000

Cancel   **Save**

As you can see from the above picture, we have set the Stateless Session Pool to use the **slsb-strict-max-pool** that ships with the default configuration

Configuring the Stateful Session Bean cache

Stateful session beans require a different implementation from the container than the stateless counterpart. There are several reasons for it:

- At first, because they maintain state, that state is associated exclusively with one session, so there is just one instance per session.
- Second, since they are bound to one session, the container must prevent any concurrent modification to that state.
- Third, because they maintain state, that state needs to be part of a clustering HA configuration.
- Last, if the instance is not accessed in a period of time, and the bean is not in use, the state may be *passivated* to disk.

For this reasons Stateful beans are hold in a **cache** instead of a pool of anonymous instances. As you can see from the following CLI query, the default cache used by Stateful Session Beans is the "**simple**" cache, which uses an indeed simple Caching mechanism that does not include **passivation** of session data to the disk:

```
/subsystem=ejb3/:read-resource(recursive=true)
    "outcome" => "success",
    "result" => {
        "default-clustered-sfsb-cache" => undefined,

        . . . .

        "default-sfsb-cache" => "simple",
        "default-stateful-bean-access-timeout" => 5000L,

    . . . .

    "cache" => {
        "simple" => {
            "aliases" => ["NoPassivationCache"],
            "passivation-store" => undefined
        },
        "passivating" => {
            "aliases" => ["SimpleStatefulCache"],
            "passivation-store" => "file"
        }
    }
}
```

 This cache can be used if you have a very limited amount of SFSBs clients in your applications, as elements won't be removed after a certain timeout either. So, you should only use this method if you can guarantee that you'll be calling the @**Remove** method of the SFSB once you're done with it.

You can switch to a more robust cache strategy by setting the "**passivating**" cache as default strategy, which will store to disk instances

```
/subsystem=ejb3/:write-attribute(name=default-sfsb-cache,value=passivating)
```

Setting the rules for passivating SFSBs

When using the passivating cache, by default SFSBs will be passivated after being idle for 300 seconds or when they exceed 100000 units. The location used for passivating SFSBs data is by default the *jboss.server.data.dir*. You can check it by issuing the following CLI query:

```
/subsystem=ejb3/file-passivation-store=file/:read-resource()
{
    "outcome" => "success",
    "result" => {
        "groups-path" => "ejb3\\groups",
        "idle-timeout" => 300L,
        "idle-timeout-unit" => "SECONDS",
        "max-size" => 100000,
        "relative-to" => "jboss.server.data.dir",
        "sessions-path" => "ejb3\\sessions",
        "subdirectory-count" => 100
    }
}
```

You can at any time change the above attributes, here's for example how to set the idle timeout to 600 seconds:

```
/subsystem=ejb3/file-passivation-store=file/:write-attribute(name=idle-timeout,value=600)
```

Conversely, here' how you can double the capacity of your passivating cache:

```
/subsystem=ejb3/file-passivation-store=file/:write-attribute(name=max-size,value=200000)
```

 Please note that the above configuration is intended to be used for non-clustered environment. In a clustered environment, you will rely on the clustered caches provided by Infinispan subsystem.

Disabling passivation for single deployments

Since EJB 3.2 there is a portable way for disabling passivation of Stateful Beans. This can be achieved either via the default *ejb-jar.xml* configuration file or by annotation directly on the Bean class. In the following example, we are disabling passivation for the Stateful Session Bean named "ExampleSFSB" by setting to **false** the passivation-capable element contained in the *ejb-jar.xml* configuration file:

```
<ejb-jar xmlns="http://xmlns.jcp.org/xml/ns/javaee"
    xmlns:xsi="http://www.w3.org/2001/XMLSchema-instance"
    xsi:schemaLocation="http://xmlns.jcp.org/xml/ns/javaee
    http://xmlns.jcp.org/xml/ns/javaee/ejb-jar_3_2.xsd"
    version="3.2">
  <enterprise-beans>
```

```xml
    <session>
      <ejb-name>ExampleSFSB</ejb-name>
      <ejb-class>com.sample.ExampleSFSB</ejb-class>
      <session-type>Stateful</session-type>
      <passivation-capable>false</passivation-capable>
    </session>
    ...
  </enterprise-beans>
</ejb-jar>
```

This is the corresponding annotation which can be applied at Class level:

```java
@javax.ejb.Stateful(passivationCapable=false)
public class ExampleSFSB {
....
}
```

Setting the Access timeout for SFSBs and Singleton beans

Stateful and Singleton Session Beans have an access timeout value specified for managing concurrent access.

> As the name implies a **Singleton bean** is a Session Bean with a guarantee that there is at most one instance per JVM in the application.

This value is the period of time that a request to a session bean method can be blocked before it will timeout. You can set the access timeout via Web Interface (EJB3 Container window) or CLI. Here's how to do it with a simple CLI command:

```
/subsystem=ejb3/:write-attribute(name=default-stateful-bean-access-timeout,value=5000)
```

The timeout value and the time unit used can also be specified using the **@javax.ejb.AccessTimeout** annotation on the SFSB/Singleton method. It can be specified on the session bean (which applies to all the bean's methods) and on specific methods to override the configuration for the bean.

Configuring EJB 3 Thread pool

WildFly 8 maintains a number of instances of Java thread objects in memory for use by Enterprise Bean services, including remote invocation, the timer service, and asynchronous invocation. The EJB Thread pool is used as first layer for client requesting EJBs, as shown by the following picture, which shows the typical invocation, chain from a remote EJB client that is done through the HTTP layer.

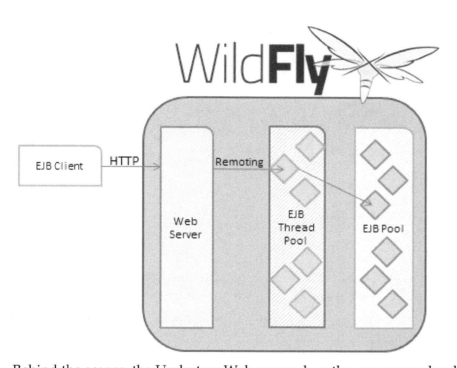

Behind the scenes, the Undertow Web server does the necessary plumbing to route the request to the EJB Thread pool using the Remoting protocol. Once that a thread instance is acquired, the call is routed to the EJB Session Bean pool where the actual methods are invoked. If the EJBs are not configured in a pool (default), a new instance for the EJB is returned on each call.

The default Thread pool executor used to serve EJB requests is a Thread pool with an **unbounded** queue. Such a Thread pool has a **core size** and a **queue** with no upper bound. When a task is submitted, if the number of running threads is less than the core size, a new thread is created. Otherwise, the task is placed in queue. If too many tasks are allowed to be submitted to this type of executor, an out of memory condition may occur.

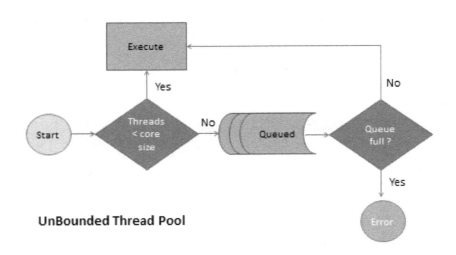

UnBounded Thread Pool

You can reach the EJB3 thread pool configuration by expanding the **Container | EJB 3** element in the left-handed menu, then select the **Thread Pools** tab as shown by this picture:

From the above window, you can configure the following parameters:

Max Threads	This element (**max-threads** attribute in CLI terms) specifies the maximum number of threads used by the EJB container for serving EJB clients.
Keepalive Timeout	This element (**keepalive-time** in CLI terms) is used to specify the amount of time that threads should be kept running when idle; if not specified, threads will run until the executor is shut down. The timeout is expressed by default in Milliseconds, though you can vary this unit by setting the Keepalive Timeout unit.
Thread Factory	This element (**thread-factory** in CLI terms) specifies the name of a specific thread factory to use to create worker threads. If not defined, an appropriate default thread factory will be used.

You can define as many EJB3 thread pools as you like: the actual pool that will be used is configured in the **Services** tab, where you can set the thread pool for all configurable services that are part of the EJB3 subsystem (Timer Service, Async Service and EJB 3 Remote Service) as shown by the following picture:

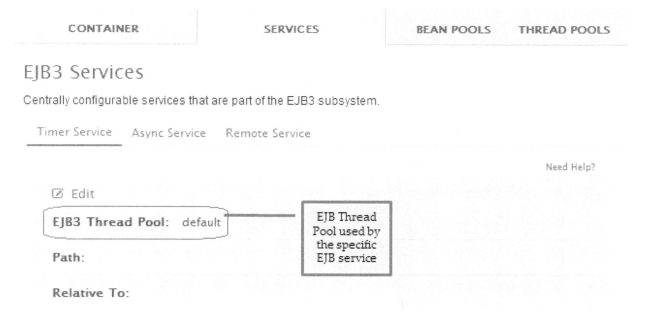

Please note that invocations on local EJBs happen on the thread of the originating client (for example a servlet whose thread semantics are configured in web subsystem). Remote invocations make use of the thread pool that's configured in the EJB3 subsystem and @Asynchronous invocations too make use of the thread pool configured in the EJB3 subsystem.

Configuring Remote EJB Transport

WildFly 8 uses the **Remoting** framework in order to provide remote access to EJBs. In the earlier release of the application server (AS7) this framework used a Socket transport (which landed on port 4447 of the application server) in order to connect the remote client and the EJB container. As we have seen in the earlier section, this communication stack is not used anymore and remote EJB clients invocations happen on the HTTP port on port 8080 using an underlying mechanism called **HTTP-upgrade**;

That's surely a good news for system administrators which will not need to configure a firewall exception to allow remote EJB access and even a better news if you are planning to deploy your application on a cloud.

The actual configuration of the remoting protocol can be checked out using the CLI with a simple **read-resource** to be issued on the remoting susbsystem:

```
/subsystem=remoting/:read-resource()
{
    "outcome" => "success",
    "result" => {
        "worker-read-threads" => 1,
        "worker-task-core-threads" => 4,
        "worker-task-keepalive" => 60,
        "worker-task-limit" => 16384,
        "worker-task-max-threads" => 16,
        "worker-write-threads" => 1,
        "connector" => undefined,
        "http-connector" => {"http-remoting-connector" => undefined},
        "local-outbound-connection" => undefined,
        "outbound-connection" => undefined,
        "remote-outbound-connection" => undefined
    }
}
```

Besides the connector -which is http-connector as we said- the transport mechanism uses a pool of XNIO threads in order dispatch calls to the EJB container. The number of core threads for the remoting worker task thread pool is determined by the element **worker-task-core-threads** while the maximum number of threads for the remoting worker task thread pool is set by the element **max-threads**. These two elements, together, are used as a constraint to prevent thread pool exaustion (see the section "Configuring the Web server Pool" for more details about the XNIO bounded thread pool)

Configuring a different Resource Adapter for your MDBs

Out of box the application server relies on HornetQ as resource adapter for messaging. Therefore you don't need any extra configuration in order to use MDBs with the default server configuration. On the other hand if you want to rely on a different Message Broker, you need to a Resource Adapter in order to communicate with it.

Let's see a concrete example. We will replace the default hornetq adapter with **ActiveMq** (http://activemq.apache.org/).

1. Start by downloading the Resource Adapter (Currently ActiveMQ resource adapter is hosted on the Maven repository (http://mvnrepository.com/artifact/org.apache.activemq/activemq-rar).

2. Once downloaded the resource adapter, you can either install it as a module, or simply deploy it as you would do for an application:

```
cp activemq-rar-5.10.0 /usr/share/wildfly-8.2.0.Final/standalone/deployments
```

3. Now, we will configure the Resource Adapter through the **resource-adapter** subsystem (The Resouce adapter configuration can be partly be completed through the Admin Console. We will need however configuring some advanced settings such as admin-objects and Connection factories; hence we suggest a direct configuration in the XML configuration file):

```
<subsystem xmlns="urn:jboss:domain:resource-adapters:2.0">
    <resource-adapters>
        <resource-adapter id="activemq">
            <archive>activemq-rar-5.10.0.rar</archive>
            <transaction-support>XATransaction</transaction-support>
            <config-property name="UseInboundSession">
                    false
            </config-property>
            <config-property name="Password">
                    defaultPassword
            </config-property>
```

```
                    <config-property name="UserName">
                            defaultUser
                    </config-property>
                    <config-property name="ServerUrl">
                            tcp://localhost:61616
                    </config-property>
                    <connection-definitions>
                            <connection-definition class-
name="org.apache.activemq.ra.ActiveMQManagedConnectionFactory" jndi-
name="java:/ConnectionFactory" enabled="true" pool-name="ConnectionFactory">
                                    <xa-pool>
                                            <min-pool-size>1</min-pool-size>
                                            <max-pool-size>20</max-pool-size>
                                            <prefill>false</prefill>
                                            <is-same-rm-override>false</is-same-rm-override>
                                    </xa-pool>
                            </connection-definition>
                    </connection-definitions>
                    <admin-objects>
                            <admin-object class-
name="org.apache.activemq.command.ActiveMQQueue" jndi-
name="java:jboss/activemq/queue/TestQueue" use-java-context="true" pool-name="TestQueue">
                                    <config-property name="PhysicalName">
                                            activemq/queue/TestQueue
                                    </config-property>
                            </admin-object>
                            <admin-object class-
name="org.apache.activemq.command.ActiveMQTopic" jndi-
name="java:jboss/activemq/topic/TestTopic" use-java-context="true" pool-name="TestTopic">
                                    <config-property name="PhysicalName">
                                            activemq/topic/TestTopic
                                    </config-property>
                            </admin-object>
                    </admin-objects>
            </resource-adapter>
    </resource-adapters>
</subsystem>
```

The most interesting part, is the ActiveMQ configuration, which relies on the default Connection settings, the **Connection Factory** configuration which exposes the ActiveMQ ConnectionFactory through the JNDI mapping "*java:/ConnectionFactory*" and two **Administered objects**: a JMS Queue bound at "*java:jboss/activemq/queue/TestQueue*" and a JMS Topic Bound at "*java:jboss/activemq/topic/TestTopic*"

4. As final step, configure your EJB3 container to use ActiveMQ resource adapter. From the EJB3 Container configuration

Edit

Stateless Session Pool:	▼
Message Driven Pool:	▼
Default Resource Adapter:	activemq
Singleton Access Timeout:	5000
Stateful Access Timeout:	5000

Cancel   Save

Chapter 6: Configure Logging

Logging is a common requirement for every middleware system that is used to trace error messages, warnings or simply write info and statistics. WildFly logging is substantially based on the J2SE built-in API named **Java UTIL Logging API** (JUL) that is included in the *java.util.logging* package.

In this chapter, we are going to learn the following topics:

- At first, we will study the default logging configuration used by the application server
- Then we will learn how to configure **Handlers** which are in charge to receive a log message and send it to a target
- Finally we will learn how to associate an Handler with a **Logger** element that binds the log to a Java package

WildFly default logging configuration

WildFly by default emits its logs both on the terminal console and on a file. The Console logging is mostly for development purposes, as you would probably start the application server as background process in a production system; therefore, we will mostly concentrate on logs that are traced to a file.

The default location for the file server log is dictated by the **jboss.server.log.dir**, which corresponds, in a standalone installation, to the folder *JBOSS_HOME/standalone/log* or, in a case of domain mode, in the folder *JBOSS_HOME/domain/log*. The number of files used varies as well according to the application server mode:

- The **standalone** installation, by default, emits logging in the file named *server.log*
- The **domain** installation emits the host controller logging in a file named *host-controller.log* which traces server activities (start/stop). The single processes, which are triggered by the host controller, are traced in a file named *process-controller.log*. Finally, each server that belongs to a domain emits loggings in the *JBOSS_HOME/domain/servers/[servername]/server.log*.

You can use the **jboss.server.log.dir** variable as first aid for configuring the location where logs are written. For example, on a standalone installation, the following command will trace the *server.log* files into the */home/user/logs* folder:

```
standalone.sh -Djboss.server.log.dir=/home/user/logs
```

When running on Domain mode, you can customize the location of your host and process controller logs by setting the *jboss.domain.log.dir* system property:

```
domain.sh -Djboss.domain.log.dir=/home/user/domainlogs
```

Besides the above quick-logging recipes, most of the time you would enter the Admin Console in order to configure the **logging** subsystem. This can be done by expanding (from within the upper **Configuration**) the **Core** left panel. From there select **"Logging"**

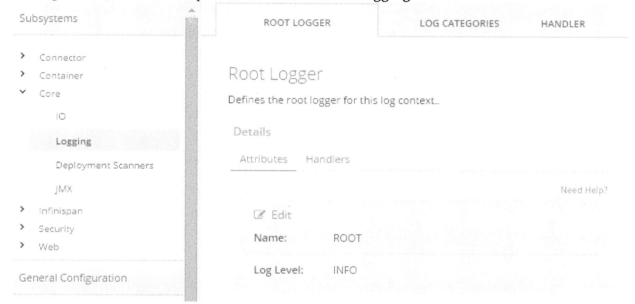

In the Logging section, you can configure the main elements that compose the WildFly logging subsystem, that is, the **Root Logger**, **Log Categories** and **Handlers**. In the following section, we will learn how to configure Handlers, which are used to capture log events and route them to a certain target. We will at first examine the existing ones and then we will show how to create new ones.

Configuring Log Handlers

An **Handler** receives a log event and export it to a destination. Out of the box, the application server has defined a **Console** Handler, which writes logs on the server console, and a **Periodic Rotating File Handler**, which writes logs (using a time based rotating policy) to a File.
By selecting the **Handler** tab in the Logging view, you can find a proof of concept of it:

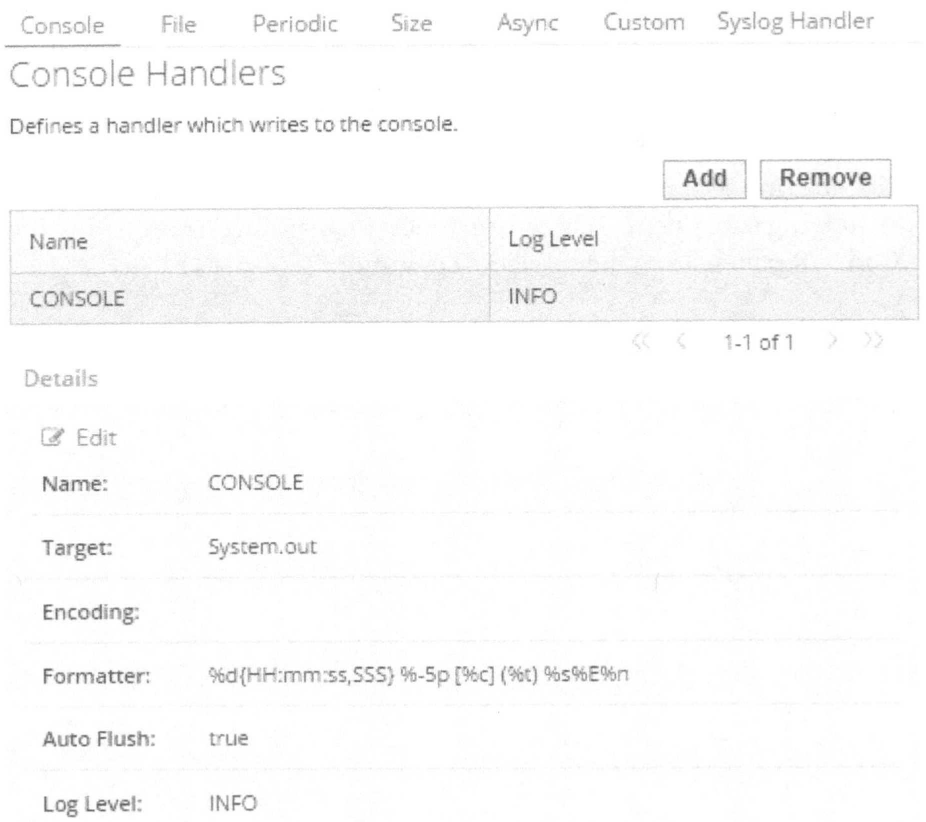

Console   File   Periodic   Size   Async   Custom   Syslog Handler

Console Handlers

Defines a handler which writes to the console.

| | | Add | Remove |

Name	Log Level
CONSOLE	INFO

≪ ＜   1-1 of 1   ＞ ≫

Details

✎ Edit

Name:	CONSOLE
Target:	System.out
Encoding:	
Formatter:	%d{HH:mm:ss,SSS} %-5p [%c] (%t) %s%E%n
Auto Flush:	true
Log Level:	INFO

As you can see from the above picture, the Handler menu contains a set of sub-options that let you create new Handlers for each of the available types. There are six types of Handlers that you can configure:

- **Console Handler**: as we said this traces logs on the server Console
- **File**: writes logs to a File without a specific (time/size) constraint
- **Periodic**: writes logs to a File by rotating logs on a time basis
- **Size**: writes logs to a File by rotating logs on a size basis
- **Async**: defines a handler that is able to use an asynchronous thread to handle its sub-handlers.
- **Custom**: allows using your own class (that extends *java.util.logging.Handler*) to trace logs.

Besides the above handlers found in the Admin console it is also possible to define a **SysLog** Handler, which is able to, trace logs according the Operating System logger (See section "Creating a SysLog Handler" later on in this chapter).

Configuring common properties of Handlers

Each Handler has obviously its own properties which are based on its nature; some properties however are common to every Log Handlers, such as the **Log Level** which is used to define the level of verbosity of logs. Message levels lower than this value will be discarded.

By entering Edit mode of any Logger you can choose the Log level which can vary from ALL (anything is logger) to OFF (which obviously turns off the logs for the Handler):

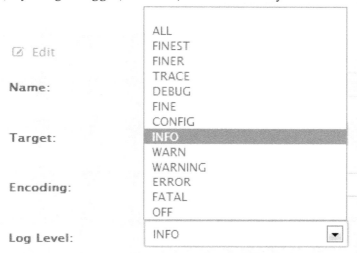

Another attribute that you can set on any Handler is the **Auto Flush** which (if set to true) immediately flushes the log event to its destination and the **Formatter**. Formatters are discussed more in detail in the section named "Configuring Log Format".

Configuring the default Rotating Handler

As we said, by default WildFly 8 ships with a Rotating Handler which daily rotates the logs in a file named *server.log*. Let's learn how to customize this Handler by selecting the "**Periodic**" option from the Handler menu:

ROOT LOGGER	LOG CATEGORIES	HANDLER

Console   File   Periodic   Size   Async   Custom

Periodic Rotating File Handlers   [Add]   [Remove]

Name	Log Level
FILE	ALL

Details   ☑ Edit

Name: FILE

Encoding:

Log Level: ALL

Formatter: %d{HH:mm:ss,SSS} %-5p [%c] (%t) %s%E%n

Suffix: .yyyy-MM-dd ──────── Determines periodic rotation policy

File Relative To: jboss.server.log.dir

File Path: server.log

Append: true

The **Suffix** is a key element of the Periodic Handler configuration as it determines how often the file is rotated. The default **yyyy-MM-dd** rotates logs daily using a pattern type *server.log.YYYY-MM-DD*. If you want to change the time rotation policy, just choose an adequate suffix, for example **yyyy-MM-dd HH** rotates the logs hourly.

The **File Path** attribute specifies where logs are written. If you have specified a **File Relative To** directory, the File Path will be treated as a relative path, otherwise (if **File Relative To** is blank) it will be the absolute path where log files will be written.

The **Log Level**, has we have already seen, defines the log level associated with the handler. Message levels lower than this value will be discarded.

Finally, the **formatter** element provides support for formatting LogRecords. The log formatting inherits the same pattern strings for layout pattern of log4j, which was in turn inspired by old C's printf function.

Formatter quick help
The string %d{HH:mm:ss,SSS} outputs the date of the logging event using the conversion included in brackets.
The string %-5pwill output the priority of the logging event
The string [%c] is used to output the category of the logging event
The string (%t) outputs the Thread that generated the logging event
The string (%M) outputs the method that generated the logging event
The string %s outputs the log message
The string %n outputs the platform dependent line separator character

Configuring a Size Rotating Handler

As we have seen, the default File Handler uses a rotation policy based on a time factor. If you want rather keep an eye on how much your file grows, then you can define a **Size Rotating** handler; this handler writes to a file, rotating the log after a the size of the file grows beyond a certain point and keeping a fixed number of backups.

In order to do that, select the **Size** option from the **Handler** File Menu and click on **Add**:

In the next popup window, enter the **Handler Name**, the **Log Level**, the **File Path** and **File Path relative to**, using the same criteria that we have learnt for the Periodic Handler. Click **Save** to persist the Handler.

As you can see from the next picture, our handler named "SIZE" has a default **Rotation Size** Policy of 2MB with a single log backup being kept as dictated by the **Max Backup** Index:

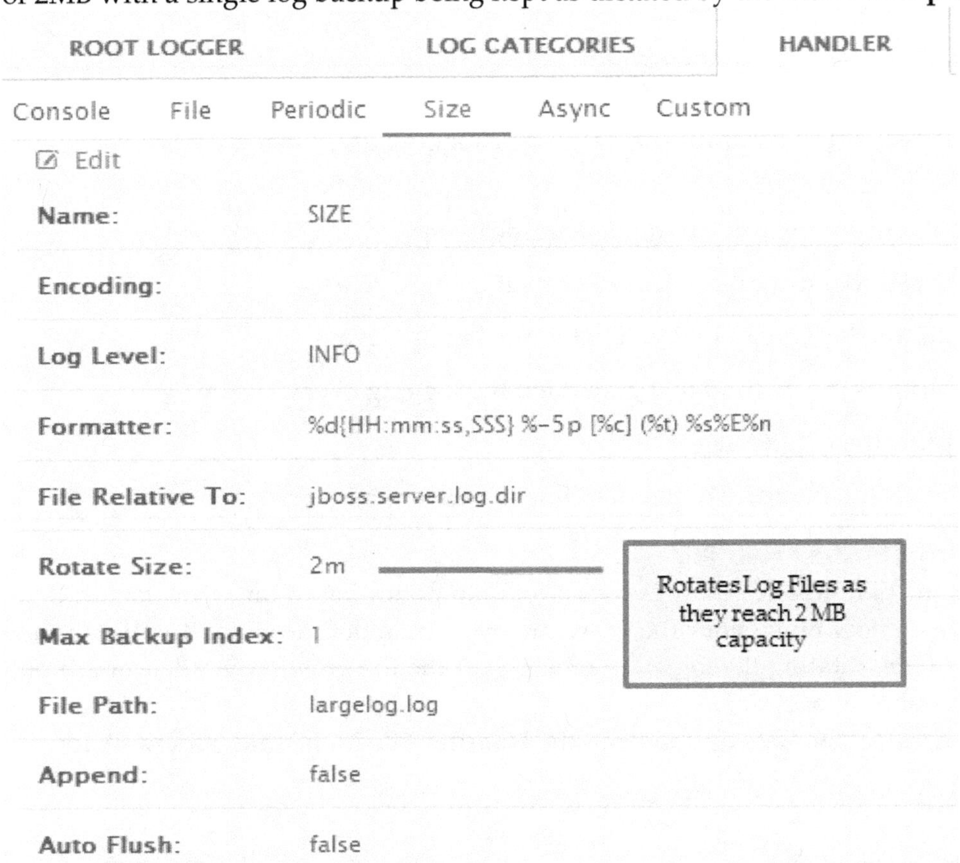

ROOT LOGGER		LOG CATEGORIES		HANDLER	
Console	File	Periodic	Size	Async	Custom

☑ Edit

Name:	SIZE
Encoding:	
Log Level:	INFO
Formatter:	%d{HH:mm:ss,SSS} %-5p [%c] (%t) %s%E%n
File Relative To:	jboss.server.log.dir
Rotate Size:	2m
Max Backup Index:	1
File Path:	largelog.log
Append:	false
Auto Flush:	false

Rotates Log Files as they reach 2 MB capacity

Your Size Handler is now configured; it however needs to be bound to a **Logger** in order to work. See the section "Configuring the Root Logger" to learn how to replace the default FILE logging policy with this one.

Creating a Custom Log Handler

If you want a full control over your logs, then you can choose to create a **Custom Handler** that extends the **java.util.logging.Handler** interface and overrides its abstract methods. In the following example, we will show how to trace logs into a MySQL database. We will use the data source connection that is contained in chapter 4. Before starting, we need to create the database tables, which will contain the logs. Here's an example which assumes that you are using MySQL as database:

```
CREATE TABLE log_table(
id integer NOT NULL PRIMARY key auto_increment,
timestamp VARCHAR(255) ,
log_level VARCHAR(255) ,
class VARCHAR(255) ,
message VARCHAR(1500));
```

Next step will be creating our custom Handler class named **com.logger.JdbcLogger** that extends the **java.util.logging.Handler** interface. The source code for the class can be collected at the following address: http://goo.gl/4fjoVY

Once you have compiled your class, pack it in a JAR file named, for example, **dblogger.jar**. Now let's create a module for this handler so start your CLI and enter the following command:

```
module add --name=org.mysql.logger --resources=Java\libs\DBLogger.jar --
dependencies=javax.api,org.jboss.logging,org.mysql
```

The above command will register a module named **org.mysql.logger** in the module structure of installation (to be precise in the *$MODULE_PATH/org/mysql/logger/main* folder) adding a *module.xml* descriptor file containing the dependencies stated in the command.

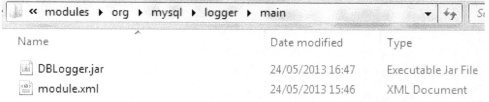

Now move to the Web console and, from the **Handler** tab menu, choose to **Add** a new custom Handler:

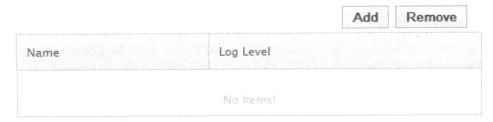

Console   File   Periodic   Size   Async   **Custom**

Custom Handlers

Defines a custom logging handler. The custom handler must extend
java.util.logging.Handler.

| | Add | Remove |

Name	Log Level

No Items!

From the popup window, enter a name for the custom Handler such as **MySQLLogHandler**, the
Log Level, the Module Name (in our example **org.mysql.logger**) and the class
com.logger.JdbcLogger.

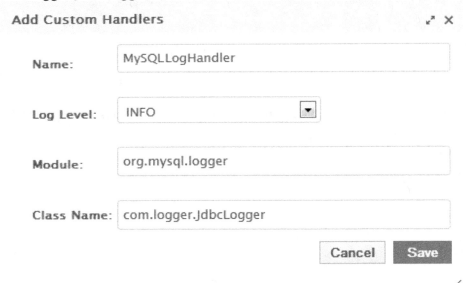

Add Custom Handlers   ⤢ ✕

Name: MySQLLogHandler

Log Level: INFO ▼

Module: org.mysql.logger

Class Name: com.logger.JdbcLogger

                              Cancel   Save

Click on **Save**. The Handler should now be enlisted among the default Handlers. We need to set
some properties in it so that the JDBC related settings are not hardcoded in the Handler class. The

properties will be automatically injected in the custom Handler class. So select the Handler "**Properties**" tab and click on the "**Add**" button:

Attributes   Properties

Add   Remove

▲ Key	Value
driverClassName	com.mysql.jdbc.Driver
jdbcUrl	jdbc:mysql://localhost:3306/mysqlschema
password	jboss
username	jboss

Last thing we need to do is adding the Handler to a Logger. For example, select the Root Logger and, in the Handler tab, add a new entry for the **MySQLLogHandler** so that the Root Logger Handler view looks like this:

Root Logger

Defines the root logger for this log context..

Details

Attributes   Handlers

Add

Name	Option
CONSOLE	Remove
FILE	Remove
MySQLLogHandler	Remove

Now we're done. Verify from your log_table that logs are being traced.

Creating a SysLog Handler

A **SysLog Handler** can be defined to log messages using the popular syslog service available on Unix/Linux System, systems. A new SysLog Handler can be added through the last tab available in the Handler menu:

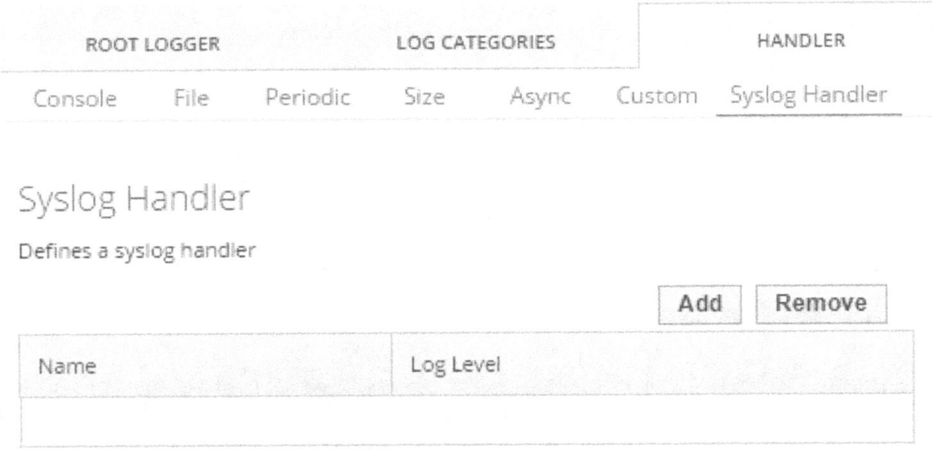

ROOT LOGGER	LOG CATEGORIES	HANDLER

Console   File   Periodic   Size   Async   Custom   Syslog Handler

Syslog Handler

Defines a syslog handler

Add	Remove

Name	Log Level

By clicking on Add, the following dialog will appear, requesting to enter the details for the Syslog Handler:

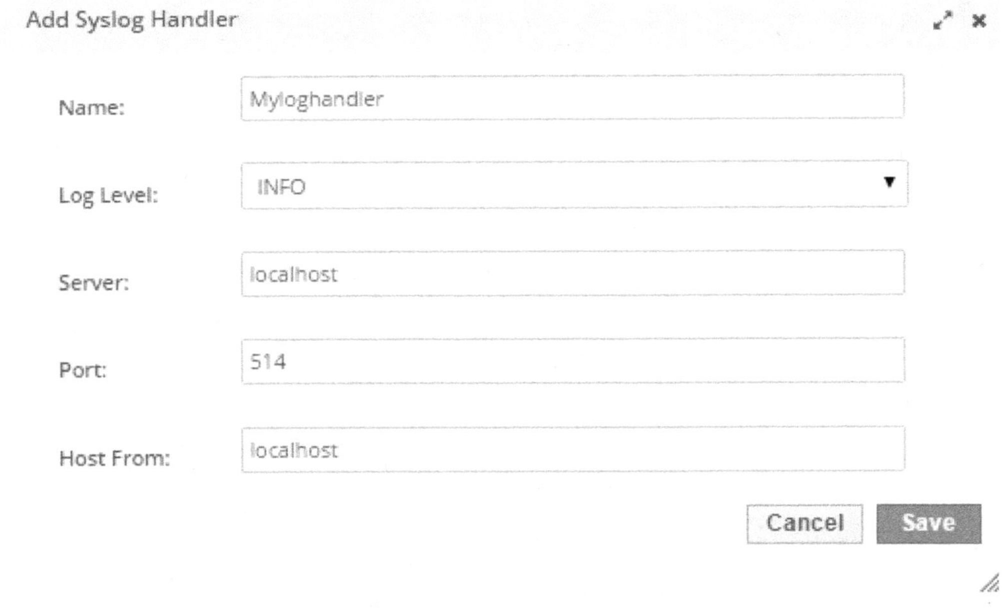

Add Syslog Handler

Name:	Myloghandler
Log Level:	INFO ▼
Server:	localhost
Port:	514
Host From:	localhost

Cancel   **Save**

The key attributes of SysLog handlers are:

Server: this is the address of the syslog server.

Port: The port the syslog server is listening on (default 514)

Host From: The name of the host the messages are being sent from. For example, the name of the
Once that you have added your Syslog Handler, and associated it to a logger, you can start
checking the log messages varies according to your Linux/Unix distribution. For example on a
CentOS system you would issue the following commands in order to tail logs:

```
sudo tail -f /var/log/messages

...

13:01:47,966 INFO  [org.jboss.as] (Controller Boot Thread) JBAS015961: Http management
interface listening on http://127.0.0.1:9990/management

13:01:47,966 INFO  [org.jboss.as] (Controller Boot Thread) JBAS015951: Admin console
listening on http://127.0.0.1:9990

13:01:47,966 INFO  [org.jboss.as] (Controller Boot Thread) JBAS015874: WildFly
8.2.0.Final "Tweek" started in 3908ms - Started 184 of 234 services (82 services

are lazy, passive or on-demand)
```

Keep in mind that you may wish to change your log rotation schedule to prevent large files. You
can do this in */etc/logrotate.conf*.

Configuring Handlers to be asynchronous

The Async Handler can be used to log events *asynchronously*. Behind the scenes, this Handler uses a
bounded queue to store events. Every time a log is emitted, the handler returns immediately after
placing events in the bounded queue. An internal dispatcher thread serves the events accumulated
in the bounded queue. An Async Handler can be added to your configuration by selecting the
"**Async**" option in the Handler Panel and clicking on the **Add** button:

ROOT LOGGER	LOG CATEGORIES	HANDLER

Console   File   Periodic   Size   Async   Custom

Async Handlers

Defines a handler which writes to the sub-handlers in an asynchronous thread. Used for handlers which introduce a substantial amount of lag.

Add   Remove

Name	Log Level
No Items!	

In the following popup window, specify the Handler name, the associated Log Level, the associated Queue Length and the action to perform, in case log messages are overflowing the Queue size (by default the Async Handler will BLOCK until there's room in the queue. You can alternatively choose to DISCARD the message):

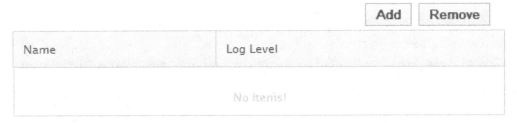

Add Async Handlers   ↗ ✕

Name: FileAsyncHandler

Log Level: INFO ▼

Queue Length: 512

Overflow Action: BLOCK ▼

Cancel   Save

Once done, click on **Save**. The Async handler will be created an included in its panel. The Async Handler is however a composite handler which attaches to other handlers to produce asynchronous logging events. Start by selecting the Handlers sub tab as shown by this picture:

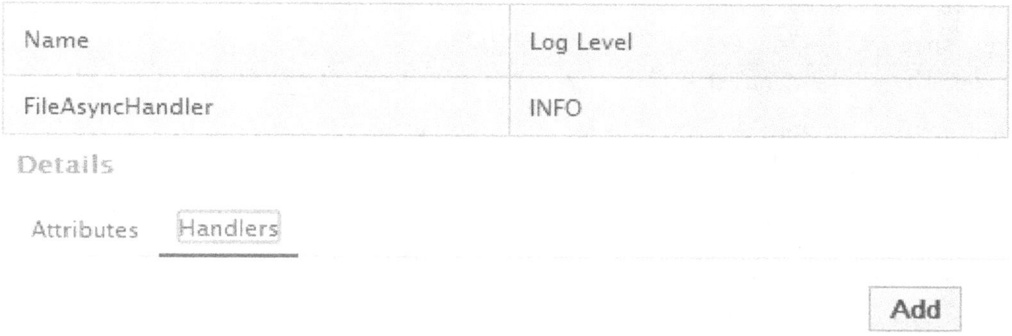

Name	Log Level
FileAsyncHandler	INFO

Details

Attributes   Handlers

Add

Now click on the **Add** button and associate the FileAsyncHandler with another existing Handler (e.g. the SIZE handler):

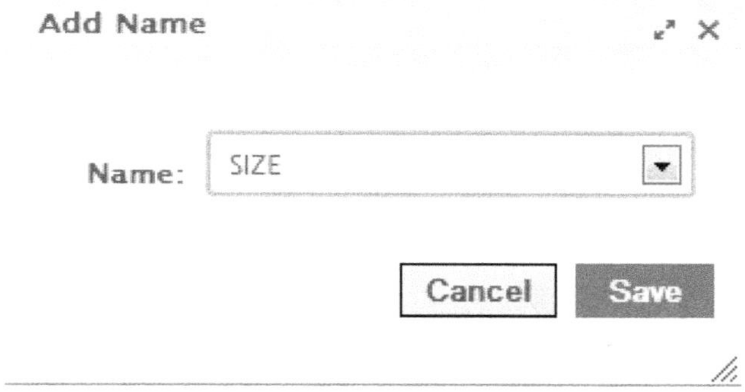

Add Name   ↗ ✕

Name: SIZE   ▼

Cancel   Save

Click **Save** in order to persist changes.

Filtering Logs

Until now, we have learnt how to filter logs using different Level of severity, so that you can increase/reduce the level of verbosity. Actually, it is also possible to specify a filter to be applied on the content of data to be logged. In order to do that, you can use a **filter expression** that is able to include/exclude log messages based on their text content.

For example, if you were to get rid of logs containing the text "IJ000906" then you could enter the following expression via CLI:

```
/subsystem=logging/periodic-rotating-file-handler=FILE/:write-attribute(name=filter-
spec,value=not(match("IJ000906")))
```

This will produce the following addition in your configuration:

```
<periodic-rotating-file-handler name="FILE" autoflush="true">
    <filter-spec value="not(match("IJ000906"))"/>
</periodic-rotating-file-handler>
```

If, on the other hand, you were to choose to log any message containing either the text "JBAS" or "JBWS022052" then you could opt for the "any" filtering expression:

```
/subsystem=logging/periodic-rotating-file-handler=FILE/:write-attribute(name=filter-
spec,value= any(match("JBAS"), match("JBWS022052"))))
```

The list of available filtering patterns can be read from the application server configuration at: https://docs.jboss.org/author/display/AS72/Logging+Configuration#LoggingConfiguration-FilterExpressions

Configuring the Root Logger

The Root logger is the ancestor of all loggers. All classes that don't have a configured logger, will inherit from the root logger. You can configure the Root logger by choosing the first tab in the **Logging** configuration panel. The Root Logger panel contains a subpanel where you can configure **Attributes** and **Handlers** for the root logger.

Configuring Root Logger Attributes:

By selecting the **Attributes** Tab, you can edit the Root Logger name and the Log Level, as shown in the following picture:

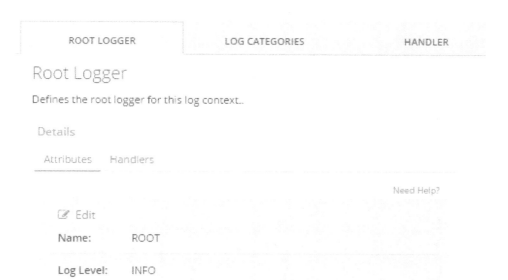

| ROOT LOGGER | LOG CATEGORIES | HANDLER |

Root Logger

Defines the root logger for this log context..

Details

Attributes   Handlers

Need Help?

✎ Edit

Name: ROOT

Log Level: INFO

By default, the Root logger has a log level of INFO, which means that will print logging messages with a priority level of INFO or higher. In order to change the Root logger level, click on the **Edit** Button and pickup from the Log Level combo box the new Log Level. Click Save. Changes to the Logger configuration will be immediately activated.

Changing the Root Logger Level has a severe impact on your applications as it will alter the verbosity of all log messages from packages that have no specific Logger attached to it.

Configuring Root Logger Handlers

By selecting the **Handlers** tab from the **Root Logger** configuration, you can configure the handlers, which are associated with the Root Logger. The following picture shows the pre-configured Root Logger handlers:

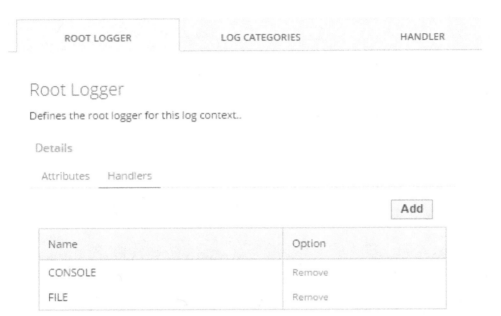

As you can see, by default the Root Logger has two Handlers associated with it:
- The **Console** logger which prints on the application server console log messages
- The **File** logger, which writes logs in the **jboss.server.log.dir** using a file name server.log.

You can add or remove Handlers to the Root logger by choosing the **Add** button on the right position, or the **Remove** buttons that are placed on the single Handlers. Let's add as an example the SIZE handler which traces logs on a file using a rotating size policy. Click on the **Add** button and select the new Handler to associate with the RootLogger:

Click **Save** and Verify that the new File Handler is enlisted in the Root Logger Details table.

Configuring Logging Categories

So far we have seen how to configure the Root Logger which is a generic Logger that is able to intercept all logs which do not belong to a specific Logger. Most of the time, you will need rather to define some specific Loggers for your application packages so that you can easily change your Logging configuration according to the characteristics of your projects. For this purpose, you will need to define **Logger Categories** which are named entities using a package-like dot-separated name such as "com.arjuna". The namespace is hierarchical and should typically be aligned with the Java packaging namespace.

You can enter the Loggers (or Categories) configurations by choosing the "**Log categories**" from the upper logging menu.

ROOT LOGGER	LOG CATEGORIES	HANDLER

Log Categories

Filter: [   ]   [Add] [Remove]

Name	Log Level
com.arjuna	WARN
jacorb	WARN
jacorb.config	ERROR
org.apache.tomcat.util.modeler	WARN
org.jboss.as.config	DEBUG
sun.rmi	WARN

«« «   1-6 of 6 » »»

Attributes   Handlers

Need Help?

✎ Edit

Name: com.arjuna

Use Parent Handlers: true

In the above panel, you can see all the categories that are already configured on your server. If you want to create a new Logger category for your packages, you need to click on the **Add** button in the Log Categories window. A simple popup will let you enter the Logger **Name** (e.g. com.sample) and the **Log Level** (default is INFO). The lower check, **Use Parent Handler** specifies whether this logger should send its output to its parent Logger (default true).

Add Log Categories   ↗ ✕

Name: | com.sample |

Log Level: | INFO   ▾ |

Use Parent Handlers: ☑

                                    Cancel   Save

Click **Save** when you are done with the changes. Logger attributes and Handlers can be added or removed just the same way we showed for the Root Logger.

Other Logging configuration files

Besides the standard logging configuration contained in your XML files, you may have noticed that there is a *logging.properties* file in the configuration directory. This file is actually generated by the application server from your logging subsystem configuration. Most of the time you should not attempt to modify this file at all; however, if you are inheriting a large JUL configuration from your applications, you might experiment using this file as a replacement for your logging subsystem configuration provided that you have removed your logging configuration from your server XML file.

Using Log4j to trace your application logs

Earlier JBoss users might remember that it was possible to use log4j as default logging system; as WildFly is based on JUL this is not possible anymore, yet you can use a feature named **Per-deployment Logging** which allows using the following configuration files on an application basis:

- logging.properties
- jboss-logging.properties
- log4j.properties
- log4j.xml
- jboss-log4j.xml

 In order to let the deployment scanner find the log configuration files, they need to be placed in an appropriate folder: EAR files should contain the configuration in the META-INF directory. On the other hand, in a WAR or JAR deployment the configuration files can be in either the META-INF or WEB-INF/classes directories.

Besides adding the log configuration file in the appropriate folder, you need to link the log library to your application: for example, in order to let your application code use log4j's module which is bundled in the application server (though not implicitly loaded by it), you can include in your META-INF/MANIFEST.MF file the following dependency:

```
Dependencies: org.apache.log4j
```

See the Chapter 9 to learn more about Classloading and modules configuration.

Disabling the core logging API

If you are planning to exclude the default logging API for your deployments, then the simplest way to achieve it is by means of setting to false the property **add-logging-api-dependencies**:

```
/subsystem=logging/:write-attribute(name=add-logging-api-dependencies,value=false)
```

When setting to false this attribute your deployments will not be processed by logging API dependencies. Another option is to use the jboss-deployment-structure.xml to exclude the logging subsystem from your deployments (See Chapter 8 "Advanced Classloading policies" for more information about it).

Reading logs from the Command Line Interface

Although log files are typically read and filtered using your operating system shell commands (such as tail or grep), the final release of WildFly enabled listing and reading the log files via the CLI as well. Gathering information from server log files is quite intuitive, for example in order to get the list of the server log files, simply execute the **list-log-files** command on the logging subsystem.

```
/subsystem=logging/:list-log-files
{
    "outcome" => "success",
    "result" => [
        {
            "file-name" => "server.log",
            "file-size" => 9695L,
            "last-modified-date" => "2014-02-13T15:46:04.365+0100"
        },
        {
            "file-name" => "server.log.2014-02-12",
            "file-size" => 9695L,
            "last-modified-date" => "2014-02-12T21:32:49.759+0100"
        }
    ]
}
```

Another interesting option for us, is the ability to display the actual log files content filtered by some parameters such as the number of lines to read (**lines** parameter) and the lines to skip (**skip** parameter) from the header. Here's how to read the first 10 lines from the server.log file:

```
/subsystem=logging/:read-log-file(name=server.log,lines=10,skip=0)
{
    "outcome" => "success",
    "result" => [
        "2014-02-13 15:04:37,017 INFO  [org.wildfly.extension.undertow] (MSC service
thread 1-2) JBAS017525: Started server default-server.",
        "2014-02-13 15:04:37,041 INFO  [org.wildfly.extension.undertow] (MSC service
thread 1-8) JBAS017531: Host default-host starting",
        "2014-02-13 15:04:37,327 INFO  [org.wildfly.extension.undertow] (MSC service
thread 1-5) JBAS017519: Undertow HTTP listener default listening on /127.0.0.1:8080",
. . . .
    ]
}
```

If you want a full read of your log file, simply provide -1 as argument to the "lines" parameter.

Chapter 7: Configuring JMS Services

This chapter discusses about the configuration of **Java Messaging Services** on WildFly 8. Out of the box, WildFly 8 ships with **HornetQ** open source messaging implementation. This new release contains a full implementation of the recent **JMS 2** specification, which includes new features such as simplified API's, shared consumers on topic subscriptions and auto closeable JMS resources.
In order to learn all about JMS configuration we will follow these steps:

- At first we will learn the building blocks of HornetQ architecture
- Next we will learn how configure JMS connections
- In the next part, we will focus on creating JMS destinations including Connection Factories and JMS Queues/Topics
- Finally, we will have a look at clustered configuration of HornetQ servers as part of a WildFly cluster

HornetQ building blocks

In terms of libraries, HornetQ is made up of just of a set of Plain Old Java Objects (POJOs) which are compiled and packaged in a set of JAR archives. Therefore one advantage of this framework is that it can be executed in many ways, either using a simple Java class or embedded into an application server, as we will see in this chapter.
In terms of building blocks, HornetQ uses the terms **Connector** and **Acceptor** to describe the incoming and outgoing connections to other JMS servers. More in detail:

- An **acceptor** defines which types of connections are accepted by the HornetQ server.
- A **connector** defines how to connect to a HornetQ server, and is used by the HornetQ client.

Acceptors and Connectors can be of two types:

- **invm-connector** which can be used by a local client (i.e. one running in the same JVM as the server)
- **netty-connector** can be used by a remote client and uses Netty over TCP for the communication (See http://netty.io for more information about Netty project)
- **http-connector** can be used by a remote client and uses Undertow Web Server to upgrade from a HTTP connection

The following picture shows a sample architecture for two HornetQ server configurations, the first one using invm connectors/acceptors and the second one running through different virtual machines using http transport libraries.

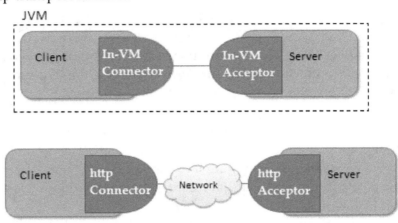

As you can see from the above picture, the connector needs to use the same transport as the acceptor so an invm acceptor can only be contacted by a client running on the same JVM while an http acceptor can only accept connections from remote JVM clients. In terms on configuration, remote connectors are the most configurable one as it can be used with a variety of API (Java NIO, Asynchronous Linux IO) and it can use TCP sockets like SSL or tunnel over HTTP or HTTPs.

Starting WildFly with JMS Services

As we said at the beginning of this book, the messaging extensions are not available with the default standalone configuration (*standalone.xml*); therefore, we need to enable one of the available messaging-aware configurations like the *standalone-full.xml* and *standalone-full-ha.xml* Hence, for example, if you plan to run JMS applications on a non-clustered standalone WildFly server, all you have to do is starting it like that:

```
standalone.sh –c standalone-full.xml
```

As for domain mode, you have to specify to use a **full** or **full-ha** profile and a corresponding socket binding group:

```
<server-group name="main-server-group" profile="full">
        <socket-binding-group ref="full-sockets"/>
</server-group>
```

Once that the server is started, move to the next section which will show you how to configure JMS services.

Configuring JMS Connections

Configuring the Acceptors and Connectors is our first stop in our journey. Having a look at the messaging subsystems, the following acceptors and connectors couples are pre-defined:

```
<connectors>
        <http-connector name="http-connector" socket-binding="http">
                <param key="http-upgrade-endpoint" value="http-acceptor"/>
        </http-connector>
        <http-connector name="http-connector-throughput" socket-binding="http">
                <param key="http-upgrade-endpoint" value="http-acceptor-throughput"/>
                <param key="batch-delay" value="50"/>
        </http-connector>
        <in-vm-connector name="in-vm" server-id="0"/>
</connectors>

<acceptors>
        <http-acceptor http-listener="default" name="http-acceptor"/>
        <http-acceptor http-listener="default" name="http-acceptor-throughput">
                <param key="batch-delay" value="50"/>
                <param key="direct-deliver" value="false"/>
        </http-acceptor>
        <in-vm-acceptor name="in-vm" server-id="0"/>
</acceptors>
```

As you already know, **acceptors** are used to configure connections, which are accepted by HornetQ servers, while **connectors** configure HornetQ client connections towards HornetQ servers.
The http-connectors, which use Undertow to reach the HornetQ provider, contain two kinds of connectors:

- **Standard http connector/acceptor**: which provide a configuration completely based on defaults
- **Throughput http connector/acceptors**: which contains a specialized configuration in order to guarantee an higher level of messaging *throughput*

Here is a description about the included parameters.

- **batch-delay**: allows HornetQ to batch up writes for a maximum of batch-delay milliseconds before sending messages. This can increase overall throughput for very small messages. It does so at the expense of an increase in average latency for message transfer.
- **direct-deliver**: when set to true, JMS message delivery is done on the same thread to which the message arrived on. This can reduce latency at the expense of a lower throughput and scalability, especially on multi-core machines.

Some additional properties, which can be configured both for Acceptors and Connectors include:

use-nio	If this is true then Java non-blocking NIO will be used. If set to false, then old blocking Java IO will be used.
host:	This specifies the host name or IP address to connect to (when configuring a connector) or to listen on (when configuring an acceptor). The default value for this property is localhost.
port	This specifies the port to connect to (when configuring a connector) or to listen on (when configuring an acceptor). The default value for this property is 5445.
tcp-no-delay	If this is true then Nagle's algorithm will be enabled. The default value for this property is true.
tcp-send-buffer-size	This parameter determines the size of the TCP send buffer in bytes. The default value for this property is 32768 bytes (32KB).
tcp-receive-buffer-size	This parameter determines the size of the TCP receive buffer in bytes. The default value for this property is 32768 bytes (32KB).
nio-remoting-threads	When configured to use NIO, HornetQ will, by default, use a number of threads equal to three times the number of cores (or hyper-threads) as reported by *Runtime.getRuntime().availableProcessors()* for processing incoming packets.

The following section shows how to add one example Property to the Acceptor configuration.

Setting custom connection properties

If you want to customize the connectors/acceptors properties, the suggested tool is the Command Line Interface, which will let you easily add or remove properties.

Here is for example how to configure the **tcp-receive-buffer-size** parameter to 65536 bytes:

```
/subsystem=messaging/hornetq-server=default/http-acceptor=http-acceptor-
throughput/param=tcp-receive-buffer-size/:add(value=65536)
```

You need to reload your server configuration in order to enable the connection attributes that you have set.

Switching to Netty sockets

If you have been using earlier versions of the application server, you might be a little surprised that the earlier **netty** connectors/acceptors are not included in the messaging configuration. As a matter of fact, netty is still a vital component of the application server infrastructure and used, behind the scenes, by several application server modules, including Undertow as well.

The general trend for the application server is however to reduce the number of ports to be used so that the configuration is simpler and you can multiplex multiple protocol using a single channel (HTTP); that makes your environment, out of the box, cloud friendly.

For these reasons, although not deprecated, netty acceptors and connectors are not configured as default anymore. You can, at any time, restore netty acceptors or connectors in your server configuration:

```
<acceptors>

    . . . .

    <netty-acceptor name="netty" socket-binding="messaging"/>
</acceptors
```

You need to be aware that netty sockets need a corresponding **socket-binding** in the server configuration:

```
<socket-binding-group name="standard-sockets" default-interface="public" port-offset="${jboss.socket.binding.port-offset:0}">
    <socket-binding name="messaging" port="5445"/>

. . . . .
</socket-binding-group>
```

> You might wonder which option works the best in your case (http or netty sockets). As we mentioned, the http solution has several administrative advantages, which are good arguments in favor of this solution. On the other hand, in terms of performance the http connectors have an initial performance penalty for upgrading the network protocol. So you should evaluate using netty sockets if you are on the hook for extreme performance.

Creating JMS Destinations

Creating Queues and Topics is next on the to-do-list. We will show how to do it both using the Administration Console and the CLI. Let's start with the **Administration console**: select the upper Configuration tab and, from the left side, expand "**Messaging**" and click on "**Destinations**":

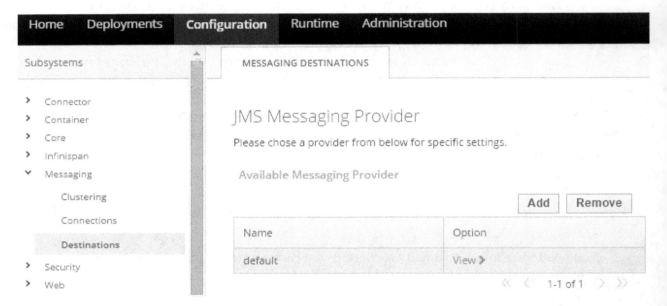

Since there is just a JMS Messaging Provider available, click on the "**View**" link which will take you to the following screen:

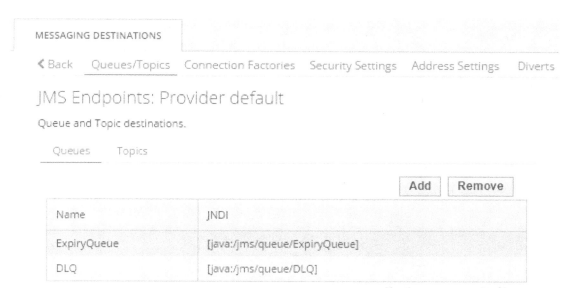

From the Messaging Destinations tab, you have access to a set of options such as:

Queue/Topics: used to add or remove JMS Queue or topics

Connection Factories: used to add or remove JMS Connection Factories

Security Settings: allows sets of permissions to be defined against Queues based on their address.

Address Settings: defines a set of attributes that are applied to one or more JMS endpoints

Diverts: allows routing messages from one destination to another without touching the application logic

In the following section we will learn how to configure a new JMS destination using the Administration Console.

Creating new Queues and Topics

By default the application server does not include any pre-defined example Queue or Topic; you can create a new JMS endpoint by selecting **Queues** or **Topics** and clicking on the "**Add**" button. (You will add new Queues if you are in the "**Queues**" Tab panel and obviously new Topics if you are in the "**Topics**" tab panel).

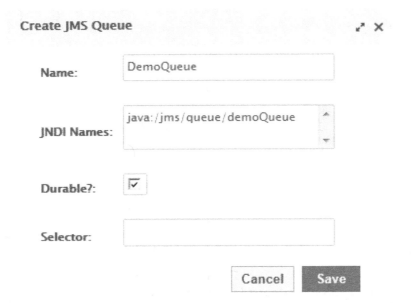

You should provide at least a Queue **Name** and a valid **JNDI name** for your Queue and optionally mark it as **Durable** or associate it with a **Selector**. Valid JNDI names need to begin with either to the "**java://**" or "**java:/jboss**".

 A queue which is tagged as "**durable**" will persist messages. It means that messages can be delivered to the consumer also in the event of server crash.

Click **Save** when done and verify that the JMS destination has been added into the Destination table:

JMS Endpoints: Provider default

Queue and Topic destinations.

Queues   Topics

| | Add | Remove |

Name	JNDI
DemoQueue	[java:/jms/queue/demoQueue]

 You can use as well the Command Line Interface to create a new Queue:

```
jms-queue add  --queue-address= jms.queue.DemoQueue --
entries=java:/jms/queue/demoQueue
```

Finally, if you are planning to use your JMS endpoint from a remote consumer, consider creating an alias for with the JNDI beginning with "**java:jboss/exported**" namespace. In our case, create an additional JNDI binding for the DemoQueue named "java:jboss/exported/jms/queue/demoQueue".

Creating Deployable JMS destinations

JMS destinations can be also be created on the fly by dropping a *–jms.xml* file in the *deployments* folder of your standalone server or packaging it along with your application. Here's an example:

```
<messaging-deployment xmlns="urn:jboss:messaging-deployment:1.0">
    <hornetq-server>
        <jms-destinations>
            <jms-queue name="ExampleQueue">
                <entry name="java:/jms/queue/ExampleQueue"/>
                <durable>true</durable>
            </jms-queue>
            <jms-topic name="ExampleTopic">
                <entry name="java:/jms/topic/ExampleTopic"/>
            </jms-topic>
        </jms-destinations>
    </hornetq-server>
</messaging-deployment>
```

Warning! Deployable resources are not manageable through the application server management interfaces therefore should be used just for development or testing purposes.

Customizing JMS destinations

The **Address Settings** option contained in the JMS Destination tab options allows defining one or more attributes which are applied to your destinations. Most of the properties that you can configure through the Admin console deal with issues caused by failures in delivery.

As you can see from the following picture, by default there is a single Address Settings definition, which uses the wildcard "#", meaning that its properties will be valid across all destinations.

‹ Back   Queues/Topics   Connection Factories   Security Settings   **Address Settings**   Diverts

Address Settings: Provider default

An address setting defines the attributes that are applied to any address that matches the address setting's name (that can contain wildcards).

Available Address Settings

| | Add | Remove |

Pattern
#

Details

☑ Edit

If you want to modify the Default Address settings click on the **Edit** link; on the other hand, if you want a specialized configuration for some addresses, click on the **Add** button. In the following example, we are creating an Address Setting, which will be applied to all JMS Queues:

Create Addressing Setting

Pattern:	jms.queue.#
Dead Letter Address:	jms.queue.DLQ
Expiry Address:	jms.queue.ExpiryQueue
Redelivery Delay:	5000
Max Delivery Attempts:	10

Cancel   **Save**

All HornetQ Queues can be referenced using the namespace "**jms.queue**" while topics can be referenced using the "**jms.topic**" namespace. That's why using the expression "**jms.queue.#**" means all Queues defined.

Here are the properties that you can set on a single destination or a group of destinations:

Dead letter address	All messages that are not delivered correctly are stored in a particular queue, so they can be parsed in a second time
Expiry Address	Messages whose time-to-live have expired are removed from the queue and sent to this expiry address
Redelivery delay	You can configure some delay time (in ms.) to let the client return in a successfully delivered state
Max delivery attempts	Defines how many times a cancelled message can be redelivered before sending to the dead-letter-address

There are several other properties which can be configured on the Address Settings: these properties are related to **Message paging** and need to be configured either by changing manually the configuration XML files or by using the CLI. (See the section "Configuring Message Paging")

Configuring Message Persistence

Configuring message persistence is a requirement for granting the reliability of messages. HornetQ persists its messages using its own high-performance journaling which, in a Linux environment (kernel 2.6), can also benefit from using **Linux's Asynchronous IO library** (AIO).

The HornetQ journal is not based on a database but it is rather made up of a set of (append-only) files of on a disk. Each file is pre-created to a fixed size and initially filled with padding. As operations are performed on the server, (e.g. add message, update message, delete message) records are appended to the journal. When one journal file is full, HornetQ creates a new one. The persistence settings are accessible from the Admin Console by selecting the "**Connections**" option contained in the **Messaging** left side menu:

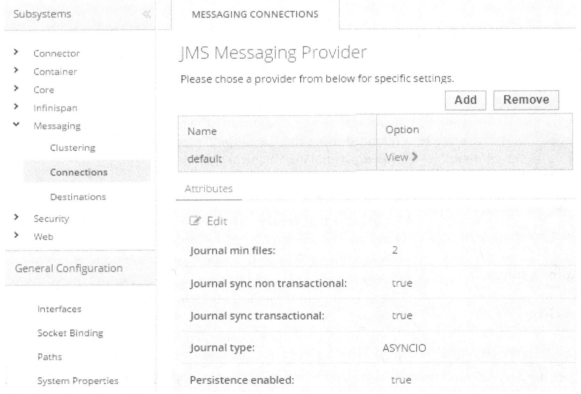

The list of configurable attributes is quite long, however we wouls like to stress the importance of the **Persistence enabled** element, which determines if messages are persisted on the journal.

According to the **Journal type** parameter, there are two types of journals that determine the input-out library to be used for message persistence.

 When choosing **NIO** HornetQ use the Java NIO journal. On the other hand, when choosing **AIO** will use the Linux asynchronous IO journal. If you choose AIO but are not running Linux (or you do not have libaio installed) then HornetQ will detect this and automatically fall back to using NIO.

The **journal-min-files** determines the minimum number of files the journal will maintain. When HornetQ starts and there is no initial message data, HornetQ will pre-create journal-min-files number of files.

Another parameter that is worth mentioning is **journal file size**, which determines the maximum size (in bytes) for journal files. All the parameters contained in this window can be also set via the CLI. For example, here's how you can set the journal file size via CLI:

```
/subsystem=messaging/hornetq-server=default/:write-attribute(name=journal-file-size,value=102400)
```

Configuring Message Paging

Although HornetQ is able to support a huge amount of messages, when the system is getting low in memory, you have to option to page them to disk. This is quite similar to the ordinary file system paging which occurs when the amount of RAM in not enough to handle all the running applications. The difference is however that, by default, HornetQ does not page messages - this must be explicitly configured to activate it.

Paging can be configured at address settings level as shown by this XML snippet:

```
<address-settings>
    <address-setting match="jms.queue.#">
        <max-size-bytes>104857600</max-size-bytes>
        <page-size-bytes>10485760</page-size-bytes>
        <address-full-policy>PAGE</address-full-policy>
    </address-setting>
</address-settings>
```

In order to enable paging you have to set the **max-size-bytes** property to the max memory allowed to a JMS address (before entering paging) and set the **address-full-policy** parameter. This must be set to PAGE for paging to enable. If the value is PAGE then further messages will be paged to disk.

If the value is DROP then further messages will be silently dropped. If the value is BLOCK then client message producers will block when they try and send further messages.

Configuring the paging folder

Each address has an individual folder where messages are stored in multiple files (page files). By default the page folder is configured through the following attributes which results in creating a folder named *pagingdir* under the *jboss.server.data.dir*:

```
/subsystem=messaging/hornetq-server=default/path=paging-directory/:write-
attribute(name=path,value=pagingdir)
```

```
/subsystem=messaging/hornetq-server=default/path=paging-directory/:write-
attribute(name=relative-to,value=jboss.server.data.dir)
```

Each file will contain messages up to a max configured size (**page-size-bytes**). The system will navigate on the files as needed, and it will remove the page file as soon as all the messages are acknowledged up to that point.

The following picture recaps the typical flow of a JMS message for different values of the **max-size-bytes** and **address-full-policy** properties:

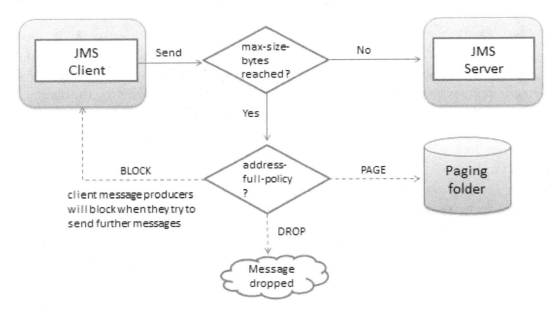

Routing Messages to other destinations

One common requirement for applications which are strongly based on messaging systems is to provide a way to route messages to other servers, without the need to perform any change in the application client logic. HornetQ offers the following options:

- **Divert** messages from one destination to another.
- Create a **Bridge** between two HornetQ servers

Although both options can be used for the same purpose, the difference between them is that a Bridge implies a connection between two HornetQ servers, whilst a message Divert operates on the *same* HornetQ server.

Diverting messages to other destinations

As we just said, message divertion operates on the *same* HornetQ server and can provide a simple yet effective way to route messages from one destination to another; besides this, a message divert is also able to perform some filtering and use a custom transformer class to transform the message's body or properties before it is diverted.

You can use the Admin Console to define a new Message Divert by selecting the **Destinations** option in the Messaging left side menu. From the Messaging Destinations choose the **Diverts** options as shown by the following picture:

MESSAGING DESTINATIONS

< Back   Queues/Topics   Connection Factories   Security Settings   Address Settings   Diverts

Diverts: Provider default .

A messaging resource that allows you to transparently divert messages routed to one address to some other address, without making any changes to any client application logic.

Add   Remove

Name	From	To

Once there, click on the **Add** button in order to add a new Divert. The following window will request to enter the **Routing Name** along with the JMS Source and Destination:

Create Divert   ↗ ✖

                                               Need Help?

Routing Name: RoutingDemo

Divert Address: jms.queue.source

Forwarding Address: jms.queue.destination

                              Cancel   **Save**

Please note that we need to refer to Queues and Topics by their core name ("**jms.queue.source**" and "**jms.queue.destination**" respectively) which is different to the Queue name that we entered during creation ("source" and "destination").

Click on **Save** in order to persist changes. Now the Message Divert will be enlisted in the main window. You can further configure your Divert by clicking on the **Edit** link, which will let you define some additional options as shown by the following window:

Routing Name: RoutingDemo

Divert Address: jms.queue.source

Forwarding Address: jms.queue.destination

Exlusive?: ☐

Filter:

Transformer Class:

Cancel   Save

The additional options available are:

Exclusive	This option determines if the divert is *exclusive*, meaning that the message is diverted to the new address, and does not go to the old address at all. If the divert is qualified as *non-exclusive*, the message continues to go the old address, and a copy of it is also sent to the new address
Filter	This is an optional filter string. If specified, only messages that match the filter expression specified will be diverted. The filter string follows the HornetQ filter expression syntax described in the HornetQ documentation (http://docs.jboss.org/hornetq/2.3.0.Final/docs/user-manual/html/filter-expressions.html).
Transformer Class	The name of a class used to transform the message's body or properties before it is diverted.

Here follows an example of **Transformer**, taken from the HornetQ documentation, which sets a property of the JMS message named "time_of_forward" to the current time, when the Transformer has been triggered:

```
package org.hornetq.jms.example;

import org.hornetq.api.core.SimpleString;
import org.hornetq.core.server.ServerMessage;
import org.hornetq.core.server.cluster.Transformer;

public class AddForwardingTimeTransformer implements Transformer
{

    public ServerMessage transform(final ServerMessage message)
    {
        message.putLongProperty(new
                          SimpleString("time_of_forward"), System.currentTimeMillis());

        return message;
    }
}
```

Creating a Bridge between two HornetQ servers

Bridges are logical software applications that allow us to connect to HornetQ servers so that it is possible to consume a message from a source queue or topic and then send them to a target queue or topic on another HornetQ server.

 Bridges are resilient to source or destination unavailability so they can be used specifically on a **Wide Area Network (WAN)**. In such a scenario, the other server could be located on a different location of your WAN, thus your bridge can help you to reconnect when the connections becomes available again.

In order to set up a bridge between two HornetQ servers, you should define:

1. On your **Source HornetQ server**, a Netty Connector which points to the target HornetQ server and a JMS Bridge element bound to that connector.
2. On your **Target HornetQ server**, a Netty Acceptor which is able to receive messages forwarded from the source HornetQ Bridge.

Of course you need to define the source and target JMS Endpoints in both HornetQ Servers.

The above tasks can be executed from within your CLI, as indicated by the following steps:

HornetQ source configuration

Log into your CLI shell and start creating a JMS Queue named:

```
jms-queue add  --queue-address= jms.queue.Record --entries= queue/queueSource
```

Now add a Connector named "netty-bridge" bound the a NettyConnectorFactory

```
/subsystem=messaging/hornetq-server=default/connector=netty-bridge/:add(factory-
class=org.hornetq.core.remoting.impl.netty.NettyConnectorFactory)
```

Then set some parameters for this Connector: at first the host name (in our example "TargetHost"):

```
/subsystem=messaging/hornetq-server=default/connector=netty-
bridge/param=host/:add(value=TargetHost)
```

Set as well the Connector port which will be used by the Bridge to connect:

```
/subsystem=messaging/hornetq-server=default/connector=netty-
bridge/param=port/:add(value=5445)
```

Now add the **Bridge definition** (named "MyBridge") which is bound to the netty-bridge and has set as forwarding address "jms.queue.Record":

```
/subsystem=messaging/hornetq-server=default/bridge=myBridge/:add(queue-
name=jms.queue.Record,forwarding-address=jms.queue.Record,static-connectors=["netty-
bridge"],retry-interval=2000)
```

Complete your HornetQ source configuration by setting some address settings for the jms.queue.Record:

```
/subsystem=messaging/hornetq-server=default/address-setting=jms.queue.Record/:add(,page-
size-bytes=10485760,address-full-policy=PAGE,max-delivery-attempts=10,max-size-bytes=-
1,dead-letter-address=jms.queue.DLQ,)
```

HornetQ target configuration

The Target configuration is much slimmer as it just requires the Acceptor and Queue configuration. Here's the Queue configuration:

```
jms-queue add  --queue-address=jms.queue.Record --entries= queue/queueTarget
```

Next, define some properties for the built-in remote Netty acceptor, named "netty". Start by setting the acceptor address (in our case 0.0.0.0 means accepting requests from any remote host):

```
/subsystem=messaging/hornetq-server=default/remote-
acceptor=netty/param=host/:add(value=0.0.0.0)
```

And add as well a port for the netty acceptor:

```
/subsystem=messaging/hornetq-server=default/remote-
acceptor=netty/param=port/:add(value=5445)
```

Complete by setting the address-settings for the target queue:

```
/subsystem=messaging/hornetq-server=default/address-setting=jms.queue.Record/:add(,page-
size-bytes=10485760,address-full-policy=PAGE,max-delivery-attempts=10,max-size-bytes=-
1,dead-letter-address=jms.queue.DLQ,)
```

Good, now your Bridge configuration is complete. You can verify by logging into the Admin console of the source HornetQ machine that the JMS Bridge has been correctly registered:

< Back   Acceptor   Connector   Connector Services   Bridges

Name	Queue	Forward
myBridge	jms.queue.Record	jms.queue.Record

Common   Connection Management

✎ Edit

Name: myBridge

Queue Name: jms.queue.Record

Forward Address: jms.queue.Record

Discovery Group:

Static Connectors: netty-bridge

Filter:

Transformer Class:

JMS Clustering

This section discusses about clustering the HornetQ messaging system. Clustering in HornetQ is done by providing multiple server instances acting like a single entity both from the consumer or producer side. The obvious advantage is that you will have an increased throughput since messages are distributed across different JMS servers.

The other important advantage of clustering is **high availability**, which allows one JMS Server to have one or more redundant servers that will be used as fallback solution in case of server failure.

This means in practice, that you will have an array of JMS Servers called **live** servers which will be used by default; then each live server can have one or more backup servers: a backup server is owned by only one live server and is not operational until failover occurs.

 Backup servers are passive JMS servers which act in passive mode, announcing its status and waiting to take over the live servers work.

In terms of high availability, since HornetQ 2.3 (that is bundled with WildFly application server), you have the choice between using a **shared store** and **data replication**.

HA with Shared Store

When using a **shared store**, both live and backup servers share the same entire data directory using a shared file system. This means the paging directory, journal directory, large messages and binding journal. The following picture depicts this case:

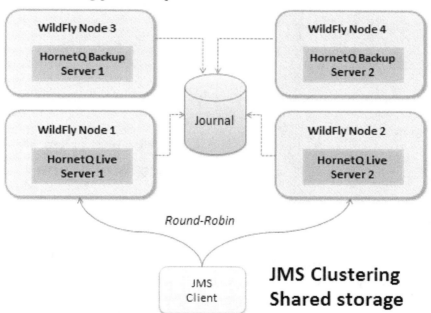

When failover occurs and a backup server takes over, it will load the persistent storage from the shared file system and clients can connect to it.

 For performance reasons it is highly recommended to use Fiber Channel or HyperSCSI to share the journal directory, instead of a file-based protocol like NFS or SMB/CIFS.

HA with data replication

When using replication, the live and the backup servers do not share the same storage and all data synchronization is done through network traffic. Therefore, all (persistent) data traffic received by the live server will be duplicated to the backup. The following picture depicts an HA configuration using data replication:

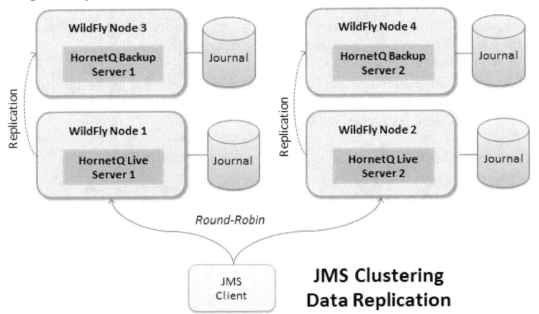

Unlike the shared store scenario, when using data replication the backup server will first need to synchronize all existing data from the live server, before becoming capable of replacing the live server should it fail. In the following example, we will show how to configure your messaging subsystem for clustering using both HA options.

Cluster core configuration

In order to configure a clustered messaging system we can go through the **Messaging** subsystem and click on the **Clustering** option, which is contained within it. The following picture shows a snapshot of this option, along with some of the configurable attributes:

MESSAGING CLUSTERING

JMS Messaging Provider

Available Messaging Provider

> Connector
> Container
> Core
> Infinispan
∨ Messaging
     Clustering
     Connections
     Destinations
> Security
> Web

General Configuration

   Interfaces
   Socket Binding
   Paths
   System Properties

			Add	Remove

Name	Option
default	View ❯

Attributes

✎ Edit

Allow failback:	true
Async connection execution enabled:	true
Backup:	false
Backup group name:	
Check for live server:	false
Cluster password:	${jboss.messaging.cluster.password:CHANGE ME!!}

The list of configurable attributes is pretty large; we will however concentrate on those needed for cluster setup. We will start with **Cluster user** and **Cluster password** credentials are used to make connections between cluster nodes. These connections are used to move messages from one node to another for load-balancing purposes. However, they can technically be used by any remote client to connect to the server, which is why you should change them from the default. If you don't change the default cluster password then a random UUID is used automatically to prevent any JMS flood attack to the HornetQ server.

Another key attribute is **Backup** specifies if the server is meant to be a backup node. If this is going to be a live server, we will specify "false" here.

The **Failover on shutdown** element, on the other hand, when set to true allows backup nodes to kick in when live servers file.

The **Shared store** attribute determines the HA mode to be used in your cluster. If we set it to true a shared storage will be used by the cluster nodes (See earlier section *"HA with Shared Store"*).

Obviously, this means that the location of the journal and paging files will have to be configured on a location where they can be accessed.

Server Discovery

Another important part of clustering is **server discovery** where servers can broadcast their connection details so clients or other servers can connect to them with the minimum of configuration.

 Server discovery uses UDP multicast to broadcast server connection settings. If UDP is disabled on your network you will have to specify explicitly a static list of servers when setting up a cluster or using a messaging client. See HornetQ documentation http://docs.jboss.org/hornetq/2.3.0.Final/docs/user-manual/html_single.

The configuration of Server Discovery can be done by clicking on the **View** link from the **Messaging Clustering** window seen in the earlier snapshot.

MESSAGING CLUSTERING

❮ Back   Broadcast   Discovery   Connections

ClusterConnections

Add   Remove

Name
my-cluster

❮❮ ❮   1-1 of 1   ❯ ❯❯

✏ Edit

Name: my-cluster

Discovery Group: dg-group1

Connector Ref: http-connector

Connection Address: jms

Duplicate Detection?: true

As you can see, the cluster communication is broken into three tabs:

- **Broadcast group**: a broadcast group is the means by which a server broadcasts connectors over the network.
- **Discovery:** describes the multicast group to listen to receive broadcast from other servers announcing their connectors.
- **Connections:** describe the virtual name of the cluster and the connector to be used. By default the http connector (Undertow) is used for managing cluster connections.

The cluster **address** determines which messages will be included in the cluster communication. In the above example, the cluster connection will load balance messages sent to address that start with jms. This cluster connection, will apply to all JMS queue and topic subscriptions since they map to core queues that start with the substring "jms".

Right now, we will not apply any change to this section which can be later optimized by setting an appropriate broadcast-period for the connector or a refresh-timeout on the discovery side.

Configuring backup nodes

Once that you have configured the backup nodes, we must replicate the same configuration contained in "Cluster core configuration" in the backup node/s with one important exception that is, we will set the **backup element to true** in the **Messaging Clustering** window

� Edit

Backup: true

Starting your cluster of HornetQ servers

Once that you have completed your cluster configuration, you can start your server live nodes and backup nodes. For example, supposing that you have configured to run your servers on different machines as standalone servers:

```
./standalone.sh -c standalone-full-ha.xml -Djboss.bind.address=IP-Node1
./standalone.sh -c standalone-full-ha.xml -Djboss.bind.address=IP-Node2
. . . .
```

If on the other hand, you are going to run your JMS Servers on the same machine, then you need to specify an additional node name and port offset:

```
./standalone.sh -c standalone-full-ha.xml -Djboss.bind.address=IP-Node -
Djboss.node.name=server1

./standalone.sh -c standalone-full-ha.xml -Djboss.bind.address=IP-Node -
Djboss.node.name=server2 -Djboss.socket.binding.port-offset=150
. . . .
```

Once that your server nodes are started, you should check on both server consoles for an (pretty verbose!) acknowledgment of the other cluster node which connected to the cluster:

```
INFO [org.hornetq.core.server] (Thread-7 (HornetQ-server-
HornetQServerImpl::serverUUID=4fac81fa-63db-11e3-8f31-298886086d39-19206925)) HQ221027:
Bridge ClusterConnectionBridge@1351db [name=sf.my-cluster.def6ca20-63db-11e3-94e6-
0d824bf89082, queue=QueueImpl[name=sf.my-cluster.def6ca20-63db-11e3-94e6-0d824bf89082,
postOffice=PostOfficeImpl [server=HornetQServerImpl::serverUUID=4fac81fa-63db-11e3-8f31-
298886086d39]]@63363e targetConnector=ServerLocatorImpl (identity=(Cluster-connection-
bridge::ClusterConnectionBridge@1351db [name=sf.my-cluster.def6ca20-63db-11e3-94e6-
0d824bf89082, queue=QueueImpl[name=sf.my-cluster.def6ca20-63db-11e3-94e6-0d824bf89082,
postOffice=PostOfficeImpl [server=HornetQServerImpl::serverUUID=4fac81fa-63db-11e3-8f31-
298886086d39]]@63363e targetConnector=ServerLocatorImpl . . . .
discoveryGroupConfiguration=null]] is connected
```

Using HA data replication for your cluster of HornetQ servers

If you are going to use data replication as **HA mode**, you should *not* include any journal/paging shared store information, rather in order to configure the live and backup servers to be a replicating pair, all you have to use is :

✐ Edit

Shared store: false

Both replication and shared store have advantages and disadvantages. Generally speaking, the shared store might bring some overhead to load the data from the shared storage, which might be well mitigated using a fast Storage Area Network (SAN). On the other hand, the advantage of shared-store high availability is that no replication happens between the live and backup nodes; this means it does not suffer any performance penalties due to the overhead of data replication during normal operation.

Configuring auto-discovery of backup Connection factories

Another tweak we might want to apply to our cluster configuration is the ability to allow failover to backup nodes, without additional Connection Factory lookups. This option is not yet included in the Administration console; in order to do that, the live ConnectionFactory needs to reference the discovery group and it must be marked with **ha**, as shown in the listing below:

```
<connection-factory name="RemoteConnectionFactory">
    <discovery-group-ref discovery-group-name="dg-group1"/>
    <entries>
        <entry name="java:jboss/exported/jms/RemoteConnectionFactory"/>
    </entries>
    <ha>true</ha>
    <client-failure-check-period>10</client-failure-check-period>
```

```
    <retry-interval>1000</retry-interval>
    <retry-interval-multiplier>1.5</retry-interval-multiplier>
    <max-retry-interval>60000</max-retry-interval>
    <reconnect-attempts>100</reconnect-attempts>
</connection-factory>
```

Within this configuration, we have set:
- **ha**: This tells the client it support HA and must always be true for failover to occur
- **retry-interval** - this is the time in ms that the client will wait after each unsuccessful reconnect to the server
- **retry-interval-multiplier** - this parameter is used to configure an exponential back off for reconnect attempts
- **reconnect-attempts** - this means how many reconnect attempts should a client make before failing, -1 means unlimited.

Chapter 8: Classloading and modules

This chapter discusses about the application server's Classloading mechanism that is an essential point for application developers and deployment administrators. Since the classloading is based on the JBoss modules project, we will at first give details about the application server modules infrastructure. In the next part of the chapter, we will learn how to solve dependencies and advanced classloading policies. Here is in detail our track:

- An introduction to the application server modules
- How to configure modules on the application server
- Configuring dependencies on other modules using WildFly deployment descriptors

What are modules ?

Class loading in WildFly 8 is quite different compared to earlier (4/5/6) versions of JBoss AS. Class loading is now based on the **JBoss Modules** project, which is a standalone implementation of a modular (non-hierarchical) class loading and execution environment for Java. In other words, rather than a single Class loader which loads all JARs into a flat class path, each library becomes a module which only links against the exact modules it depends on, and nothing more. It implements a thread-safe, fast, and highly concurrent delegating class loader model, coupled to an extensible module resolution system, which combine to form a unique, simple and powerful system for application execution and distribution.

So returning to our initial question, a module is a logical grouping of resources (like classes and configuration files) used for class loading and dependency management. Depending on the way modules are packaged, we can identify two different types of modules:

Static Modules: these modules are installed as a tree of directories in the application server's *modules* directory. Each module contains one or more JAR files and a configuration file (*module.xml*) that defines its unique name. All the libraries which are contained in WildFly distribution are static modules and include both the application server core libraries and the Java EE APIs. You can also install as static module third party libraries, which are used across your applications.

Modules are *only* loaded when required. This usually only occurs when an application is deployed that has explicit or implicit dependencies.

Dynamic Modules: these modules are created and loaded by the application server when a library (e.g. EAR, JAR,WAR) is deployed. The name of a dynamic module is derived from the name of the deployed archive. Because deployments are loaded as modules, they can also configure dependencies and be used as dependencies by other deployments.

Configuring static modules

WildFly statically loads its modules based on a module path environment variable named **JBOSS_MODULEPATH**. This variable defaults to the *JBOSS_HOME/modules* folder therefore this is the standard location where you can find WildFly 8 core modules:

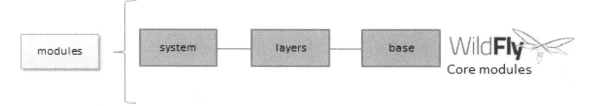

By setting the **JBOSS_MODULEPATH**, you can specify additional paths for your modules. Here's an example: (Linux users):

```
JBOSS_MODULESPATH=/usr/libs/custom-modules:$JBOSS_HOME/modules
```

 You can alternatively boot the server using the **-mp** switch which by default uses the path specified by JBOSS_MODULESPATH variable.

The above behavior makes it relatively straightforward to define a common repository for your WildFly installations: in the following example, there's a shared module repository in */var/lib/modules* and a corresponding symbolic link in each distribution pointing to the common repository:

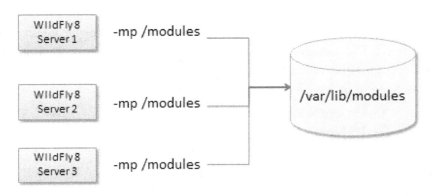

Shared library modules

/modules -> /var/lib/modules

How to install a new module

By configuring an application under the modules folder is the most flexible option as it allows defining the exact dependencies contained in your library. In addition, it allows defining different library versions (e.g. two different implementations of JSF API) which are qualified as **slots**.

You can install new modules at the root of your JBOSS_MODULESPATH therefore allowing a clear distinction between the base distribution modules and your own libraries:

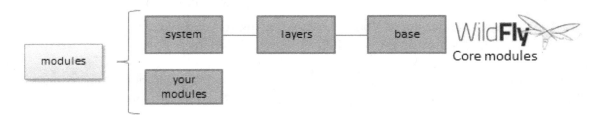

The first step for installing a module is obviously creating a path for your module. The choice of the path name is up to you; however, you need to include a **"main"** folder at the end of your path structure which will contain the module's default libraries and its configuration file.

Example: How to install Jython library as a module

Let's see as an example how to install the Jython libraries which can be used as a Java interpreter for the Python language. In order to do that, you just need to have your library jar file ready (*jython-standalone-2.5.2.jar*). Then launch *jboss-cli* script and issue the following command:

```
module add --name=org.jython --resources=/usr/libs/jython-standalone-2.5.2.jar --dependencies=javax.api
```

This will create the following module structure under *JBOSS_HOME/modules*

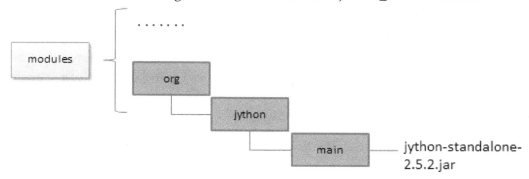

The **module add** command will create as well the following ***module.xml*** configuration file:

```
<module xmlns="urn:jboss:module:1.1" name="org.jython">
<resources>
  <resource-root path="jython-standalone-2.5.2.jar"/>
</resources>
<dependencies>
  <module name="javax.api"/>
</dependencies>
</module>
```

This basically says that the module is bound to the name "org.jython" and has a dependency on the javax.api module.

How to use an installed module in your application

In order to use this module in your applications you have to trigger a dependency on the module. This can be done by adding into the *META-INF/MANIFEST.MF* file a:

Dependencies: [modulename]

Example:

```
Dependencies: org.jython
```

Please note that the module name does not have to match with the package name of the library. The actual module name is specified in the *module.xml* file by the **name** attribute of the module element.

You are not limited to use a single dependency in your Manifest file, as you can add multiple dependencies separated by a comma. For example, here is how to configure a multiple dependency towards two modules (org.jython and log4j):

```
Dependencies: org.jython,org.apache.log4j
```

In case your application is contained in an Enterprise Archive, if you want that your dependency is exported to all submodules you can add the **export** keyword to your EAR's Manifest file. For example, here is how to export jython and log4j dependencies to other submodules contained in an Enterprise Archive:

```
Dependencies: org.jython,org.apache.log4j export
```

How to turn your modules in a global module

The above dependency strategy is the default and recommended one for your applications. It is however also possible to define a module as a global module, which means that it will be accessible to all deployments without adding any entry to the application Manifest file. This can be done by is done by expanding the **Container** left side option (from the Configuration upper tab) and selecting the EE subsystem. Click on Add to create a new global module and enter the Module name and slot:

Create Module   ⤢ ✕

Name: `org.apache.log4j`

Slot: `main`

Cancel   Save

Click on **Save** to persist your configuration. This results in the following global module definition:

☑ Edit

Isolated Subdeployments?:   false

Global Modules

	Add	Remove

Name	Slot
org.apache.log4j	main

Please note that from this screen you can also define the global setting for the **Isolated Subdeployment** behavior flag which by default (false) means the subdeployments can see classes belonging to other subdeployments within the .ear (More about it in the section "Configuring classloading isolation").

Configuring dynamic modules

Anything in WildFly is a module, therefore if you deploy a library into the AS (for example by dropping it into the deployments folder) then it's automatically elected as a module. You will not be able to use all the flexible options contained in *module.xml* yet, in some circumstances, it can be useful. As an example, you can drop a JDBC driver into the deployment folder and it will be automatically deployed and a module created out of it.

How to use dynamic modules in your applications

You can use a dynamic module in your applications just the same way we have seen for installed module. The only thing we need to know is the actual module name.

Here's the rule to determine the module name: applications that are packaged as top-level archives (such as WAR, JAR, and SAR) are assigned the following module name:

```
deployment.[archive name]
```

For example, a Web application named WebExample1.war will be deployed as module name:

```
deployment.WebExample1.war
```

Therefore, you can reference this module with the following entry in *MANIFEST.MF*

```
Dependencies: deployment.WebExample1.war
```

On the other hand, on applications that contain nested deployments (such as the EAR archive), every single archive will be assigned a module name using this classification:

```
deployment.[ear archive name].[sub deployment archive name]
```

So, the same Web application, if contained in the archive *EnterpriseApp.ear*, will be deployed with the name:

```
deployment.EnterpriseApp.ear.WebExample1.war
```

Configuring module Dependencies

So far we have seen how to install a new module and how to specify that an application is dependent on that module. The previous example does not cover all aspects of application dependencies; actually, the application server recognizes two types of dependencies: explicit and implicit.

- The Java EE core libraries are qualified as **implicit** dependencies, so they are automatically added to your application when the deployer detects their usage.
- The other module libraries need to be **explicitly** declared by the user in the application's Manifest file or in a custom descriptor file named *jboss-deployment-structure.xml*.

Implicit dependencies

Implicit dependencies include two sets of core modules, which are added to your application without an explicit dependency assertion. The first set of module, include the following core modules, which are *automatically* added to your applications:

Implicit dependencies (1)

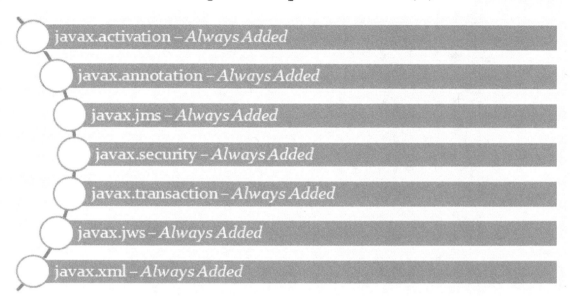

- javax.activation – *Always Added*
- javax.annotation – *Always Added*
- javax.jms – *Always Added*
- javax.security – *Always Added*
- javax.transaction – *Always Added*
- javax.jws – *Always Added*
- javax.xml – *Always Added*

The second set of implicit dependency is added *on a condition* and includes almost all modules that are based on configuration files or annotations. For example, the **javax.ejb** dependency is triggered if the user annotates the class with an EJB annotation (e.g. @Stateless) or if the *ejb-jar.xml* file is included in the application.

Implicit dependencies (2)

- javax.ejb – *Condition: annotation / ejb-jar.xml*
- org.jboss.resteasy – *Condition: JAX-RS annotation*
- javax.persistence – *Condition: annotation / persistence.xml*
- org.hibernate – *Condition: annotation / persistence.xml*
- org.jboss.as.web – *Condition: archivio .war*
- org.jboss.as.weld – *Condition: weld.xml*

Explicit dependencies

Modules, which are not qualified as implicit dependencies, need to be declared by the user. In our initial example, the org.jython is mentioned in the Manifest file therefore the application server will link the library to the application.

```
Dependencies: org.jython
```

If you need a fine grained control over your dependencies and classloading policies you can use the file *jboss-deployment-structure.xml* which is an application server custom descriptor discussed in the next section of this chapter.

Advanced Classloading policies

The first common usage of the *jboss-deployment-structure.xml* file is to set application dependency against modules. The advantage of using this file (compared to the Manifest's entry) is that you can define dependencies across top-level deployments and subdeployments.

In the following example, we have defined a top-level dependency (The file *itextpdf-5.4.3.jar* which has been added in the deployments folder) which is exported to all submodules of an Enterprise Archive (ear):

```
<jboss-deployment-structure>
  <deployment>
    <dependencies>
      <module name="deployment.itextpdf-5.4.3.jar" export="TRUE"/>
    </dependencies>
  </deployment>
</jboss-deployment-structure>
```

If we want a more restrictive policy, we can include the dependency just for the sub-module named *myapp.war* which is included in the EAR:

```
<jboss-deployment-structure>
  <sub-deployment name="myapp.war">
   <dependencies>
     <module name="deployment.itextpdf-5.4.3.jar" />
   </dependencies>
  </sub-deployment>
</jboss-deployment-structure>
```

The above examples are using deployment-based dependencies; you can however reference your modules installed in the *modules* folder as in the following example where we are referencing log4j libraries:

```
<jboss-deployment-structure>
  <deployment>
    <dependencies>
      <module name="org.apache.log4j" export="TRUE"/>
    </dependencies>
   </deployment>
</jboss-deployment-structure>
```

If you need to provide a fine-grained control over your dependencies, you can exclude/include some packages from your dependencies. Let's take as an example the following application which is composed of these artifacts:

```
MyApp.ear
|
|-- MyWebApp.war
|
|-- lib/itextpdf-5.4.3.jar
```

As it is, you don't need configuring the *jboss-deployment-structure.xml* to use the itext classes, which are picked up from the lib folder. However, what if you want to select which packages to use of included itext library? That can be done by defining the itext library as a module and include a filter in it, which excludes for example the *com/itextpdf/awt/geom* package:

```
<jboss-deployment-structure>
   <sub-deployment name="MyWebApp.war">
    <dependencies>
      <module name="deployment.itextpdf-5.4.3.jar" />
    </dependencies>
   </sub-deployment>
   <module name="deployment.itextpdf-5.4.3.jar" >
    <resources>
     <resource-root path="itextpdf-5.4.3.jar" >
        <filter>
        <exclude path="com/itextpdf/awt/geom" />
      </filter>
    </resource-root>
    </resources>
   </module>
</jboss-deployment-structure>
```

How to prevent your modules from being loaded

In this second section, we will show how to exclude some modules from being loaded by WildFly. Here's for example how to prevent your application to use dom4j libraries and use the XOM (http://www.xom.nu/) object module which we have installed as module name "org.xom":

```
<jboss-deployment-structure>
   <deployment>
      <exclusions>
         <module name="org.dom4j" />
      </exclusions>
      <dependencies>
         <module name="org.xom" />
      </dependencies>
   </deployment>
</jboss-deployment-structure>
```

As a footnote, please be aware that you can use the **slot** parameter in the module name in order to specify a dependency against a particular release of a module. In the following example we want to replace the default (main) implementation of the **com.mysql** module with the one contained in the slot named "**1.26**". Here's the view of the com.mysql folder under your modules tree:

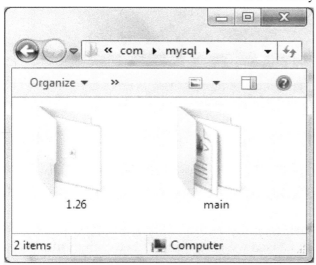

This is the corresponding configuration needed to use the slot 1.26 for your JDBC Driver:

```
<jboss-deployment-structure>
    <deployment>
        <exclusions>
            <module name="com.mysql" />
        </exclusions>
        <dependencies>
            <module name="com.mysql" slot="1.26" />
        </dependencies>
    </deployment>
</jboss-deployment-structure>
```

 Please note that the slot name does not have to be a version number, you can use any name of your like as long it does exist in your module file system.

How to prevent a subsystem from being loaded

Another feature of the *jboss-deployment-structure.xml* file is the ability to prevent the classloader to use a subsystem included in the application server. In the following example, we are excluding the resteasy subsystem that is used for consuming REST Messages:

```
<jboss-deployment-structure>
    <deployment>
     <exclude-subsystems>
        <subsystem name="resteasy" />
     </exclude-subsystems>
    </deployment>
</jboss-deployment-structure>
```

Please note that if the exclude-subsystem is specified for the top-level archive, it will be inherited by sub deployments, unless the sub deployments specify their own (possibly empty) list.

Configuring classloading isolation

The *jboss-deployment-structure.xml* can be used also to configure the application server classloading policy. The default policy, which is used to solve conflicts between multiple versions of the same class, is the following:

- The highest priority is given to modules, automatically loaded by the container (e.g. the Java EE APIs).
- Next, libraries that are indicated by the user either using the MANIFEST.MF mechanism (Dependencies:) or the *jboss-deployment-structure.xml* file).
- Then, libraries that are packed within the application itself, such as classes contained in *WEB-INF/lib* or *WEB-INF/classes*.
- Finally, libraries that are packed within the same EAR archive (in the EAR's lib folder).

Now that we are aware about the default classloading policies, let's see a concrete example.
The following application (myapp.ear) includes libraries: an EJB archive, a Web application and an utility library in the *lib* folder.

```
myapp.ear
   |
   |--- web.war
   |
   |--- ejb.jar
   |
   |--- lib/utility.jar
```

What is the default behavior of the server's classloader in this example?

- WEB application classes are able to use the EJB classes
- EJB classes are not able to see the WEB application classes (which are loaded by a different classloader as per Java EE specification).
- Both WEB classes and EJB classes are able to use the utility.jar

By setting to true the **ear-subdeployments-isolated** (default false), you can alter this behavior:

```
<jboss-deployment-structure>
  <ear-subdeployments-isolated>true</ear-subdeployments-isolated>
</jboss-deployment-structure>
```

Here is the new behavior now:

- WEB application classes are not able to use the EJB classes
- EJB classes are still not able to see the WEB application classes (the ear-subdeployments-isolated has no effect on this archive)
- Both WEB classes and EJB classes are still able to use the *utility.jar* (the ear-subdeployments-isolated has no effect on the archives in the lib folder)

As a final note, you should be aware that, as per Java EE specification, you can alter the default name for the shared libraries (lib) by adding a library-directory element in your application.xml:

```
<library-directory>mylibs</library-directory>
```

Sticking to Java EE compatibility

Using the Dependencies declaration in your Manifest file is a custom classloading strategy adopted by WildFly and JBoss AS 7. That's a quite powerful add-on, yet if you are on the hook for Java EE portability you should evaluate using the **Class-Path** Manifest entry in your artifacts. This can be used within an EAR to set up dependencies between sub deployments and also to allow modules access to additional jars deployed in an ear that are not sub deployments and are not in the EAR/lib directory. Here's for example how to state a dependency to the *utility.jar* library which is packaged in your EAR archive:

```
Manifest-Version: 1.0
Class-Path: utility.jar
```

As you can see, one important difference with the WildFly Dependencies strategy is that Java EE's Classpath needs to directly reference an artifact; therefore, if you plan to upgrade your libraries you need to keep your Manifest file in sync. Besides this, the biggest downside of this approach is that you can only use libraries that are packaged along with your application, whilst the Dependencies option can reference modules which are loaded anywhere from the application server.

Chapter 9: Clustering

Clusters in an application server enhance scalability and availability, which are related concepts. In order to achieve the benefits of clustering, you need to manage the configuration of several components like the clustering transport at first, the replication/distribution of data across cluster members and the techniques used to balance load between nodes. As you can imagine, there is a lot of ground to cover so we will start right away with the list of topics that follows:

- Which are the WildFly clustering building blocks
- Configuring application server for clustering in standalone mode and domain mode
- Configuring the cluster Transport libraries
- Configuring Cluster Caches using Infinispan subsystem

In the next chapter, we will provide some complimentary information that is essential to balance the load of Web applications.

WildFly clustering building blocks

The following picture shows the clustering building blocks from a component-centric viewpoint:

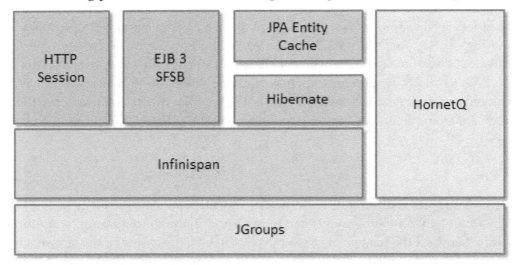

As you can see, there the backbone of WildFly clustering is the **JGroups** library, which provides a reliable multicast system used by cluster members to find each other and communicate.

Multicast is a protocol where data is transmitted simultaneously to a group of hosts that have joined the appropriate multicast group. You can think about multicast as a radio or television streaming where only those tuned to a particular frequency receive the streaming.

Next comes **Infinispan**, which is a data grid platform that is used by the application server to keep in sync the application data in the cluster by means of a replicated and transactional JSR-107 compatible cache. Infinispan is used both as a Cache for standard session mechanisms (HTTP Sessions and SFSB session data) and as advanced caching mechanism for JPA and Hibernate objects (aka second level cache).

Clustering standalone nodes

As we already know, the application server includes the following standalone configurations that are cluster-aware:

- *standalone-ha.xml*
- *standalone-ha-full.xml*

Therefore, in order to start a cluster of application servers in cluster mode you have to select one of these configurations. Additionally, you need to specify a server node's name if your cluster nodes are going to be bound to on the same IP Address.

Clustering standalone servers on different machines

The first and simpler use case is a clustering configuration where each server is bound on a different IP Address; that's usually the case of an installation on different machines. In the following example, the first cluster node is started on a machine bound at the IP Address **192.168.10.1** and the second one at the IP Address **192.168.10.2**:

```
standalone.bat -b 192.168.10.1 -c standalone-ha.xml
standalone.bat -b 192.168.10.2 -c standalone-ha.xml
```

The following picture summarizes our clustering configuration:

WildFly Cluster - one AS installation per host

Clustering standalone servers on the same machine

In the second use case, we are going to start more than one AS instance on the same machine; in order to avoid conflicts, we need to specify a server node name on each server JVM and a port-offset for the second (and eventually other nodes). For this purpose, we will use the **jboss.node.name** and **jboss.socket.binding.port-offset** as shown by the following code:

```
standalone.bat -c standalone-ha.xml -Djboss.node.name=nodeA

standalone.bat -c standalone-ha.xml -Djboss.node.name=nodeB -Djboss.socket.binding.port-offset=150
```

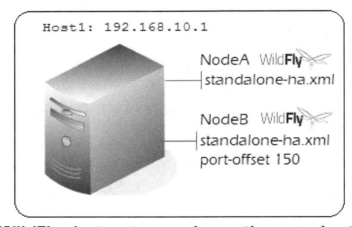

WildFly cluster - two nodes on the same host

Configuring a cluster of domain nodes

In the second chapter, we have learnt that the domain configuration is federated in a single file named *domain.xml*. Within this file, there are four built-in profiles namely:

- The **default** profile, which can be used for non-clustered environments
- The **ha** profile for clustered environments
- The **full** profile which includes the messaging extension to the default profile
- The **full-ha** profile which includes both the messaging extension and the clustering capabilities

Therefore, in order to use clustering you have to make sure that your server groups are using one cluster aware profile, such as the "**ha**" and "**full-ha**". You can check your server groups' profile by manual inspection of your *domain.xml* or entering in the **Domain** tab of the Admin Console and selecting the **Server Groups** option contained in the Server panel:

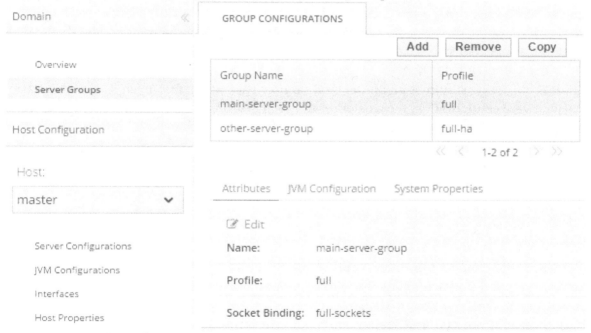

As you can see, by default, the *main-server-group* is bound to a "**full**" profile, while the *other-server-group* uses a "**full-ha**" profile. In order to select a different profile, click on the "**Edit**" lower link.

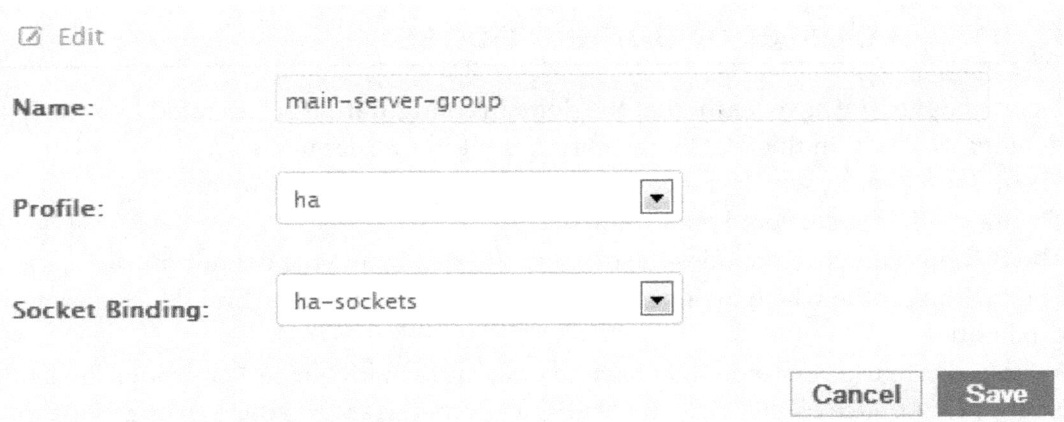

Name: main-server-group

Profile: ha ▼

Socket Binding: ha-sockets ▼

Cancel **Save**

As you can see from the above picture, we have selected an "**ha**" profile and the corresponding "**ha-sockets**" SocketBinding for our main-server-group.

You will be advised that a server restart is necessary in order to acknowledge the changes. At domain restart, the server nodes which are part of the main-server-group will be able to deliver clustered applications.

Enabling clustering services

WildFly clustering service is an on-demand service. This means that, even if you have started a cluster aware configuration, the cluster service won't start until you deploy a cluster-aware application. Enabling clustering for your applications can be achieved in different ways depending on the type of application you are going to deploy:

If you are deploying a **Web based application**, then you need to declare it as "distributable" in the *web.xml* configuration file to have your HTTP session state replicated across the cluster:

```
<web-app>
  <distributable />
</web-app>
```

If you are deploying an **EJB based application**, clustering services will start *automatically* and you do not need any special annotation or XML configuration element. In the earlier versions of the application server, you used to demarcate your EJB with the annotation **@org.jboss.ejb3.annotation.Clustered** to trigger clustering services, as in the following example:

```
@Stateful
@Clustered
public class ClusteredStatelefulBean { … }
```

This annotation is **now deprecated** and will be ignored by the application server (and the same stands for the <clustered>true</clustered> element that you could include into the *jboss-ejb3.xml* deployment descriptor). So ultimately, with the new release of the application server, the state of your Stateful Bean is automatically replicated across cluster nodes without any effort from your side.

Configuring the Cluster transport

The backbone of JBoss clustering is the **JGroups** library, which provides the communication between members of the cluster using a multicast transmission. The JGroups API handles the communication between nodes in the cluster using a set of reliable communication protocols.
The protocol stack contains a number of protocol layers in a bidirectional list. All messages sent and received over the channel have to pass through all protocols. Every layer may modify, reorder, pass or drop a message, or add a header to a message.
Here's an example of the default Protocol stack which uses **UDP** (default) as transport protocol:

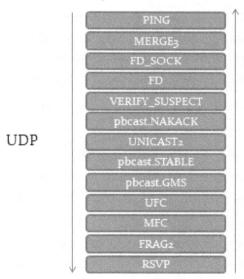

Configuring the Transport Properties
You can configure the transport JGroups properties by expanding the **Core** element from the left side menu and selecting the option **JGroups** as showed by the following picture:

From there, click on **View** on the Protocol stack configuration that you will be using. In our case, we will go through the (default) UDP protocol stack. Each protocol stack has its own **Transport** properties and a list of **Protocols** used for the communication. We will start discussing about the Transport properties which are depicted by the following picture:

The following table includes a short description for all the Transport protocol properties:

Type	The protocol stack used. Default is UDP.
Socket Binding	The socket binding specification for this protocol layer. It is used to specify IP interfaces and ports for communication.
Diagnostics Socket	This is the diagnostics socket binding used for probing the communication in the cluster.
Is Shared?	If true, the underlying transport is shared by all channels using this stack.
Machine	The machine (i.e. host) identifier for this node. Used by Infinispan topology-aware consistent hash.
Site	The site (i.e. data centre) identifier for this node. Used by Infinispan topology-aware consistent hash.
Rack	The rack (i.e. server rack) identifier for this node. Used by Infinispan topology-aware consistent hash.

A protocol stack with UDP as transport protocol is typically used with clusters whose members run in the same subnet. If running across subnets, an admin has to ensure that IP multicast is enabled across subnets. It is often the case that IP multicast is not enabled across subnets. In such cases, the stack has to either use UDP without IP multicasting or other transports such as TCP.

Besides using the Admin Console, a quick way to change the default stack to TCP for all clustering services can be achieved by issuing the following CLI command:

```
/subsystem=jgroups/:write-attribute(name=default-stack,value=tcp)
```

Configuring the Protocol Properties

You can access the JGroups Protocols panel by selecting the **Protocols** sub-tab contained in the JGroups panel:

< Back   Protocols   Transport

Protocols: Stack udp

The configuration of protocols within a protocol stack. The order of protocols does matter.

Append   Remove

Type
PING
MERGE3
FD_SOCK
FD_ALL

In this window, you can add or remove new protocols to your communication Stack. Adding new protocols can enhance the reliability of your communications while reducing the performance of your network transmission and vice versa.

By selecting a single Protocol, you can pinpoint the single properties used by the protocols in the **Properties** panel contained in the lower part of the GUI. For example, in the following screenshot we have customized two properties of the **MERGE3** Protocol that is used to discover cluster subgroups. This Protocol uses the properties *min_interval* and *max_interval* to determine the minimum and maximum interval between each info message sent across the cluster node:

JGROUPS

< Back   Protocols   Transport

PING

MERGE3

FD_SOCK

Attributes   Properties

[Add]   [Remove]

▲ Key	Value
max_interval	30000
min_interval	10000

If, on the other hand, you are more familiar with the CLI, you can direct your commands to the jgroups subsystem in order to tune your protocols. In the following example, we are setting the UNICAST3 protocol to send and receive buffer to (respectively) 50000000 bytes and 1280000 bytes, open the CLI and issue the following commands:

```
/subsystem=jgroups/stack=udp/protocol=UNICAST3/property=ucast_recv_buf_size/:add(value=50
000000)
/subsystem=jgroups/stack=udp/protocol=UNICAST3/property=ucast_send_buf_size/:add(value=12
80000)
```

 If you want to learn more about the single Protocols and their properties, check out the JGroups documentation available at: http://www.jgroups.org/manual-3.x/html/protlist.html.

Configuring Clustering Caches

The second building block of WildFly clustering is **Infinispan**, which is an advanced Data Grid Platform that can be used to cache and synchronize cluster data across its members. The Infinispan subsystem contains two main elements in it:

- **Cache Containers**: this component is a Cache Manager that acts as container for a set of Infinispan caches.
- **Individual Caches**: these caches are used by the application software to store cluster data which is maintained across the cluster.

In order to explore Infinispan subsystem, you have to navigate to the Admin Console and expand the **Infinispan** label, as shown by the following picture, which shows the list of available Cache containers:

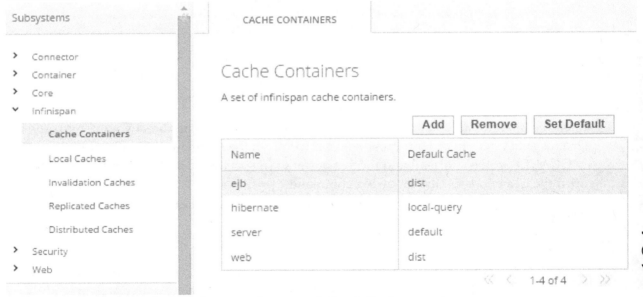

As you can see, out of the box there are four pre-defined Cache containers:
- The **ejb** Cache Container used for replication of Stateful EJB Session data
- The **hibernate** Cache Container used as foundation for second level entity cache by JPA/Hibernate
- The **server** Cache Container used as general purpose replication of objects in a cluster
- The **web** Cache Container used for replication of HTTP sessions

The above cache containers are used internally by the application server, however you can define new ones (clicking on the Add button) for the purpose of having your own replicated/distributed cache solution.

The **Set Default** button, on the other hand, can be used to configure the default cache to be used, when no cache is otherwise specified.

Configuring Cache Container Attributes

Once that you have selected a single Cache, you can define, through the **Details** section, the single **Attributes** and **Transport** parameters of the Cache. Here are for example the Attributes of the "**ejb**" cache:

Attributes   Transport   Aliases

☞ Edit

Name: ejb

Default Cache: dist

Start:

JNDI Name:

Eviction Executor:

Replication Queue Executor:

Listener Executor:

The **Default Cache** attribute controls the cache to be used by the Cache container. In this example, the Default Cache is set to "dist" which points to a **Distributed Cache** (more about the different type of caches in next section). The **Start** attribute configures the cache container start mode, which can be EAGER (immediate start) or LAZY (on-demand start).

> If you are deploying an application which initializes at startup a Cache (e.g. Hibernate 2LC) you need to setup this attribute to **EAGER** to avoid an application startup failure.

The **JNDI** attribute controls the assigned JNDI name for the cache container.

Here's for example how to use the Web cache container in your Enterprise Applications

```
@Resource(lookup="java:jboss/infinispan/container/web")
private CacheContainer container;
```

The **eviction-executor** attribute references a Thread pool executor from the threads subsystem. It controls the allocation and execution of runnable tasks to handle *evictions*. You should consider configuring this attribute if you make a regular use of cache evictions in order to keep control over the amount of memory available.

The **replication-queue-executor** attribute references as well a Thread pool executor and controls the allocation and execution of runnable tasks to handle *asynchronous* cache operations. By default, the web and ejb cache containers use an asynchronous replication mechanism, therefore you should consider setting this attribute if you have a consistent amount of data to be replicated.

The **listener-executor** attribute references also a defined Thread pool executor and governs the allocation and execution of runnable tasks in the replication queue. You should consider using it if you are emitting frequent notifications to asynchronous listeners.

 Please note that in order to create the Thread pool executors used by Infinispan you need first to enable the **threads** subsystem. (See *"The threads subsystem"* in the Appendix of the book).

In the following example, we have at first defined a **Bounded Thread Pool** named "Custom Executor" (You can reach this screen by expanding the **Core** panel and entering the **Thread Pools** section):

THREAD FACTORIES	THREAD POOLS

Queless   Blocking Queless   Unbounded   Bounded   Blocking Bounded

Bounded Pools

A set of bounded queue thread pools.

Add   Remove

Name	Max Threads
CustomExecutor	25

《 〈 1-1 of 1 〉 》

The **Thread pool** is then referenced in the Cache Container's attributes by the **Eviction Executor**
Property:

☑ Edit

Name: ejb

Default Cache: repl

Start: ▼

JNDI Name:

Eviction Executor: CustomExecutor

Configuring the Cache Container Transport

In the beginning of this chapter, we have learnt the core cluster transport configuration that is
carried out by the JGroups library. Besides the core transport settings, you can also specialize the
transport settings just for a *single* Cache container. In order to do that, from your Cache container
details panel, select the **Transport** tab as shown by the following screen:

☑ Edit

Is transport defined?: true

Stack:

Executor:

Lock Timeout (ms):   60000

Cluster:

In this screen, you can configure the following Cache container attributes:

Stack	The Stack attribute defines the JGroup Stack to be used for transport. By default UDP is used, however if you have requirements that are incompatible for this stack (e.g. some cluster nodes on a different subnetwork) you can fine-tune the cache transport to use TCP.
Executor	The Executor attribute governs the Thread pool to be used for Cache transport.
Lock Timeout	The Lock Timeout attribute configures the time-out to be used when obtaining locks for the transport.
Cluster	This attribute configures the name of the group communication cluster. This is the name which will be seen in debugging logs.

If you are seeing the following exception in your logs you should consider tuning the Lock Timeout attribute:

```
Caused by: org.infinispan.util.concurrent.TimeoutException: Unable to acquire lock after
[60 seconds] on key [178328] for requestor [Thread[http-10.226.32.128-5000-
Processor10,5,main]]! Lock held by [(another thread)
```

Caching strategies

Infinispan caches can opt for different caching strategies:

- **replicated-cache:** This element is used by caches that replicate its state across all nodes of the cluster.

- **distributed-cache:** This element is used by caches that distribute its state across a set of nodes of the cluster. It is the default for ejb and web applications.
- **invalidation-cache:** This element is used by caches that simply send an invalidation message to other nodes of the cluster.

Using a replicated cache

In a replicated cache, all nodes in a cluster hold all keys i.e. if a cache entry exists on one nodes, it will also exist on all other nodes. The Replication strategy is the simplest way to guarantee high availability to your cluster; as soon as your application is modifying a session attribute (e.g. a *session.setAttribute* for a web application), the change is propagated across all nodes of the cluster.

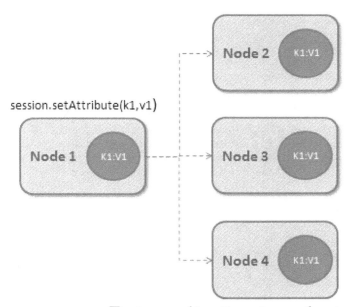

Data replication in a cluster

The replication strategy proves to be an efficient mechanism for clustered applications that *mostly read* data, or for applications that are distributed over a limited number of cluster nodes (Infinispan recommends 10 as a reasonable upper bound on the number of replicated nodes).

Using a distributed cache

When using cache distribution, cache entries are copied to a fixed number of cluster nodes (2, by default) regardless of the cluster size. Distribution uses a consistent hashing algorithm to determine which nodes will store a given entry and can be used to enable your clusters to achieve "linear scalability". The number of copies represents a trade-off between performance and durability of data. The more copies you maintain, the lower performance will be, but also the lower the risk of losing data due to server outages. You can use the **owners** parameter (default 2) to define the number of cluster-wide replicas for each cache entry. Here's how to set this parameter to 3 for the "ejb" Cache container:

```
/subsystem=infinispan/cache-container=ejb/distributed-cache=dist/:write-
attribute(name=owners,value=3)
```

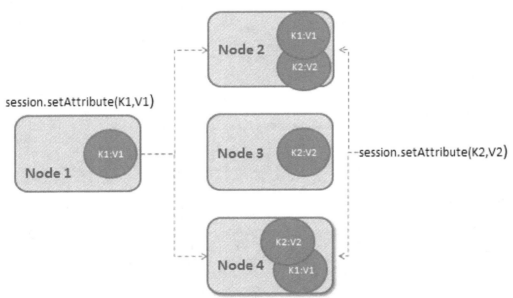

Data distribution in a cluster (owners = 3)

Using an invalidation cache

When using this cache mode no data is actually shared among the cluster nodes. Instead, notifications are sent to all nodes when data changes, causing them to evict their stale copies of the updated entry. By using invalidation, you can achieve the following benefits:

1. Each cluster node looks up for changes only when needed (e.g. when the application requests a data fetching which has been marked as *dirty*).
2. The network traffic does not lead to network congestion as the invalidation messages contain a very little data payload.

As you can see from the following picture, the invalidation cache is used by **hibernate** Cache Container for caching Entities:

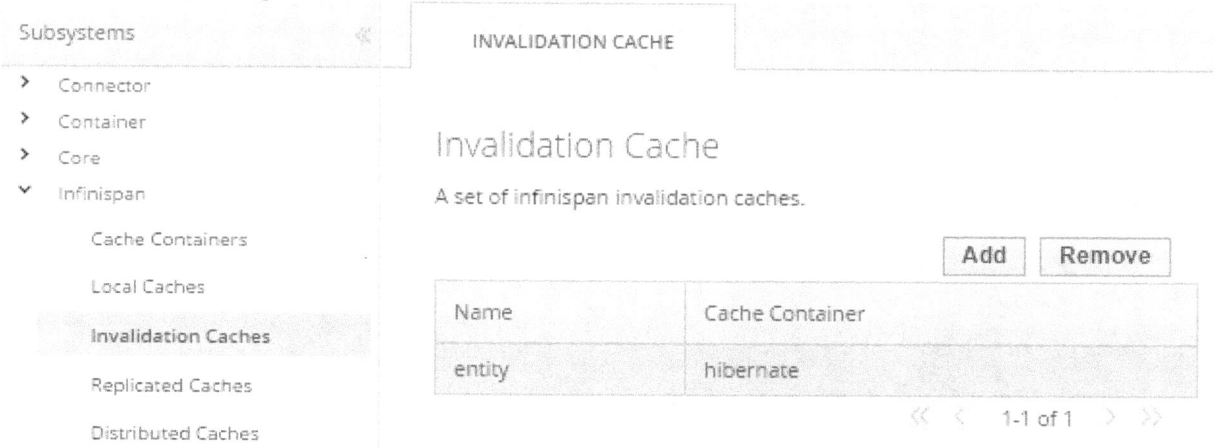

As a matter of fact, hibernate uses this cache as part of the **second level cache** mechanism in order to have data accessible *locally* rather than having to go to the database to retrieve it every time this is needed. When an Entity is updated/deleted, an invalidation message is sent across cluster nodes to inform that data for that Entity has changed which must therefore be reloaded on its next access.

Controlling the amount of data to be stored in memory

You can control the amount of data to be cached by hibernate by entering in the **Details** of the **Entity** cache container. For example, if you want to have control over the amount of items to be contained in your cache, you can select the **Eviction** sub tab and define the following properties:

		Add	Remove

Name	Cache Container
entity	hibernate

Attrs	Locking	Trans	Eviction	Expiration	Store	File Store	JDBC Store	Rmt Store

✏ Edit

Is eviction defined?:	true
Eviction Strategy:	LRU
Max Entries:	10000

The **Max Entries** parameter controls the maximum number of items to be held in memory, while you can choose among the following eviction strategies: 'UNORDERED', 'FIFO', 'LRU', 'LIRS' and 'NONE' (to disable eviction).

 LIRS is a variation of the LRU algorithm that addresses weak access locality shortcomings of LRU. For more information about it, please refer to http://dl.acm.org/citation.cfm?id=511334.511340.

If you want a control over your Cache data expiration then you can select the **Expiration** sub-tab and configure the **Max Idle** parameter in order to have control over the maximum idle time a cache entry will be maintained in the cache, in milliseconds.

Using a Local cache

The last type of Caching strategy is **local caching** that is used for caching Hibernate/JPA queries; this means that, by default, the query cache is configured so that queries are only cached locally. Alternatively, you can configure Hibernate/JPA query caching to use replication if a set of conditions are met:

- The query used are quite expensive
- The query are very likely to be repeated in different cluster nodes
- The query is unlikely to be invalidated out of the cache (Note: Hibernate must aggressively invalidate query results from the cache each time any instance of one of the Entity classes involved in the query's WHERE clause changes. All such query results are invalidated, even if the change made to the Entity instance would not have affected the query result)

By default a maximum number of 10000 Entries can be stored locally by this cache, as you can see from the Details panel of the local-query

| | Add | Remove |

Name	Cache Container
local-query	hibernate

<< < 1-1 of 1 > >>

Attributes   Locking   Trans   Eviction   Expiration   Store   File Store   JDBC Store   Rmt Store

Edit

Is eviction defined?:   true

Eviction Strategy: LRU

Max Entries: 10000

Configuring the Timestamp cache

The last cache that is included in the "hibernate" Cache Container is named **timestamp-cache**. The timestamp-cache keeps track of the last update timestamp for each table (this timestamp is updated for any table modification). Any time the query cache is checked for a query, the timestamp-cache is checked for all tables in the query. If the timestamp of the last update on a table is greater than the time the query results were cached, the entry is removed and the lookup is a miss.

By default, the timestamps cache is configured with asynchronous replication as clustering mode. Since all nodes of the cluster must store all the timestamps relative to table changes, local or invalidated cluster modes are not allowed. For the same reason, no eviction or expiration is allowed for timestamp caches either.

Managing the Cache Storage

The default replication and distributed caches which are included in the Infinispan subsystem both use a file system as data store. In order to configure the FileStore properties of your Cache, select the **FileStore** details of your cache (in our example the "dist" cache):

And here's an explanation to the single attributes that you can configure:

shared	Indicates that the file store is shared among different cache instances. Setting this to true prevents repeated and unnecessary writes of the same data to the cache loader by different cache instances
preload	If true, when the cache starts, data stored in the cache loader will be pre-loaded into memory. Can be used to provide a "warm-cache" on startup, however there is a performance penalty as startup time is affected by this process.
passivation	When set to true, the cache will enforce entry passivation and activation on eviction in a cache. Cache passivation is the process of removing an object from in-memory cache and writing it to a secondary data store on eviction. Cache Activation is the process of restoring an object from the data store into the in-memory cache when it's needed to be used. In both cases, when passivation is set to true, configured cache will be used to read from the data store and write to the data store.
fetch-state	Determines whether or not to fetch the persistent state of a cache when joining a cluster. If cache store is configured to be shared, since caches access the same cache store, fetch persistent state is ignored.

purge	Empties the specified cache loader when the cache starts up.
singleton	When set to true enables modifications to be stored by only one node in the cluster, the coordinator. Essentially, whenever any data comes in to some node it is always replicated(or distributed) so as to keep the caches in-memory states in sync; the coordinator, though, has the sole responsibility of pushing that state to disk.

Some additional properties like **path** (the location where the file store is persisted) or **relative-to** (the root path where the cache will be persisted) can be set using the CLI, like in the following example where we are setting the FileStore path:

```
/subsystem=infinispan/cache-container=ejb/distributed-cache=dist/file-
store=FILE_STORE/:write-attribute(name=path,value=filestorepath)
```

Using a JDBC Cache store

The default file cache store is a good approach for many basic clustering scenarios. However, bear in mind the following limitations:

- Usage on shared filesystems such as NFS, Windows shares, and other similar technologies, should be avoided as these do not implement proper POSIX file locking, and can cause data corruption
- Filesystems are inherently not transactional, so when attempting to use your cache in a transactional context, failures when writing to the file (which happens during the commit phase) cannot be recovered

A valid alternative approach can be using a **JDBC cache store**, which persists data in a relational database using a JDBC driver. There are three implementations of the JDBC cache store, which are as follows:

- JdbcBinaryCacheStore
- JdbcStringBasedCacheStore
- JdbcMixedCacheStore

The **JdbcBinaryCacheStore** is a standard JDBC based solution that can store any type of key for your entries. This can be obtained by storing all the Map buckets (slot of array elements) as rows into the database table. This provides greater flexibility, at the price of coarse-grained access granularity and inherent performance.

The **JdbcStringBasedCacheStore** implementation will store each entry within a row in the table (rather than grouping multiple entries into a row). This assures a better granularity and performance than JdbcBinaryCacheStore, but it requires that all cache keys are Strings.

Finally, **JdbcMixedCacheStore** is a hybrid implementation which, based on the key type, delegates to either JdbcBinaryCacheStore or JdbcStringBasedCacheStore, so you have the best of both worlds.

Example: Defining a JDBC Cache Store

Although the Admin console includes a subpanel which is dedicated to **JDBC Cache store**, it is more convenient to use the Command Line Interface in order to quickly configure it and have access to the different JDBC implementations available.

In the following example, we will learn how to create a Binary keyed JDBC store: the first thing you need to do is replacing the current file store for your cache. For example, supposing you want to operate on the "web" cache container, start by issuing this command:

```
/subsystem=infinispan/cache-container=web/replicated-cache=repl/file-
store=FILE_STORE/:remove
```

Next step will be adding the Binary keyed JDBC store which is bound, in this example, to the default ExampleDS Datasource, using a set of three fields to store data:

```
/subsystem=infinispan/cache-container=web/replicated-cache=repl/binary-keyed-jdbc-
store=BINARY_KEYED_JDBC_STORE:add(datasource=ExampleDS,binary-keyed-table={"id-column" =>
{"name" => "ID_COLUMN","type" => "VARCHAR(255)"},"data-column" => {"name" =>
"DATA_COLUMN","type" => "BINARY"},"timestamp-column" => {"name" =>
"TIMESTAMP_COLUMN","type" => "BIGINT"}})
```

Reload your configuration for changes to take effect.

Controlling Passivation of HTTP Sessions

Besides using Infinispan Cache Manager settings, Web application can configure passivation of HTTP Sessions using some directive which can be included on application basis into the *jboss-web.xml* file. These directives have been included mostly for backward compatibility with earlier versions of the application server yet they introduce the concept of passivating session data, which can be restored later. Let's see a concrete example:

```
<jboss-web>
    <max-active-sessions>100</max-active-sessions>
</jboss-web>
```

In this example, if session creation would cause the number of active sessions to exceed 100 active sessions, then the oldest session known to the Session Manager will passivate to make room for the new session.

Please note that <passivation-config/> element (and its subelements) used in the earlier releases of the application server have been deprecated therefore you shouldn't add anything else for fine tuning your HTTP Session passivation.

Chapter 10: Load balancing applications

This chapter discusses about the other key aspect of clustering, which is **load balancing**. As the point of access to Java EE application is traditionally the web tier, we will cover mostly how to balance request across your Web applications using a set of software components. Later on, we will show also how to balance request for EJB applications. Here is in detail what we will discuss:

- At first, we will learn how to configure and install the Apache Tomcat **mod_jk**, which was the *de facto* load balancer solution in earlier application server versions and can still be used in WildFly 8 clusters.
- Next, we will learn how to configure and install the newer **mod_cluster** library, which buys you additional capabilities in terms of dynamicity.
- In the last part of this chapter, we will shortly review the configuration needed for balancing remote calls to clustered Enterprise Java Beans.

Configuring Apache mod_jk

Mod_jk has been in the past years the most-used solution for fronting JBoss AS with Apache web server. All requests first come to the Apache web server. The Apache web server accepts and processes any static resource requests, such as requests for HTML pages or graphical images. Then, with the help of mod_jk, the Apache web server redirects requests for any JSP or Servlet component to a JBoss Web server instance(s).

The main advantage of keeping using this library is that it has been solidly tested in productions in countless projects and that, although it lacks in dynamicity (as we will see in a minute), for a simple and static cluster configuration it is just what you need to get running.

Configuring Apache Web server side

In order to install mod_jk, as first step download the latest stable Apache mod_jk connectors from http://tomcat.apache.org/download-connectors.cgi .Once completed the download, copy the connector to the modules folder of your Apache 2 distribution:

```
cp mod_jk.so $APACHE_HOME/modules
```

Now modify your Apache Web server configuration file (*httpd.conf*) by adding a single line at the end of it:

```
Include conf/mod-jk.conf
```

Now create the file *mod-jk.conf* in your Apache configuration folder. This file will contain the mod_jk configuration including the web context we are going to route from Apache to WildFly.

```
LoadModule jk_module modules/mod_jk.so
# Where to find workers.properties
JkWorkersFile conf/workers.properties
# Where to put jk logs
JkLogFile logs/mod_jk.log
# Set the jk log level [debug/error/info]
JkLogLevel info
# Mount your applications
JkMount /myapp/* loadbalancer
JkShmFile logs/jk.shm
```

Here is a description for the most important settings:

The **LoadModule** directive references the mod_jk library you have downloaded. You must indicate the exact same name with the "modules" file path prefix.

The **JkMount** directive tells Apache which URLs it should forward to the mod_jk module. In the above file, all requests with URL path /myapp/* are sent to the mod_jk load-balancer.

The **JkWorkersFile** references in turn the cluster configuration and thus contains the (static) list of nodes that are part of the Web farm. The worker file, named *workers.properties*, follows here:

```
worker.list=loadbalancer,status
# Define Node1
worker.node1.port=8009
worker.node1.host=localhost
worker.node1.type=ajp13
worker.node1.lbfactor=1
# Define Node2
worker.node2.port=8159
worker.node2.host=localhost
worker.node2.type=ajp13
worker.node2.lbfactor=1
# Load-balancing behavior
worker.loadbalancer.type=lb
worker.loadbalancer.balance_workers=node1,node2
worker.loadbalancer.sticky_session=1
worker.status.type=status
```

The above configuration can be used for example on a cluster of nodes running on localhost with a port offset of 150 for the second node (hint: you can use a Domain mode configuration with the ha/full-ha profile for quickly testing this example).

Configuring WildFly to receive AJP requests

Done with mod_jk, now let's move to WildFly configuration. From the Admin Console expand the **Web** subsystem, select the default Web server by clicking on **View**. From there you will see the list of listeners (HTTP,AJP,HTTPs) which are configured. Select the **AJP** tab and verify that the ajp listener is included in the configuration:

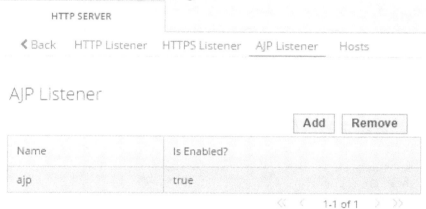

If you cannot find it or you have accidentally deleted it, you can create a new AJP listener by clicking on the Add button. The AJP listener is bound requires a socket binding, which can be found by browsing into its attributes as shown by the following picture:

HTTP SERVER

❮ Back   HTTP Listener   HTTPS Listener   AJP Listener   Hosts

Request parse timeout:	0
Resolve peer address:	false
Scheme:	
Send buffer:	
Socket binding:	ajp
Tcp backlog:	
Tcp keep alive:	
Url charset:	UTF-8
Worker:	default
Write timeout:	

The "ajp" socket binding needs to be present as well into the Socket Binding configuration of your server and default to port 8009. For example, if you have using the ha-sockets in your cluster:

```
<socket-binding-group name="ha-sockets" default-interface="public">
    <socket-binding name="ajp" port="${jboss.ajp.port:8009}"/>
    . . . .
</socket-binding-group>
```

Assumed that you have started two nodes with a 150 port offset, the following ports will be engaged on your system:

```
netstat -an | find "8009"
TCP 127.0.0.1:8009 0.0.0.0:0 LISTENING
netstat -an | find "8159"
TCP 127.0.0.1:8159 0.0.0.0:0 LISTENING
```

So with the above configuration, all incoming requests accepted by Apache Web server for the Web context "myapp" will be transparently routed to WildFly Web server.

Configuring mod_cluster

Mod_cluster is an HTTP-based load balancer which, like mod_jk, can be used to forward a request to a set of application server instances. The key difference compared with mod_jk is that the communication channel follows a different direction: instead of a single one-way direction connection from the Web server to the application server, mod_cluster uses a back channel from backend server to httpd. As the information is pushed from the server side, it can carry critical information such as cluster nodes lifecycle information and load balancing information. This in turn buys you the following benefits:

In terms of **configuration**:

- The httpd side does not need to know cluster topology in advance, so the configuration is dynamic and not static
- As a consequence you need very little configuration on the httpd side

In terms of **load balancing**:

- You have an improved load balancing as main calculations are done on the backend servers, where more information is available
- You have a fine grained web application lifecycle control

Installing mod_cluster

Since mod_cluster ships bundled with an Apache Web server vanilla distribution there are several versions of it, each one fit for a different operating system. In the following example, we will install the Linux 64 bit bundle as a proof of concept; anyway, we will highlight which are the key configuration points so that you can adapt it to any platform. Download at first the bundle named mod_cluster from http://www.jboss.org/mod_cluster/downloads.

As we said, this package contains the mod_cluster binary modules and the Apache httpd server precompiled for your operating system. The version we will use (mod_cluster-1.2.6.Final-linux2-x64-ssl.tar.gz) can be fully installed to /opt by executing:

```
sudo tar xvfz mod_cluster-1.2.6.Final-linux2-x64.tar.gz -C /
```

Now you can start the Apache Web server with mod_cluster bundled by issuing:

```
sudo /opt/jboss/httpd/sbin/apachectl start
```

Point the browser to localhost and you should see the 'It works!' message. This means that Apache Web server (with bundled mod_cluster) has started successfully. Now in next section let's move to the application server side.

Configuring WildFly for mod_cluster

WildFly 8 by default includes the mod_cluster subsystem in the *standalone-ha.xml* and *standalone-full-ha.xml* hence you don't need any particular tweak to the server configuration to get started.

 Actually, some configuration changes are needed if your machine or your network does not support multicasting (please refer to the section *"Troubleshooting mod_cluster"* for more information about it).

You can have a look at mod_cluster configuration by opening the Admin Console and selecting the **mod_cluster** option, which is contained in the **Web** subsystem:

Subsystems ≪	MOD_CLUSTER
> Connector	mod_cluster Subsystem
> Container	The modcluster configuration.
> Core	
> Infinispan	
> Security	Advertising Sessions Web Contexts Proxies SSL Networking
∨ Web	
Web Services	✎ Edit
mod_cluster	Load Balancing Group:
Servlets	Balancer:
HTTP	
General Configuration	Advertise Socket: modcluster
	Advertise Key:
Interfaces	Advertise: true

Within this panel, you can configure the mod_cluster elements that are logically grouped in the following items:

- **Advertising**: containing the configuration which is related to mod_cluster advertising mechanism
- **Sessions**: containing the Sticky session policy to use in your cluster (by default is on)
- **Web Contexts**: the Web application contexts to be published on the Web server
- **Proxies**: this can be used if the default Advertising mechanism needs to be replaced by a list of server proxies
- **SSL**: this can be used to cipher mod_cluster communication
- **Networking**: containing low level configuration of the socket transmission used by mod_cluster

Testing your configuration

The default http configuration contained in your mod_cluster bundle includes an administration console bound at the **mod_cluster_manager** Web Context on port 6666, therefore you can test your cluster configuration by pointing to: http://localhost:6666/mod_cluster_manager.
In our example, the mod_cluster manager displays the following information about all the application server nodes that have been discovered through multicast announcements:

Auto Refresh show DUMP output show INFO output

Node nodeA (192.168.10.1:8080)

Enable Contexts Disable Contexts

Balancer: mycluster, Domain: , Flushpackets: Off, Flushwait: 10000, Ping: 10000000, Smax: 1, Ttl: 60000000, Elected: 9, Read: 8406,

Virtual Host 1:

Contexts:

```
/ClusterWebApp, Status: ENABLED Disable
```

Aliases:

```
default-host
localhost
example.com
```

Node nodeB (192.168.10.2:8080)

Enable Contexts Disable Contexts

Balancer: mycluster, Domain: , Flushpackets: Off, Flushwait: 10000, Ping: 10000000, Smax: 1, Ttl: 60000000, Elected: 0, Read: 0, Tra

Virtual Host 1:

Contexts:

```
/ClusterWebApp, Status: ENABLED Disable
```

Aliases:

```
default-host
localhost
example.com
```

As you can see, in the mod_cluster manager page you have plenty of useful information, such as the number of hosts that are currently active (in our example, two nodes) and the web context that are available.

By default, all web contexts are mounted automatically (not requiring an explicit mount as for mod_jk), but you can, at any time, exclude or include them by clicking on the **Disable/Enable** link, which is placed next to the web context. In the section named *"How to configure mod_cluster to exclude one Web context"*, it is described how to exclude web context declaratively.

A deep look into mod_cluster configuration

Up to now, we have started our cluster using a pre-packaged bundle, which is good for building your muscles; in this section, we will go through the configuration of mod_cluster, so that you can learn how to apply it also to your existing Apache Web server.

Start by opening Apache configuration file, *httpd.conf* file. The first thing we need to know is the list of modules which are needed for proper communication between httpd and WildFly:

```
LoadModule proxy_module modules/mod_proxy.so
LoadModule proxy_ajp_module modules/mod_proxy_ajp.so
LoadModule slotmem_module modules/mod_slotmem.so
LoadModule manager_module modules/mod_manager.so
LoadModule proxy_cluster_module modules/mod_proxy_cluster.so
LoadModule advertise_module modules/mod_advertise.so
```

The first two modules should be already part of your Apache configuration so just make sure they are not commented. As for the other ones, they are included in the mod_cluster bundle, so all you have to do is copying them to your Apache's **modules** folder:

```
cp mod_slotmem.so $HTTPD_HOME/modules/
cp mod_manager.so $HTTPD_HOME/modules/
cp mod_proxy_cluster.so $HTTPD_HOME/modules/
cp mod_advertise.so $HTTPD_HOME/modules/
```

On the other hand, verify that the **mod_proxy_balancer** module is commented out; otherwise it is going to conflict with mod_cluster load balancer:

```
# LoadModule proxy_balancer_module modules/mod_proxy_balancer.so
```

With the modules in place, we will add the mod_cluster configuration which is essentially broken in two parts:

- One part that defines the virtual IP address and port to be used by Mod-Cluster Management Protocol (MCMP). In the default bundle this uses the loopback address and port 6666
- One part which is used for the administration interface of mod_cluster

```
<IfModule manager_module>
  Listen 127.0.0.1:6666
  ManagerBalancerName mycluster
  <VirtualHost 127.0.0.1:6666>

    <Location />
      Order deny,allow
      Deny from all
      Allow from 127.0.0
    </Location>

    KeepAliveTimeout 300
    MaxKeepAliveRequests 0

    AdvertiseFrequency 5
    EnableMCPMReceive

    <Location /mod_cluster_manager>
        SetHandler mod_cluster-manager
        Order deny,allow
        Deny from all
        Allow from 127.0.0
    </Location>

  </VirtualHost>
</IfModule>
```

Here are some details about the core configuration parameters:

ManagerBalancerName: That is the name of balancer to use when the application server doesn't provide a balancer name (default: mycluster).

AdvertiseFrequency: Time between the multicast messages advertising the IP and port (default 10 seconds).

EnableMCPMReceive: Allows the VirtualHost to receive mod_cluster Protocol Message (MCPM) from nodes. You need one EnableMCPMReceive in your in the VirtualHost configuration to allow mod_cluster to work.

If you followed our guidelines chances are that you are happily running your mod_cluster; just in case you are not that lucky, the next section will try to fix most common issues.

Troubleshooting mod_cluster

The first and obvious thing you should check is that you don't have a firewall that prevents your multicast messages to be received. The ports you are going to investigate are the UDP port 23364 and the multicast address 224.0.1.105.

If you are running a Linux/Unix box it's likely that you have stricter security requirements. So chances are that **iptables** or **selinux** are blocking your messages. You have several option, start by disabling (as root) iptables to see if that's the problem:

```
# /etc/init.d/iptables stop
```

Next, we will weaken Selinux security policy by setting it to permissive mode. In Fedora Core and RedHat Enterprise, edit as root the file /etc/selinux/config. Look for the following line:

```
SELINUX=enforcing
```

This need to be set to permissive in order to enable traffic from other machines:

```
SELINUX=permissive
```

Reboot your machine to take effect. Once that you have identified that the source of the problem is the firewall configuration, you can refine the security policies so that you only enable mod_cluster and WildFly traffic:

```
/sbin/iptables -I INPUT 5 -p udp -d 224.0.1.0/24 -j ACCEPT -m comment --comment
"mod_cluster traffic"
/sbin/iptables -I INPUT 6 -p udp -d 224.0.0.0/4 -j ACCEPT -m comment --comment "WildFly
Cluster traffic"
```

Additionally, you need to allow also intra-cluster communication. For example supposing your cluster nodes are bound on the 192.168.1 subnet and are using the (default) UDP stack:

```
/sbin/iptables -I INPUT 9 -p udp -s 192.168.1.0/24 -j ACCEPT -m comment --comment
"cluster subnet for inter-node communication"
```

Check multicast communication

If your firewall rules are properly configured you should then verify that multicasting is working correctly. That can be done by starting a multicast test chat which is part of the JGroups distribution.

```
cd modules\system\layers\base\org\jgroups\main
```

Now execute the McastReceiverTest class passing as argument the multicast address and port:

```
java -classpath jgroups-3.4.5.Final.jar org.jgroups.tests.McastReceiverTest -mcast_addr
224.0.1.105 -port 23364
```

Once started the receiver, start as well the server using the following shell:

```
java -classpath jgroups-3.4.5.Final.jar org.jgroups.tests.McastSenderTest -mcast_addr
224.0.1.105 -port 23364
```

The McastSenderTest will start a prompt where you can type in messages. If multicast is working properly you should see the message printed out also in the McastReceiverTest window, as shown by the following picture:

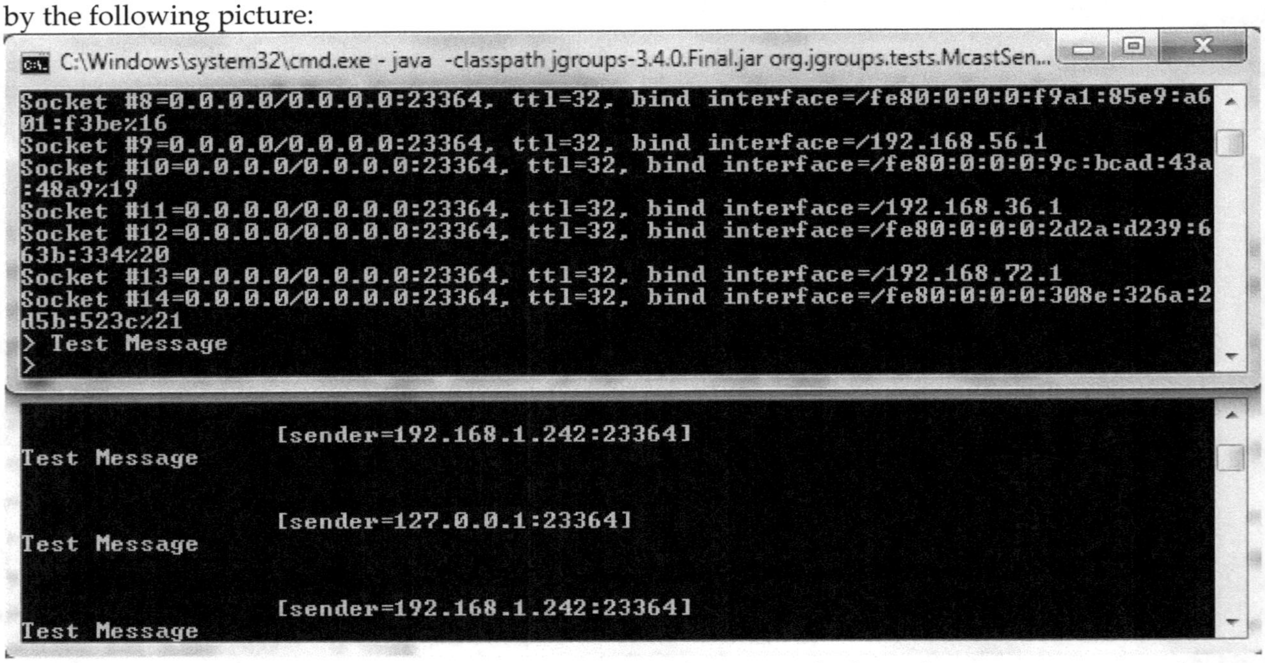

If the multicast communication test fails, chances are that your platform does not support multicast; this is a known issue of some Window systems like Vista. In such a scenario, you should stick to static configuration which is detailed in the section "*Using static mod_cluster configuration*".

Switch additional display

Another useful debugging option can be enabled in your configuration by setting the **AllowDisplay** to on:

```
AllowDisplay On
```

By setting this option to on, you will have some detail about the single modules that are needed to run mod_cluster, therefore you can identify the potential source of an issue:

mod_cluster/1.2.0.Final

start of "httpd.conf" configuration

```
mod_proxy_cluster.c: OK
mod_sharedmem.c: OK
Protocol supported: http AJP https
mod_advertise.c: OK
```

Server: localhost
Server: localhost VirtualHost: 127.0.0.1:6666 Advertising on Group 224.0.1.105 Port 23364 for http://127.0.0.1:6666 every 10 seconds
end of "httpd.conf" configuration

Auto Refresh show DUMP output show INFO output

Node 4e6189af-0502-3305-8ff3-fad7fee8b516 (ajp://127.0.0.1:8009):

Enable Contexts Disable Contexts
Balancer: mycluster,LBGroup: ,Flushpackets: Off,Flushwait: 10000,Ping: 10000000,Smax: 26,Ttl: 60000000,Status: OK,Elected: 0,Read: 0,Tr
0,Connected: 0,Load: 100

Advanced mod_cluster configuration

The configuration that we have learnt so far assumes some defaults such as:
- Multicast communication protocol
- Web context enabled by default
- Sticky sessions

Although it might be perfectly ok to rely on these defaults, you should be also able to deal with alternative scenarios. The following sections discuss about them in detail.

Using static mod_cluster configuration

One of the main advantages of mod_cluster over the older mod_jk library is that mod_cluster allows to configure dynamically the list of cluster nodes (by means of server advertisement) which can be changed without a cluster stop.

Server advertisement allows worker nodes to dynamically discover and register themselves with proxy servers. If multicast is not available or server advertisement is disabled then worker nodes must be configured with a static list of proxy server addresses and ports.

Luckily, switching to static configuration is not difficult to configure. All you have to do is entering the **mod_cluster** panel (available by expanding the **Web** subsystem) and selecting the **Proxies** option as shown in the following picture:

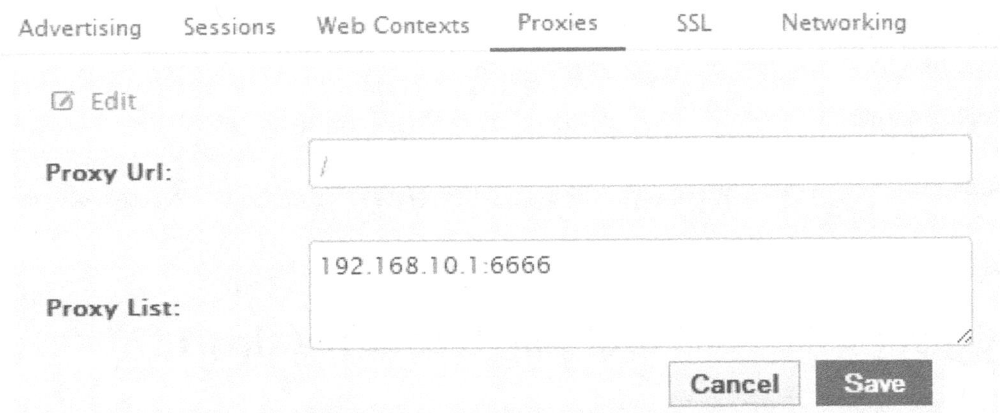

| Advertising | Sessions | Web Contexts | Proxies | SSL | Networking |

☑ Edit

Proxy Url:

```
/
```

Proxy List:

```
192.168.10.1:6666
```

Cancel   Save

The key attribute that you need to set is **Proxy List** (**proxy-list** in CLI terms) which needs to include the (comma-separated) list of httpd proxies. In the above example, we suppose that the httpd proxy is bound at the IP address 192.168.10.1 and port 6666.

The same action can be performed via CLI using the following command:

```
/subsystem=modcluster/mod-cluster-config=configuration/:write-attribute(name=proxy-list,value=192.168.10.1:6666)
```

How to configure mod_cluster to exclude one Web context

When using mod_cluster, by default, all web contexts which are deployed on WildFly nodes are accessible through the list of httpd proxies. You can either change this behavior or you can rather choose to disable selectively some web context. Out of the box, some Web contexts are already disabled, such as the Root Web application and the server console. In order to configure the Web Context exclusion, navigate to the Web Contexts tab, contained in the mod_cluster panel:

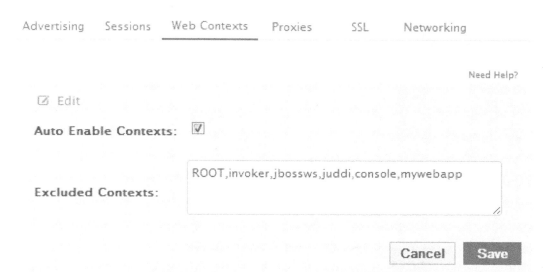

As you can see from the above picture, you can use the **Auto Enable Contexts** to enable/disable automatic Web context inclusion and the **Excluded Contexts** to exclude selectively one Web application.

Here's the corresponding CLI action to disable the above Web contexts:

```
/subsystem=modcluster/mod-cluster-config=configuration/:write-attribute(name=excluded-contexts,value=ROOT,invoker,jbossws,juddi,console,mywebapp)
```

In turn to disable auto Context loading you can use the following CLI command:

```
/subsystem=modcluster/mod-cluster-config=configuration/:write-attribute(name=auto-enable-contexts,value=false)
```

Configuring Sticky Sessions with mod_cluster

The term "**sticky session**" refers to the feature of many load balancing solutions to route the requests for a particular session to the same physical machine that serviced the first request for that session.

In a clustered WildFly environment, calls between nodes in the cluster are, by default, balanced using the **jvmRoute** parameters, which is automatically generated for you at server startup. Sticky sessions can be enabled using the **Sticky Session** parameter (which by default is true) contained in the **Sessions** tab of the mod_cluster panel:

Advertising   Sessions   Web Contexts   Proxies   SSL   Networking

☑ Edit

Sticky Session: true

Sticky Session Force: false

Sticky Session Remove: false

The other two parameters included are:

Sticky Session Force: when set to "Yes" returns an error if the request can't be routed according to JVMRoute. If set to "no" routes it to another node. Default: "false".

Sticky Session Remove: when set to "Yes", session information is removed in case of failover ". Default: "false".

Configuring Metrics

A key feature of mod_cluster is the ability to use server-side load metrics to determine how best to balance requests. The built-in configuration of mod_cluster distributes HTTP requests based on the **CPU** load on the nodes of the cluster:

```
<subsystem xmlns="urn:jboss:domain:modcluster:1.2">
      <mod-cluster-config advertise-socket="modcluster" connector="ajp">
            <dynamic-load-provider>
                   <load-metric type="cpu"/>
            </dynamic-load-provider>
      </mod-cluster-config>
</subsystem>
```

On the other hand, earlier versions of WildFly shipped with another default metric named **BusyConnectorsLoadMetric:**

```
<mod-cluster-config advertise-socket="modcluster" connector="ajp">
      <dynamic-load-provider>
            <load-metric type="busyness"/>
      </dynamic-load-provider>
  </mod-cluster-config>
```

The metric 'busyness' was used to represent the thread pool usage, in earlier versions of the application server. This doesn't translate cleanly to the current Web server (Undertow) architecture. It now represents number of currently being processed requests. You are supposed to set capacity explicitly on this metric.

You can mix and match the metric types to achieve custom load balancing policies. The list of metrics which are available are:

- **cpu**: metric based on CPU load
- **mem**: metric based on System memory usage
- **heap:** metric based on Heap memory usage as a percentage of max heap size
- **sessions:** metric based on the number of web sessions
- **requests:** metric based on the amount of requests/sec
- **send-traffic:** metric based on the amount of outgoing requests traffic
- **receive-traffic:** computes metric based on the amount of incoming requests POST traffic
- **busyness:** computes metric based on the percentage of connector Threads from the Thread Pool that are busy servicing requests.
- **connection-pool:** computes metric based on the percentage of connections from a JCA connection pool that are in use.

In order to add new metrics you can use the Command Line Interface or edit directly the XML configuration file. For example, supposing we want to add a couple of dynamic metrics, based respectively on cpu and memory:

```
/subsystem=modcluster/mod-cluster-config=configuration/dynamic-load-
provider=configuration/load-metric=cpu-metric/:add(type=cpu,capacity=1.0,weight=2)
```

```
/subsystem=modcluster/mod-cluster-config=configuration/dynamic-load-
provider=configuration/load-metric=heap-metric/:add(type=heap,capacity=1.0,weight=1)
```

The most important factors when computing load balancing are the **weight** and **capacity** properties.

- The **weight** indicates the impact of a metric with respect to the other metrics. In the first example, the CPU metric will have twice the impact on the sessions that have a load factor metric of 1.
- The **capacity**, on the other hand, can be used for a fine-grained control on the load metrics. By setting a different capacity to each metric, you can actually favor one node instead of another while preserving the metric weights.

In order to make easier the addiction of new server side metrics you can use the CLI in graphical mode which greatly helps choosing the metric type and its attributes as shown here:

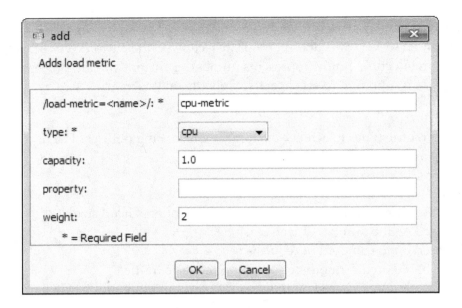

Configuring HA for remote EJB clients:

Configuring load balancing for remote EJB applications is not done by means of external tools but uses the file *jboss-ejb-client.properties* (must be available in the client application's classpath) to specify the list of server nodes where the clustered EJBs are available. This file contains the list of nodes that will be used to route the client request.

One key difference with earlier versions of the application server is that WildFly relies on a feature named **HTTP Upgrade** of the Web container (Undertow) in order to dispatch calls to the EJBs. What happens in practice is that you will not use any more to the default port 4447 for the remote communication but rather Undertow's default port (8080).

Supposing that we have started a cluster of two nodes on the same machine (localhost) using a port-offset of 200, here's your suggested *jboss-ejb-client.properties:*

```
remote.connectionprovider.create.options.org.xnio.Options.SSL_ENABLED=false
remote.connections=node1,node2
remote.connection.node1.host=localhost
remote.connection.node1.port = 8080
remote.connection.node1.connect.options.org.xnio.Options.SASL_POLICY_NOANONYMOUS=false
remote.connection.node1.username=userejb1
remote.connection.node1.password=mypassword
```

```
remote.connection.node2.host=localhost
remote.connection.node2.port = 8280
remote.connection.node2.connect.options.org.xnio.Options.SASL_POLICY_NOANONYMOUS=false
remote.connection.node2.username=userejb2
remote.connection.node2.password=mypassword
```

Behind the scenes, the EJB client API project does the necessary plumbing to request Undertow to switch to JBoss Remoting protocol while communicating on that HTTP port. Undertow thus switches transparently the protocol to Remoting and the rest of the communication happens as if it was the usual invocation on the Remoting port.

Chapter 11: Server Management with the CLI

The Command Line Interface is a management tool, which can be used to govern every aspect of your server configuration. Within this chapter, we will have a closer look at its syntax and commands including advanced recipes for server administrators. Here is our checklist:

- We will start by reviewing the Command Line start up options available for standalone and domain server modes
- Next, we will cover how to construct the Command Line commands
- Learnt the basics, we will go through a set of advanced concepts
- Finally, we will learn how to use the CLI in graphical mode

Starting the Command Line

The CLI startup script is located in the application server's home *bin* folder and it is named *jboss-cli.bat* (Linux users, as well, will use the *jboss-cli.sh* equivalent).

By launching the shell script, you will start with a disconnected session. You can connect at any time using the **connect**[standalone/domain controller] command, which by default, connects to a server controller located at localhost on port 9990.

```
C:\wildfly-8.2.0.Final\bin>jboss-cli.bat


You are disconnected at the moment. Type 'connect' to connect to the
server or 'help' for the list of supported commands.
[disconnected /] connect
Connected to standalone controller at localhost:9990
```

If you invoke the CLI using the **--help** flag you can see a brief summary of its options which includes the following ones:

```
jboss-cli.sh/jboss-cli.bat [--help] [--version] [--controller=host:port]
                [--connect] [--file=file_path]
                [--commands=command_or_operation1,command_or_operation2...
                [--command=command_or_operation]
                [--user=username --password=password]
                [--no-local-auth]
```

The first option we will discuss about is the **--connect** flag (or **–c**) which will let you connect automatically and can be combined with the **--user** and **--password** if you are connecting to a remote server host:

```
C:\wildfly-8.2.0.Final\bin>jboss-cli.bat --connect 192.168.10.1 --user=admin1234 -
password=password1234!
Connected to standalone controller at 192.168.10.1:9990
```

Another interesting option that is worth exploring is the **--file** option which allows executing script files written using the CLI syntax or even other scripting languages:

```
C:\wildfly-8.2.0.Final\bin>jboss-cli.bat --file=myscript.cli
```

Commands can be also injected in no-interactive way using the **--command** and **--commands** flags, which include a comma, separated list of commands:

```
C:\wildfly-8.2.0.Final\bin>jboss-cli.bat --commands="connect,deploy Utility.jar"
```

Restoring your server configuration using the CLI

The CLI can be your lifesaver tool in case you have damaged your server configuration, for example by deploying artifacts which are not usable at the moment. In such a scenario, you can start the application server adding the *--admin-only* flag as follows:

```
./standalone.sh --admin-only
```

This will cause to open administrative interfaces and accept management requests, but not start other runtime services or accept end user requests.

Once that you have completed the changes in the configuration, you can resume the normal application behavior by issuing, from the Command Line Interface, the following command which sets to false the **admin_only** mode and reloads the configuration:

```
[standalone@localhost:9990 /] reload --admin-only=false
```

Using the CLI

One of the most interesting features of the CLI is its embedded intelligence, which helps us to find the correct spelling of resources and commands, by simply pressing the Tab key. You can even use it to find out the parameters needed for a particular command, without the need to go through the reference documentation.

For example, by entering the **/subsystem=** command and pressing Tab, the CLI will show you all the subsystems which are available in the application server:

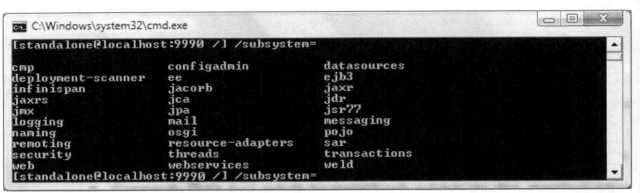

After you are done with the node path, adding ':' at the end of the node path and pressing the Tab key will print all the available operation names for the selected node:

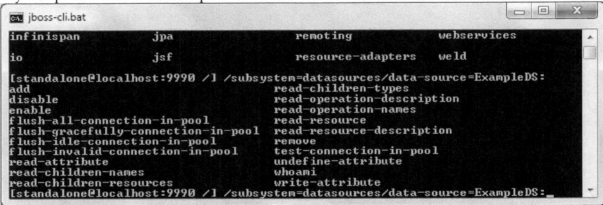

Once that you have chosen the operation, (in our example, **write-attribute** which will vary one attribute for one particular resource) add '(' after the operation name and press the Tab key.

```
C:\Windows\system32\cmd.exe

deployment-scanner   jdr                 pojo               undertow
ee                   jmx                 remoting           webservices
ejb3                 jpa                 resource-adapters  weld
infinispan           jsf                 sar
io                   logging             security
jaxrs                mail                threads
[standalone@localhost:9990 /] /subsystem=datasources/
data-source       jdbc-driver      xa-data-source
[standalone@localhost:9990 /] /subsystem=datasources/data-source=ExampleDS:write
-attribute(
name=     value=
[standalone@localhost:9990 /] /subsystem=datasources/data-source=ExampleDS:write
-attribute(
```

Choose the parameter name and specify its value after '='. Finally, when all the parameters have been specified, add ')' and press enter to issue the command. In the above command, we managed to set one key attribute of the default Datasource of the application server.

Commands which can be used against the CLI can be divided into two broad categories:

- **Operations**: These include the resource path (address) on which they are executed. (Ex. /subsystem=naming:jndi-view which displays the JNDI tree of the application server)
- **Commands**: These don't include the resource path and they can, thus, execute an action independently from the path of the current resource (e.g.: read-config-as-xml which displays the XML configuration file).

In the next section, we will provide some more details on the syntax for creating CLI commands.

Build up the CLI commands

So far we have already built and executed some CLI commands, however in order to reach every resource of the application server we need to learn the exact syntax expected by the CLI interpreter. All CLI operation requests allow for low-level interaction with the server management model. They provide a controlled way to edit server configurations. An operation request consists of three parts:

- an address, prefixed with a slash (/).
- an operation name, prefixed with a colon (:).
- an optional set of parameters, contained within parentheses (()).

Determine the resource address

The server configuration is presented as a hierarchical tree of addressable resources. Each resource node offers a different set of operations. The address specifies which resource node to perform the operation on. An address uses the following syntax:

```
/node-type=node-name
```

node-type is the resource node type. This map to an element type in the server configuration. **node-name** is the resource node name. This map to the name attribute of the element in the server configuration.

Separate each level of the resource tree with a slash (/). So for example, the following CLI expression identifies the http default listener, which is part of the undertow subsystem:

```
/subsystem=undertow/server=default-server/http-listener=default
```

Performing operations on resources

Once you have identified a resource, you can perform operations on the resource. An operation uses the following syntax:

```
:operation-name
```

So for example, you can query the list of available resources for your nodes by adding the *read-resource* command at the end of it:

```
/subsystem=undertow/server=default-server/http-listener=default/:read-resource()
{
    "outcome" => "success",
    "result" => {
        "buffer-pool" => "default",
        "enabled" => true,
        "max-post-size" => 10485760L,
        "socket-binding" => "http",
        "worker" => "default"
    }
}
```

If you want to query for a specific attribute of your node, you can use the *readAttribute* operation instead; for example here's how to read the "enabled" attribute from the http listener:

```
/subsystem=undertow/server=default-server/http-listener=default/:read-
attribute(name=enabled) {
    "result" => true
}
```

The CLI is not however just about querying attributes of the application server; you can also set attributes or create resources. For example, if you were to vary the http port of the http connector, then you have to use the corresponding *write-attribute* on the http's socket binding interface as shown here:

```
/socket-binding-group=standard-sockets/socket-binding=http/:write-
attribute(name=port,value=8280)
{
    "outcome" => "success",
    "response-headers" => {
        "operation-requires-reload" => true,
        "process-state" => "reload-required"
    }
}
```

Besides these operations that we have seen so far, (which are available on every resource of your subsystems) there can be special operations which can be performed *exclusively* on one resource. For example, within the naming subsystem, you are able to issue a *jndi-view* operation, which will display the list of JNDI bindings

```
/subsystem=naming/:jndi-view
{
    "outcome" => "success",
    "result" => {"java: contexts" => {
        "java:" => {
            "TransactionManager" => {
                "class-name" => "com.arjuna.ats.jbossatx.jta.TransactionManagerDelegate",
                "value" =>
"com.arjuna.ats.jbossatx.jta.TransactionManagerDelegate@afd978"
            },
        . . . .
}
```

Advanced CLI features

Having mastered the basics of the CLI, it is time to move on to more advanced features. The following sections will teach you how to:

- Use the batch mode to execute multiple CLI commands

- Use batch deployments to execute multiple resource deployments
- Take snapshots of your configuration using the CLI
- Auditing CLI commands
- Applying patches to your server installation

Using CLI batch mode

We have already learnt how to execute multiple CLI commands by including them in a file. The batch mode can be either used interactive mode or in files and allows the execution of multiple CLI commands as an atomic unit. It is quite like a transaction, so that if any of the commands or operations fails, the changes are rolled back. On the other hand, if the execution ends without any error, changes are committed into the configuration.

 You cannot include navigation commands as part of a batch, therefore commands like cd, pwd, or help are excluded, because they do not result in any change into the server configuration.

In order to start batch mode you need to demarcate your session using the **batch** command. If you are running the CLI in interactive mode, you will notice that the prompt is now be marked by the character "#".

Then, in order to terminate your batch session, you have to use the **run-batch command**. Here's an example session:

```
[standalone@localhost:9990 /] batch
[standalone@localhost:9990 /#] deploy MyApplication.jar
[standalone@localhost:9990 /#] /system-property=myprop:add(value=myvalue)
[standalone@localhost:9990 /#] run-batch
```

Another handy command is **list-batch**, which can be executed during a batch session to get the list of pending batch commands:

```
standalone@localhost:9990 /] list-batch
#1 deploy MyApplication.jar
#2 /system-property=myprop:add(value=myvalue)
```

Advanced batch commands

If you are executing your batch scripts in interactive mode, you might need to edit or interrupt your batch session and continue it later. For this purpose, when running in batch mode you are allowed to use some extra commands such as **holdback-batch**, which creates a savepoint to your batch execution:

```
[standalone@localhost:9990 / #] undeploy myproject.war
#1 undeploy myproject.war
[standalone@localhost:9990 / #] holdback-batch
```

In order to continue your batch of commands, you can issue the **batch** command again.

It is also possible to create multiple savepoints by adding an unique name to your holdback-batch command as follows:

```
[standalone@localhost:9990 /# ] holdback-batch step1
Later on, you can continue the execution, by specifying the holdback name:
[standalone@localhost:9990 /] batch step1
```

The list of available batch commands does not end here. For the sake of completeness we will list them all here, in case you need some extra power to your batches:

batch	Starts a batch of commands. When the batch is paused, reactivates the batch.
list-batch	Lists the commands that have been added to the batch.
run-batch	Executes the currently active batch of commands and exits batch mode.
holdback-batch	Saves the currently active batch and exits the batch mode, without executing the batch. The held back batch can later be re-activated, by executing "batch"
clear-batch	Removes all the existing command lines from the currently active batch. The CLI stays in the batch mode after the command is executed.
discard-batch	Discards the currently active batch. All the commands added to the batch will be removed, the batch will be discarded and the CLI will exit the batch mode
edit-batch-line	Replaces an existing line from the currently active batch, (with the specified line number) with the new one.
remove-batchline	Removes an existing line specified with line number argument from the currently active batch.
move-batch-line	Moves an existing line from the specified position to the new position, shifting the lines between the specified positions.

Using batch deployments

Batch deployments have been introduced specifically to make it easier to install/uninstall complex applications; a batch deployment consists of a JAR file with .cli extension containing a set of applications to be deployed plus one deploy and one undeploy configuration file. Things will be easier with an example: suppose that we are going to manage three applications named *app1.war*, *app2.war* and *app3.war*. Let's bundle them all in a file named *batchdeploy.cli* using the jar tool:

```
$ jar cvf batchdeploy.cli app1.war app2.war app3.war
```

Now let's create a file named **deploy.scr** which contains the deployment order:

```
deploy app1.war
deploy app2.war
deploy app3.war
```

As a final step, create a file named **undeploy.scr**, which contains the undeployment order as well:

```
undeploy app1.war
undeploy app2.war
undeploy app3.war
```

Now update your cli archive including the above two scripts:

```
$ jar uvf batchdeploy.cli deploy.scr undeploy.scr
```

As a result, you should expect the following CLI archive breakdown:

```
$ jar -tf test.cli
app1.war
app2.war
app3.war
deploy.scr
undeploy.scr
```

Now you can deploy this archive by issuing

```
[standalone@localhost:9990 /] deploy test.cli
#1 deploy app1.war
#2 deploy app2.war
#3 deploy app3.war
```

Undeploying is easy as well and requires adding the **--path** flag, otherwise the deployer will look for a deployed application using the CLI script file name:

```
[standalone@localhost:9990 /] undeploy --path=test.cli
#1 undeploy app1.war
#2 undeploy app2.war
#3 undeploy app3.war
```

Auditing CLI commands

Tracing commands which are sent across the native management interface might be required if you want to keep an adequate level of security in your system. By default the CLI commands are not audited, however it just takes a minute to enable them. Log into the console and point to the management's core service to reach the logger's audit log as follows:

```
/core-service=management/access=audit/logger=audit-log:write-
attribute(name=enabled,value=true)
```

Logging is done in JSON format and by default is directed into the *data/audit-log.log* file of your application server base directory.

You can specify a custom format for your CLI auditing commands or, as an alternative, direct your auditing commands to your operating system logger. Consult the EAP 6.2 documentation if you need additional information about auditing CLI: https://access.redhat.com/site/documentation/en-US/JBoss_Enterprise_Application_Platform/6.2/html/Administration_and_Configuration_Guide/About_a_Management_Interface_Audit_Logging_Formatter.html

Applying patches to your configuration

The patch command is a new feature that has been introduced in WildFly 8 (and in the release 6.2 JBOSS EAP) in order to provide a simple and effective way to apply application server patches.

As an example, we will download the patch used to **upgrade from the release 8.1.0 of the application server to the 8.2.0**. You can download it from the same location where the application server is available, that is http://www.wildfly.org

The following picture shows the download link and description for the patch:

Version	Date	Description	License	Size	Format
8.2.0.Final	2014-11-20	Java EE7 Full & Web Distribution	LGPL	126 MB	⬇ ZIP
				113 MB	⬇ TGZ
		Update Existing 8.1.0.Final Install	LGPL	62 MB	⬇ ZIP
		Minimalistic Core Distribution	LGPL	15 MB	⬇ ZIP
		Application Server Source Code	LGPL	36 MB	⬇ ZIP

So download the patch zip file labeled as "*Updated Existing 8.X.X. Final Install*". In order to apply the 8.2.0 patch just unzip the patch bundle in a folder of your like

```
unzip wildfly-8.2.0.Final-update.zip
```

Now we will show how to apply patching it to in offline mode. Launch the CLI when WildFly is shut down:

```
jboss-cli.bat
You are disconnected at the moment. Type 'connect' to connect to the server or '
help' for the list of supported commands.
[disconnected /]
```

Now in "disconnected mode" execute the following command (adjust the path to the location where you have unzipped the patch):

```
[disconnected /] patch apply c:\patch8.2\wildfly-8.2.0.Final.patch
{
"outcome" : "success",
"result" : {}
}
```

Please notice that the patch installation might find some conflicts, which prevent the installation. In this case, first review the conflicts. If you find them not critical (might be for example the README.txt file in the deployments folder!) just choose **the --override-all** in order to solve any conflicts:

```
[disconnected /] patch apply c:\patch8.2\wildfly-8.2.0.Final.patch --override-all
```

You can follow the same guidelines for installing the patch in **online** mode; just you will be warned that the server needs a **restart**:

```
{
"outcome" : "success",
"response-headers" : {
"operation-requires-restart" : true,
"process-state" : "restart-required"
}
}
```

When the server is restarted, check from the server logs that the new 8.2.0 version has been correctly installed:

```
18:01:12,857 INFO [org.jboss.as] (Controller Boot Thread) JBAS015951: Admin console
listening on http://127.0.0.1:9990

18:01:12,983 INFO  [org.jboss.as] (Controller Boot Thread) JBAS015874: WildFly
8.2.0.Final "Tweek" started in 4010ms - Started 290 of 403 services (181 services are
lazy, passive or on-demand)
```

Patch rollback can be executed in either online or offline modes as specified above. The steps are the same as applying a patch, although instead a **rollback** command is used instead of the **apply** command:

```
[standalone@localhost:9990 /] patch rollback --reset-configuration=true
{
"outcome" : "success",
"response-headers" : {
"operation-requires-restart" : true,
"process-state" : "restart-required"
}
}
```

Next, issue a shutdown/restart command for the patch to take effect:

```
[standalone@localhost:9990 /] shutdown --restart=true
```

Taking snapshots of your configuration

The configuration of the application server is pretty much like a database; actually, every change that is applied into the configuration is persisted in the *standalone_xml_history* folder (the same applies for the domain file named *domain_xml_history*).

Within these folders you will normally find a set of files which are part of the application server history:

standalone.initial.xml: This file contains the original configuration that was used the first time you successfully booted the application server. It is the only file which does not get overwritten.

standalone.boot.xml: This file contains the configuration that was used for the last successful boot of the server. This gets overwritten every time we boot the server successfully.

standalone.last.xml: This file gets overwritten each time a change is committed to the configuration. If you happen to corrupt your server configuration and you want to restore to the latest save point, this is the file to pickup.

Besides the above three files, *standalone_xml_history* contains a directory called *current* which at boot is be empty. As you apply configuration changes, this folder will contain the latest 100 configuration version in the format *standalone.vX.xml* (where X is the change version).

As you restart the application server, the current folder is emptied and its content is timestamped using the format *YYYYMMDD-HHMMSSMS*. These timestamped folders are kept for 30 days.

The last element within the standalone_xml_history is the *snapshot* folder where you can find the server configuration's snapshot created by you, using the Command Line Interface.

In order to take a snapshot of the configuration, just issue the **take-snapshot** command and the CLI will back up your configuration:

```
[standalone@localhost:9990 /] :take-snapshot
{
    "outcome" => "success",
    "result" => "C:\\wildfly-
8.2.0.Final\\standalone\\configuration\\standalone_xml_history\\snapshot\\20131108-
171642235standalone.xml"
}
```

You can check the list of available snapshots by using the **list-snapshots** command:

```
[standalone@localhost:9990 /] :list-snapshots
{
    "outcome" => "success",
    "result" => {
        "directory" => "C:\\wildfly-
8.2.0.Final\\standalone\\configuration\\standalone_xml_history\\snapshot",
        "names" => [
            "20131108-171642235standalone.xml",
            "20131108-171803638standalone.xml"
        ]
    }
}
```

You can delete a particular snapshot using the **delete-snapshot** command, which requires the snapshot name as parameter. Suppose we would need to delete the snapshot we've just created:

```
[standalone@localhost:9990 /] :delete-snapshot(name="20131108-171642235standalone.xml")
{"outcome" => "success"}
```

Running the CLI in graphical mode

Up to now we have used the Command Line in terminal mode which, thanks to the auto completion functionality, does not require a steep learning curve. There's however an even more intuitive way to run the Command Line and generate scripts, that is the **graphical mode**. The CLI graphical mode can be activated by passing the **--gui** switch to the jboss cli script, as shown:

```
jboss-cli.bat --gui
```

A java graphical application will display, containing on the left side the list of server resources and on the upper side the command being built:

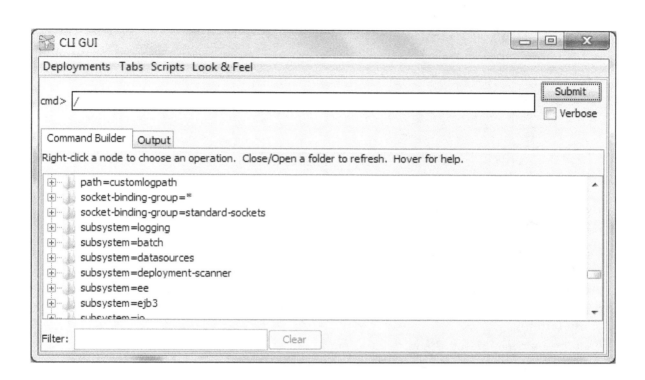

The Command Line Interface in graphical mode does not require using the connect command since, by default, connects to the server address and port specified in the file *jboss-cli.xml*.

By using the CLI in graphical mode you can just navigate through the application server module and then right click on the node you want to operate with. Here's gor example how to get a dump of the JNDI tree:

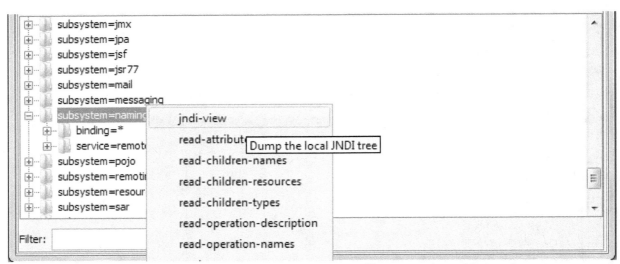

Once selected the command (when necessary the GUI will prompt for additional parameters to be set), the command will be included in the upper text box and can be executed by clicking on the Submit button:

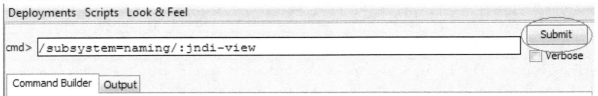

Adding new resources in graphical mode

If you paid attention to the list of resources contained in the graphical CLI, you should have discovered, for each resource, one element containing the value "=*" as shown by the following picture:

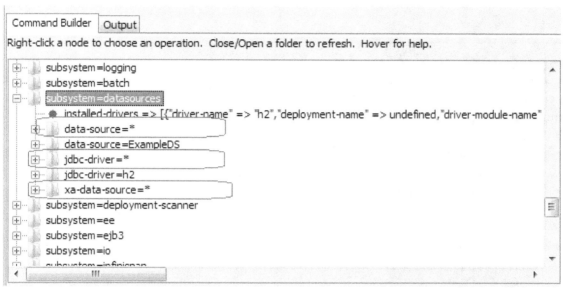

These paths which are marked with an "*" can be used to create new resources. So in the above example, if you were to create a new Datasource, you could right click on the "data-source=*" element and select "**Add**" from the list of options:

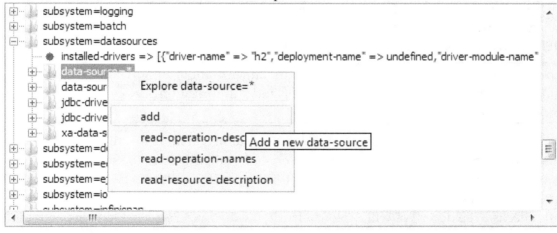

Chapter 12: Securing WildFly

This chapter introduces WildFly security infrastructure and methods for securing the applications running on the top of it. As security is a quite complex topic, which needs a former introduction to the basic concepts, we will follow this schedule:

- At first we will discuss about the key components of WildFly security, introducing the concepts of Security Domains and Security Realms
- Then we will learn how to create Login modules, which are associated with a Security Domain.
- Next we will cover Role Based Access Control which is a new core feature of WildFly 8
- Last, we will discuss about configuring Secure Sockets Layers to encrypt the transmission of your HTTP channel.

Introducing Security

Security is a key component of the application server security subsystem. All security configuration is managed centrally by the domain controller of a managed domain, or by the standalone server. WildFly security is based on the concept of security domain.

> A **Security Domain** consists of configurations for authentication, authorization, security mapping, and auditing. It implements Java Authentication and Authorization Service (JAAS) declarative security.

A security domain therefore performs all the authorization and authentication checks before a request reaches the borders of the application server. In order to work the security domain relies on the concept of **Security Realm**. The Realm job is to respond to callbacks based on a supplied username and return either the users password or a hash of their password allowing the transport specific checks to be done. We will explore Security Realms and Security Domains with the following schedule:

- Configuring Security Realms and Security Domains
- Creating Login modules for securing
- Configuring Secure Sockets Layers to encrypt the transmission of your HTTP channel.

Configuring Security Realms

Since a Security Domain relies on the concept of **Security Realm**, we will learn at first how Security Realms are configured. Out the of box, the application server defines the following Security Realms:

- The **ManagementRealm**: which is used to secure access to the Management interfaces(CLI/Web console)
- The **ApplicationRealm**: which is used to secure access to your applications

In the next section, we will enter into the details of each Realm and we will learn how to customize its configuration.

The Management Realm

The **ManagementRealm** is used to control the management instruments of the application server. Out of the box, the Management Realm is based on a simple authentication and authorization mechanism which stores the user credentials on the files *mgmt-users.properties* and group mappings in the file *mgmt-groups.properties* as shown by the following configuration snippet:

```
<security-realm name="ManagementRealm">
   <authentication>
      <local default-user="$local" />
      <properties path="mgmt-users.properties" relative-to="jboss.server.config.dir" />
   </authentication>
   <authorization map-groups-to-roles="false">
      <properties path="mgmt-groups.properties" relative-to="jboss.server.config.dir" />
   </authorization>
</security-realm>
```

The CLI management interfaces relies on the **local** mechanism which means that any user connecting from a local host will be granted a guest access named "$local" which does not requires a password in order to access the CLI.

The Web interface and remote CLI clients, on the other hand, require username / password authentication in order to access the Management interfaces. The user's details will be loaded by default from the file *mgmt-users.properties* which is located in the *JBOSS_HOME/standalone/configuration* or *JBOSS_HOME/domain/configuration* depending on the running mode of the server.

The Application Realm

The **ApplicationRealm** is used to secure applications that are exposing services such as EJBs for example. Here is the default configuration of the ApplicationRealm:

```
<security-realm name="ApplicationRealm">
   <authentication>
     <local default-user="$local" allowed-users="*" />
     <properties path="application-users.properties"
                 relative-to="jboss.server.config.dir" />
   </authentication>
   <authorization>
     <properties path="application-roles.properties"
                 relative-to="jboss.server.config.dir" />
   </authorization>
</security-realm>
```

The ApplicationRealm configuration is slightly more complex than the ManagementRealm since it is used both for authentication and authorization of service invocations.

- The **authentication** process is pretty similar to the ManagementRealm realm counterpart since it allows a guest authentication (named $local) for local application clients. The only difference is that users are taken from the file named *application-users.properties* located in *JBOSS_HOME/standalone/configuration* or *JBOSS_HOME/domain/configuration* depending on the running mode of the server.
- The **authorization** process, on the other hand, relies on the file named *application-roles.properties*, which is located as well in the server's configuration folder.

Since Application Realms are able to define an identity for the server, they can be used for both *inbound* connections to the server and *outbound* connections being established by the server.

A typical example of it is the Remoting subsystem, which is used to drive your connections towards the EJB container and by default, is bound to the ApplicationRealm:

```
<subsystem xmlns="urn:jboss:domain:remoting:2.0">
    <http-connector name="http-remoting-connector" connector-ref="default" security-
realm="ApplicationRealm"/>
</subsystem>
```

You can add users in the default **ApplicationRealm** by running the *add-user.sh* script and selecting "Application User" as option. Check the section *"Adding new Application users"* later on for an example of application user creation.

WildFly Security Domains

The other key component of the application server security is the **Security Domain** which defines all the authentication and authorization policies to be used by the application server. The security domain in turn contains **login modules** that implement the Security Domain's principal authentication and role-mapping behavior. Security domains are defined into the **security** subsystem which, out of the box, contains already a few security domains: here is the first one:

```
<subsystem xmlns="urn:jboss:domain:security:1.2">
    <security-domains>
        <security-domain name="other" cache-type="default">
            <authentication>
                <login-module code="Remoting" flag="optional">
                    <module-option name="password-stacking" value="useFirstPass" />
                </login-module>
                <login-module code="RealmDirect" flag="required">
                    <module-option name="password-stacking" value="useFirstPass" />
                </login-module>
            </authentication>
        </security-domain>
        // . . . . .
    </security-domains>
</subsystem>
```

The **other** security domain is a basic security domain that can be used for our first experiments with the **ApplicationRealm**. As you can see, this domain defines a couple of login modules named respectively: "Remoting" and "RealmDirect".
  - o The **Remoting** login module is used internally when authentication requests are received over a Remoting connection (usually an EJB call).
  - o The **RealmDirect** is triggered when the request did not arrive over a Remoting connection (e.g. when logging into a Web application).

Besides the "other" security domain, you can find also other two security domains named respectively **jboss-ejb-policy** and **jboss-web-policy**. These domains define the default authorization modules that should be used if none is found in the application security domain. As they are used internally by Security Framework (named PicketBox), most of the time, you shouldn't care about these domains at all. We include them here for your reference:

```
<security-domain name="jboss-web-policy" cache-type="default">
    <authorization>
        <policy-module code="Delegating" flag="required" />
    </authorization>
</security-domain>
<security-domain name="jboss-ejb-policy" cache-type="default">
    <authorization>
        <policy-module code="Delegating" flag="required" />
    </authorization>
</security-domain>
```

Security under the hood

If you paid attention to the definition of the built-in login modules, you should have noticed the **flag** attribute which controls the overall behavior of the authentication stack:

```
<login-module code="RealmDirect" flag="required">
```

This attribute can be set to the following values:

- **Required** - The LoginModule is required to succeed. If it succeeds or fails, authentication continues to proceed down to the LoginModule list.
- **Requisite** - The LoginModule is required to succeed. If it succeeds, authentication continues down the LoginModule list. Should it fail, control immediately returns to the application (authentication does not proceed down the LoginModule list).
- **Sufficient** - The LoginModule is not required to succeed. If it does succeed, control immediately returns to the application (authentication does not proceed down the LoginModule list). Should it fail, authentication continues down the LoginModule list.
- **Optional** - The LoginModule is not mandatory to succeed. If it succeeds or fails, authentication continues to proceed down the LoginModule list.

The overall authentication succeeds only if all *required* and *requisite* LoginModules are successful. If no required or requisite LoginModules are configured for an application, then at least one *sufficient* or *optional* LoginModule must succeed. In the following sections, we will show how to add a Security Domain for securing your applications using some built-in login modules such as:

- **RealmDirect** login module: used to store users and roles in simple text files
- **Database** login module: used to store credentials in a relational database
- **LDAP** login module: used to store the users and roles in a directory tree such as OpenLdap.

Using the RealmDirect login module

The RealmDirect is one of the simplest login modules and is used, as we said, for authenticating the current request if that did not occur in the Remoting login module.

```
<login-module code="RealmDirect" flag="required">
        <module-option name="password-stacking" value="useFirstPass"/>
</login-module>
```

The advantage of using this login module is that you don't need to provide any backing store configuration as the Security Domain will just delegate it to the Realm. Actually, the user and roles storage for RealmDirect are contained in the **ApplicationRealm**:

```
<security-realm name="ApplicationRealm">
    <authentication>
        <local default-user="$local" allowed-users="*"/>
        <properties path="application-users.properties"
                    relative-to="jboss.server.config.dir"/>
    </authentication>
    <authorization>
        <properties path="application-roles.properties"
                    relative-to="jboss.server.config.dir"/>
    </authorization>
</security-realm>
```

The **RealmDirect** login module contains just an option in it, the **password-stacking** which can be used if multiple login modules are chained together in a stack.

If you don't want to delegate to the ApplicationRealm for the user/roles file names location, you can add the usersProperties and rolesProperties to your login module as shown by the following example:

```
<module-option name="usersProperties"
        value="${jboss.server.config.dir}/custom-users.properties"/>
 <module-option name="rolesProperties"
        value="${jboss.server.config.dir}/custom-roles.properties"/>
```

Adding new Application users

Having described the available configuration options, it is now time to add some users into our **ApplicationRealm** so that the RealmDirect login module will use them for authentication. In order to do that, you can use the *add-user.sh* (or *add-user.bat* for Windows) mentioning to create a new

Application User and entering the credentials and the group (in our case the "Manager" group) to whom the user belongs to:

```
What type of user do you wish to add?
 a) Management User (mgmt-users.properties)
 b) Application User (application-users.properties)
(a): b


Enter the details of the new user to add.
Using realm 'ApplicationRealm' as discovered from the existing property files.
Username : francesco
Password recommendations are listed below. To modify these restrictions edit the
 add-user.properties configuration file.
 - The password should not be one of the following restricted values {root, admin,
administrator}
 - The password should contain at least 8 characters, 1 alphabetic character(s), 1
digit(s), 1 non-alphanumeric symbol(s)
 - The password should be different from the usernamePassword :
Password :
What groups do you want this user to belong to? (Please enter a comma separated
list, or leave blank for none)[   ]: Manager
```

The above user will be added into the **application-users.properties** using the following format:

```
username=HEX( MD5( username ':' realm ':' password))
```

so, in our example it will be:

```
francesco=b6deaea47caf6a533cc8c60fe372063d
```

And its role into will be added as clear text into **application-roles.properties** :

```
francesco=Manager
```

Defining the roles into your applications

Once you have defined the server security stack, it is time to secure your applications with it. The steps required will be different depending if you are securing a Web application or an EJB application.

1. Web applications:

Web applications configure their security in two different points: in the Java EE configuration file (*web.xml*) you will declare which role will map a set of URL patterns. On the other hand, in the *jboss-web.xml* configuration file we will declare which Security Domain will be used to verify the login credentials entered by the user (in our example, the "other" Security Domain). Here's the *web.xml*:

```
<web-app>
    . . .
    <security-constraint>
        <web-resource-collection>
            <web-resource-name>HtmlAuth</web-resource-name>
            <description>application security constraints</description>
            <url-pattern>/*</url-pattern>
            <http-method>GET</http-method>
            <http-method>POST</http-method>
        </web-resource-collection>
        <auth-constraint>
            <role-name>Manager</role-name>
        </auth-constraint>
    </security-constraint>
    <login-config>
        <auth-method>BASIC</auth-method>
        <realm-name>UserRoles simple realm</realm-name>
    </login-config>
    <security-role>
        <role-name>Manager</role-name>
    </security-role>
</web-app>
```

And here's the *jboss-web.xml* configuration file which needs to be placed into the *WEB-INF* folder of your web application:

```
<jboss-web>
    <security-domain>java:/jaas/other</security-domain>
</jboss-web>
```

2. EJB applications:

In order to secure EJB applications you can either use XML configuration files or applying Java EE annotations such as **@javax.annotation.security.RolesAllowed** combined with JBoss annotations like **@org.jboss.ejb3.annotation.SecurityDomain** to specify the Security Domain which will be used to protect your applications.

In the following example, we are restricting access to the EJB named SafeEJB using the role **Manager** that we have earlier defined:

```
import org.jboss.ejb3.annotation.SecurityDomain;
import javax.annotation.security.RolesAllowed;


@Stateless
@SecurityDomain("other")
@RolesAllowed( { "Manager" })
public class SafeEJB {

 . . . . . .

}
```

Annotations can also be applied at method level as shown in the following example:

```
@RolesAllowed( { "Manager" })
public void persistData() {

 . . . .

}
```

Database Login module

The Database Login Module is a **Java Database Connectivity-based (JDBC)** login module that supports authentication and role mapping. You can use this login module if you have your username, password and role information stored in a relational database, which is accessible by means of a Datasource.

The first obvious thing that you need to perform is creating the database tables that will you're your user credentials. For this purpose, we will use MySQL with which we have already worked in the chapter 4 of this book.

Open up a MySQL shell and select your database at first:

```
use mysqlschema
```

Now issue the following sql commands that will create two tables and insert one user (username "admin", password "admin") which is bound to the "Manager" role:

```
CREATE TABLE USERS(login VARCHAR(64) PRIMARY KEY, passwd VARCHAR(64));
CREATE TABLE USER_ROLES(login VARCHAR(64), role VARCHAR(32));
INSERT into USERS values('admin', 'admin');
INSERT into USER_ROLES values('admin', 'Manager');
```

Now create a data source named "**java:jboss/datasources/MySQLDS**" following the instructions contained in Chapter 4. In order to secure your application we need to add a security domain to your security subsystem: we will call this Security Domain **DBLogin:**

```
<subsystem xmlns="urn:jboss:domain:security:1.2">
    <security-domains>
        <security-domain name="DBLogin">
            <authentication>
                <login-module code="Database" flag="required">
                    <module-option name="dsJndiName" value="java:jboss/datasources/MySQLDS" />
                    <module-option name="principalsQuery"
                                   value="select passwd from USERS where login=?"/>
                    <module-option name="rolesQuery"
                                   value="select role,'Roles' from USER_ROLES where login=?"/>

                </login-module>
            </authentication>
        </security-domain>
    </security-domains>
</subsystem>
```

As you can see from the highlighted section, your login module references the Datasource we have formerly created, where credentials are stored. The application security configuration follows the same guidelines as in RealmDirect, that is, you will state your URLs/Role mappings in *web.xml* and in your *jboss-web.xml* you will reference the DBLogin module:

```
<jboss-web>
    <security-domain>java:/jaas/DBLogin</security-domain>
</jboss-web>
```

On the other hand, EJB applications will use the **@org.jboss.ejb3.annotation.SecurityDomain** to reference your DBLogin module:

```
@Stateless
@SecurityDomain("DBLogin")
@RolesAllowed( { "Manager" })
public class SafeEJB {
 // . . . .
}
```

Using encrypted database passwords

The login module showed so far stores password in the database using clear text. For greater security rather than storing passwords in plain text, a one-way hash of the password can be stored (using an algorithm such as MD5) in a similar fashion to the *etc/passwd* file on a UNIX system. This has the advantage that anyone reading the hash won't be able to use it to log in. However, there is no way of recovering the password should the user forget it, and it also makes administration slightly more complicated because you also have to calculate the password hash yourself to put it in your security database. This is not a major problem though. To enable password hashing in the database login module, you need to include the following highlighted module options:

```
<login-module code="Database" flag="required">
    <module-option name="dsJndiName" value="java:/jboss/datasources/MySQLDS" />
    <module-option name="principalsQuery"
                value="select passwd from USERS where login=?"/>
    <module-option name="rolesQuery"
                value="select role, 'Roles' from USER_ROLES where login=?"/>
    <module-option name="password-stacking" value="useFirstPass"/>
    <module-option name="hashAlgorithm" value="MD5"/>
    <module-option name="hashEncoding" value="base64"/>
</login-module>
```

This indicates that we want to use MD5 hashes and use base64 encoding to covert the binary hash value to a string. The application server will now calculate the hash of the supplied password using these options before authenticating the user, so it's important that we store the correctly hashed information in the database. If you're on a UNIX system or have Cygwin installed on Windows, you can use **openssl** to hash the value. For example supposing you want to hash the password "smith":

```
$ echo -n "admin" | openssl dgst -md5 -binary | openssl base64
ISMvKXpXpadDiUoOSoAfww==
```

On the other hand, you can use the **Base64Encoder** class that is part of PicketBox modules as follows:

```
C:\wildfly-8.2.0.Final\modules\system\layers\base\org\picketbox\main>java -classpath
picketbox-4.0.20.Final.jar org.jboss.security.Base64Encoder admin MD5
[ISMvKXpXpadDiUoOSoAfww==]
```

Now you can update your database password so to use an encrypted password:

```
update USERS set passwd = 'ISMvKXpXpadDiUoOSoAfww==' where login ='admin';
```

LDAP Login module configuration

In this section, we will show how to use **OpenLDAP** as repository for authentication. We will assume that you have the following LDAP configuration in *slapd.conf*:

```
database        bdb
suffix "dc=jboss,dc=com"
rootdn "uid=root,dc=jboss,dc=com"
# Cleartext passwords, especially for the rootdn, should
# be avoid.  See slappasswd(8) and slapd.conf(5) for details.
# Use of strong authentication encouraged.
rootpw          secret
```

 A **suffix** is a node of the directory tree associated with a particular set of data.

The **rootdn** entry is the Distinguished Name (DN) for a user who is unrestricted by access controls for operations on the LDAP directory. The rootdn user can be thought of as the root user for the LDAP directory.

Now login into the LDAP server using the root userid and the password secret. The following picture uses the JXplorer tool (http://jxplorer.org/) to log into the OpenLDAP tree:

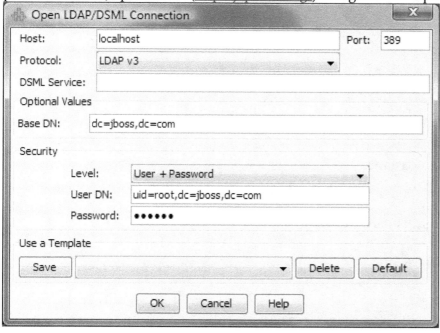

Once logged, you need to load the following *jboss.ldif* file, which contains just an user named "admin" which is granted a role "Manager":

```
dn: dc=jboss,dc=com
objectclass: top
objectclass: dcObject
objectclass: organization
dc: jboss
o: MCC

dn: ou=People,dc=jboss,dc=com
objectclass: top
objectclass: organizationalUnit
ou: People

dn: uid=admin,ou=People,dc=jboss,dc=com
objectclass: top
objectclass: uidObject
objectclass: person
uid: admin
cn: Manager
sn: Manager
userPassword: secret

dn: ou=Roles,dc=jboss,dc=com
objectclass: top
objectclass: organizationalUnit
ou: Roles

dn: cn=Manager,ou=Roles,dc=jboss,dc=com
objectClass: top
objectClass: groupOfNames
cn: Manager
description: the JBossAS7 group
member: uid=admin,ou=People,dc=jboss,dc=com
```

This will generate the following LDAP tree :

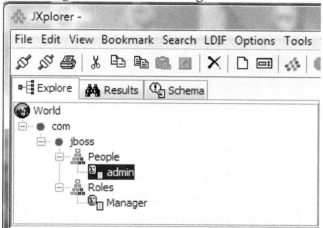

Now in order to use LDAP for Authentication, you can use the **LdapExtended** Login module, entering the values of the **bindDN** and **bindCredential** contained in *slapd.conf*.

Here follow our **LDAPAuth** security domain:

```
<security-domain name="LDAPAuth">
    <authentication>
        <login-module code="LdapExtended" flag="required">
            <module-option name="java.naming.factory.initial"
value="com.sun.jndi.ldap.LdapCtxFactory" />
            <module-option name="java.naming.provider.url" value="ldap://localhost:389" />
            <module-option name="java.naming.security.authentication" value="simple" />
            <module-option name="bindDN" value="uid=root,dc=jboss,dc=com" />
            <module-option name="bindCredential" value="secret" />
            <module-option name="baseCtxDN" value="ou=People,dc=jboss,dc=com" />
            <module-option name="baseFilter" value="(uid={0})" />
            <module-option name="rolesCtxDN" value="ou=Roles,dc=jboss,dc=com" />
            <module-option name="roleFilter" value="(member={1})" />
            <module-option name="roleAttributeID" value="cn" />
            <module-option name="searchScope" value="ONELEVEL_SCOPE" />
            <module-option name="allowEmptyPasswords" value="true" />
        </login-module>
    </authentication>
</security-domain>
```

Within our login module, we need at first to specify the organization unit containing the users, through the **baseCtxDN** option and as well the organization, which contains the roles through the **rolesCtxDN**.

The **baseFilter** option is a search filter used to locate the context of the user to authenticate.

The **roleFilter** is as well a search filter used to locate the roles associated with the authenticated user.

The **searchScope** sets the search scope to one of the strings. ONELEVEL_SCOPE searches directly under the named roles context.

Finally the **allowEmptyPasswords**: It is a flag indicating if empty (length==0) passwords should be passed to the LDAP server.

Auditing Security Domains

Security auditing enables tracing events that happen within the security subsystem. The auditing mechanism is part of the Security Domain, along with authentication and authorization that we have already learnt. In order to enable auditing of your security subsystem you need formerly to associate it with a module: for this purpose, you can use one of the included ones, or implement your own module. The simplest way to associate your Security Domain with a module is by means of the Admin Console. Once selected your **Security Domains** panel, choose which Security Domain you want to configure (click on the **View** Link).

Then, enter in the **Audit** screen where you can Add or Remove Provider Modules.

In the following screen we have added a built-in Security Auditing Provider Module named **LogAuditProvider** that uses the *org.jboss.security.audit.providers.LogAuditProvider* to audit security in the *audit.log* file in the *log* subfolder within the JBOSS_HOME directory.

‹ Back   Authentication   Authorization   Mapping   Audit

Security Domain: jboss-ejb-policy

Authentication configuration for this domain. Can either be classic or jaspi.

| | Add | Remove |

Code	Flag	
LogAuditProvider	required	

Securing the Management Interfaces with Login Modules

So far we have learnt how to configure several login modules which can be used to store user name and passwords on a relational database or on a directory service. The same JAAS-based login modules can be used as well as authorization schema for your management interfaces. For example, suppose you want to use the **DBLogin** security domain to control access to the **management interfaces**. As you can see, it's simply a matter of replacing the authentication schema contained in the ManagementRealm with a **jaas** element pointing to the DBLogin security domain:

```
<security-realms>

    . . . .

    <security-realm name="ManagementRealm">
            <authentication>
                <jaas name="DBLogin"/>
            </authentication>
    </security-realm>
</security-realms>
```

One side effect of removing the "local" authentication schema from your ManagementRealm is that you will be prompted for username and password also when connecting from a local CLI client:

```
[jboss@localhost bin]$ ./jboss-cli.sh -c
Username: admin
Password:
```

Securing the Management Interfaces with LDAP

If you don't want to rely on JAAS based login modules, you can directly specify your LDAP Connection settings from within your Security Realm. This has the evident advantage that you can apply any extra level of security on your Realm, for example by encrypting the communication. As a proof of concept, we will show how to create a Security Realm which is based on the LDAP directory tree that we have formerly used for the JAAS based login module:

```
<management>
    <security-realms>
        <security-realm name="LdapRealm">
            <authentication>
                <ldap connection="ldap_connection" base-dn="ou=People,dc=jboss,dc=com">
                    <username-filter attribute="uid" />
                </ldap>
            </authentication>
        </security-realm>
```

So as first step, we have created a new **Security Realm** named "**LdapRealm**". Within the authentication section, we have included the **base-dn** for connecting to the Directory service and the attribute used to filter the username ("uid").

What happens under the hoods is that a first connection is made to LDAP to perform a search using the supplied user name to identity the distinguished name of the user. Then a subsequent connection is made to the server using the password supplied by the user - if this second connection is a success then authentication succeeds.

The Security Realm named LdapRealm is then referenced in the **management-interfaces** section, which needs and **outbound connection** to the LDAP Server and a search base connection string:

```
<management-interfaces>
    <management-interfaces>
        <http-interface security-realm="LdapRealm" http-upgrade-enabled="true">
            <socket-binding http="management-http"/>
        </http-interface>
<outbound-connections>
    <ldap name="ldap_connection" url="ldap://127.0.0.1:389" search-dn="uid=admin,ou=People,dc=jboss,dc=com" search-credential="secret" />
</outbound-connections>
</management>
```

Configuring Role Based Access Control

In the earlier version of the application server (AS7) the administrative control on users was done in a fairly simple "all or nothing" schema which just allowed full management of the application server to any user part of the Management realm. The new release of the application server allows using **Role-Based Access Control (RBAC)** where administration users can be mapped to one or more standard role. In security terms by **role** we mean a set of permissions. Permissions, on the other hand, include a set of actions and constraints (on data and resources) that can be allowed or denied to users.

The element, which controls the current management policy, is defined in the **access-control** stanza, which by default is set to use the "**simple**" access control style:

```
<management>
. . .

        <access-control provider="simple">
            <role-mapping>
                <role name="SuperUser">
                    <include>
                        <user name="$local"/>
                    </include>
                </role>
            </role-mapping>
        </access-control>
</management>
```

With the default settings, all management users are granted the **SuperUser** role which has complete access to all resources and operations of the server with no restrictions. This role is equivalent to the administrator users of earlier versions of JBoss AS 7 and EAP 6 (6.0 and 6.1).

By turning on RBAC allows a "separation of duties" for management users making it easy for an organization to spread responsibility between individuals or groups without granting unnecessary privileges. RBAC thus ensures the maximum possible security of your servers and data while still providing a good level of flexibility for configuration, deployment, and management.

Out of the box, seven Roles are defined each one with different permissions on the server resources. The following table contains the list of the server roles and the permissions which are granted to them:

Monitor	Users of the Monitor role have the fewest permissions and it is meant for users who need to track and report the performance of the server. Monitor users cannot modify server configuration nor can they access sensitive data or operations.
Operator	Users of the Operator role have all the permissions of the Monitor role plus the ability to start/stop servers or pause/resume JMS destinations. The Operator role is a good choice for users who are responsible for the physical/virtual hosts where application servers are running. Operators cannot modify server configuration or access sensitive data or operations.
Deployer	The Deployer role has the same permissions as the Monitor, but can modify configuration and state for deployments and any other resource type classified as an application resource.
Maintainer	Users of the Maintainer role have access to view and modify runtime state of the server plus the ability to configure resources and execute operations on which are not classified as *sensitive* resources. Thus, the Maintainer role is the general-purpose role that does not have access to sensitive data and operation.
Administrator	The Administrator role has unrestricted access to all resources and operations on the server except the audit logging system. Administrator is the only role (besides the SuperUser) that has access to sensitive data and operations. This role can also configure the access control system.
Auditor	The Auditor role has all the permissions of the Monitor role and can also view (but not modify) sensitive data, and has full access to the audit logging system. The Auditor role is the only role other than SuperUser that can access the audit logging system. Auditors cannot modify sensitive data or resources. Only read access is permitted.
SuperUser	The SuperUser has all permissions on all resources and operations on the application server

Enabling RBAC

Now that we have covered the basics of roles and permissions we will turn on Role Based access Control. In order to do that, you can either update the server's XML file manually replacing:

```
<access-control provider="simple">
```

With:

```
<access-control provider="rbac">
```

or (suggested approach) use the CLI and issue the following command:

```
| /core-service=management/access=authorization/:write-attribute(name=provider,value=rbac)
```

Now we will create a few users specifying just username and password:

```
$ add-user.sh
What type of user do you wish to add?
 a) Management User (mgmt-users.properties)
 b) Application User (application-users.properties)
(a): a


Enter the details of the new user to add.
Using realm 'ManagementRealm' as discovered from the existing property files.
Username : f.marchioni
. . .
Password :
Re-enter Password :
What groups do you want this user to belong to? (Please enter a comma separated
list, or leave blank for none)[  ]:
About to add user 'f.marchioni' for realm 'ManagementRealm'
Is this correct yes/no? yes
```

You can create a few more users following the same approach; for example create an user named **wildoperator** and another one **wilddeployer.** (Just follow the same procedure that we showed for the first user). The expected outcome should be in your *mgmt-groups.properties* the following list of users with no groups associated right now:

```
f.marchioni=
wildmonitor=
wilddeployer=
```

Now we will map the above users stored to some server Roles. Let's start first with the user named "f.marchioni" and, in order to boost my ego, let's bind it to the **SuperUser** Role. This can be done by digging into the */core-service=management/access=authorization* path:

```
/core-service=management/access=authorization/role-
mapping=SuperUser/include=f.marchioni/:add(type=USER,name=f.marchioni)
```

Now, in order to assign the Monitor and Deployer roles, we will at first define them as follows:

```
/core-service=management/access=authorization/role-mapping=Monitor/:add
/core-service=management/access=authorization/role-mapping=Deployer/:add
```

Now we will grant to the other two users respectively the **Monitor** and **Deployer** Role:

Page 261

```
/core-service=management/access=authorization/role-
mapping=Monitor/include=wildmonitor/:add(type=USER,name=wildmonitor)
```

```
/core-service=management/access=authorization/role-
mapping=Deployer/include=wilddeployer/:add(type=USER,name=wilddeployer)
```

Reload your configuration before logging in. After committing the above changes your configuration should look like this:

```
<access-control provider="rbac">
    <role-mapping>
        <role name="SuperUser">
            <include>
                <user name="$local" />
                <user alias="f.marchioni" name="f.marchioni" />
            </include>
        </role>
        <role name="Deployer">
            <include>
                <user alias="wilddeployer" name="wilddeployer" />
            </include>
        </role>
        <role name="Monitor">
            <include>
                <user alias="wildmonitor" name="wildmonitor"/>
            </include>
        </role>
    </role-mapping>
</access-control>
```

Now login into the Admin Console in order to verify the changes. As first attempt, login using the SuperUser (f.marchioni). Once logged, check out from the upper right corner your current Role:

You can also check, from the **Administration** upper tab, the list of available users and the Roles that have been granted to them:

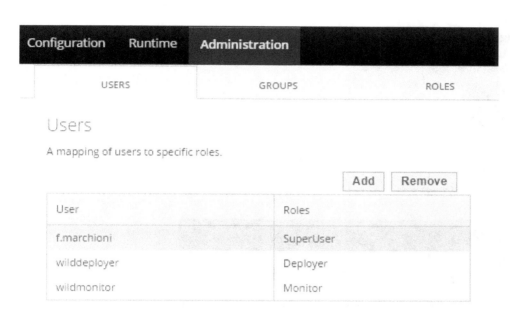

Being a SuperUser grants you every permission over the server configuration: have a quick turnaround on the console and verify it. Besides this, if you are a SuperUser you are also able to switch to any other Role by clicking on the "**Run as ..**" link. This will lead you to the following screen where you can temporarily change the capability of your users to a different Role:

Now let's change user and login with the **wildmonitor** user. Again, verify the Role from the right corner:

Being a user with Monitor Role grants you just an overview on the server status: for example, by selecting the upper **Runtime** tab you can select **Overview** from the **Server** option, which shows the server status:

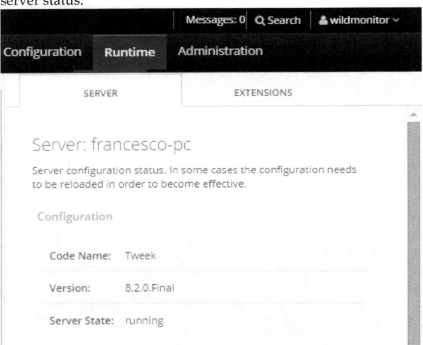

You will find that the Monitor Role grants you some additional information such as JVM, Datasource and Transaction statistics. On the other hand, some critical data, such as a JNDI tree view is forbidden and it's obviously forbidden any change to the server configuration.
Now let's test our third user, the "wilddeployer". Logout with the former user and then login as "wilddeployer". Again check your Role from the right information corner:

As you can see from a quick look into **Manage Deployments** option (available in the **Deployments** tab), this user is capable of managing deployments of your applications and any other resource type enabled as an application resource.

WildFly 8.2.0.Final | Messages: 0   Q Search | wilddeployer ∨

| Home | **Deployments** | Configuration | Runtime | Administration |

DEPLOYMENTS

Deployments

Currently deployed application components.

Available Deployments

Filter: [ ] | Add | Remove | En/Disable | Replace |

▶ demo.war   ✔

Using groups

So far, we have defined individual users and assigned a role to those users. If the user has not been granted a role, he/she can still operate with that role, provided that he/she is part of a group (that has been granted that role). Let's see a concrete example:

```
What type of user do you wish to add?
 a) Management User (mgmt-users.properties)
 b) Application User (application-users.properties)
(a): a

Enter the details of the new user to add.
Using realm 'ManagementRealm' as discovered from the existing property files.
Username : wildmaintain
```

```
. . .
Password :
Re-enter Password :
What groups do you want this user to belong to? (Please enter a comma separated
list, or leave blank for none)[  ]: Admin in-training
```

In example given above, we have created an user named "wildmaintain" and included it as part of the "**Admin in-training**" group. Now let's login in the Admin Console as SuperUser and select the **Group** tab which is available once you have selected the Administration upper tab.

USERS	GROUPS	ROLES

Groups

A mapping of groups to a specific roles.

	Add	Remove

Group	Roles

《 ‹ › 》

Fine, now click on the **Add** button, which will let you define a new Group. Enter the same group name that we have granted to our former user (Admin in-training) and check the "Maintainer" Role:

	Name
Group:	Admin in-training
Realm:	
Type:	Include ▾

	Name
☐	Administrator
☐	Auditor
☐	Deployer
☑	Maintainer
☐	Monitor
☐	Operator
☐	SuperUser

Roles:

[Cancel] [Save]

The expected outcome in our configuration will be the following role, which includes not an user but a group, the "Admin in-training".

```
<role name="Maintainer">
      <include>
             <group name="Admin in-training"/>
      </include>
</role>
```

Now log in the console using the "wildmaintain" user and check that you have been granted the Maintainer role:

As a Maintainer user, you will be able to manage the Runtime state of your server and its deployments, yet you will not be able to read or write sensitive information from your configuration; for example if you jump into the DataSource security settings: you won't be able to catch the user/password credentials to the DB:

Name	JNDI	Enabled?
ExampleDS	java:jboss/datasources/ExampleDS	✔

Selection

Attributes   Connection   Security   Properties   Pool   Validation

  ☑ Edit

Username: 🔒

Password: 🔒

Defining Scoped Roles for Domain mode

So far, we have just seen a standalone server view of the RBAC. When running in Domain mode you generally speak in terms of Server Groups and Hosts and RBAC makes no exception to it. As a matter of fact, when running in domain mode, you can configure Scoped roles which are Administrative roles that are based on standard roles but are constrained to a particular set of managed domain hosts or server groups. More in detail:

Host-scoped roles: a role that is host-scoped restricts the permissions of that role to one or more hosts. This means access is provided to the relevant /host=*/ resource trees but resources that are specific to other hosts are hidden.

Server-Group-scoped roles: a role that is server-group-scoped restricts the permissions of that role to one or more server groups. Additionally, the role permissions will also apply to the profile, socket binding group, server config and server resources that are associated with the specified server-groups. Any sub-resources within any of those that are not logically related to the server-group will not be visible to the user.

In order to define scoped roles, you need to start your server in domain mode and enable as well RBAC for your current profile by issuing:

```
/core-service=management/access=authorization/:write-attribute(name=provider,value=rbac)
```

Next, elect as SuperUser one of your users defined so far:

```
/core-service=management/access=authorization/role-
mapping=SuperUser/include=f.marchioni/:add(type=USER,name=f.marchioni)
```

Now log in the Admin console using your SuperUser (Only users in the SuperUser or Administrator roles can manage Scoped Roles) and select the upper **Administration** tab. Now select the **Roles** tab; you will see that this tab now includes an additional link named "**Scoped Roles**".

USERS	GROUPS	ROLES

Role Mangement

Standard Roles   Scoped Roles

Administrative roles that are based on standard roles but are constrained to a particular set of managed domain hosts or server groups.

			Members	Add	Remove
Name	Based On	Type	Scope	Include All	

We will now define a Server-Group-scoped roles which allows users running that Role to administer just one Server Group, the **main-server-group**. For this purpose select "**Scoped Roles**" and click on **Add**.

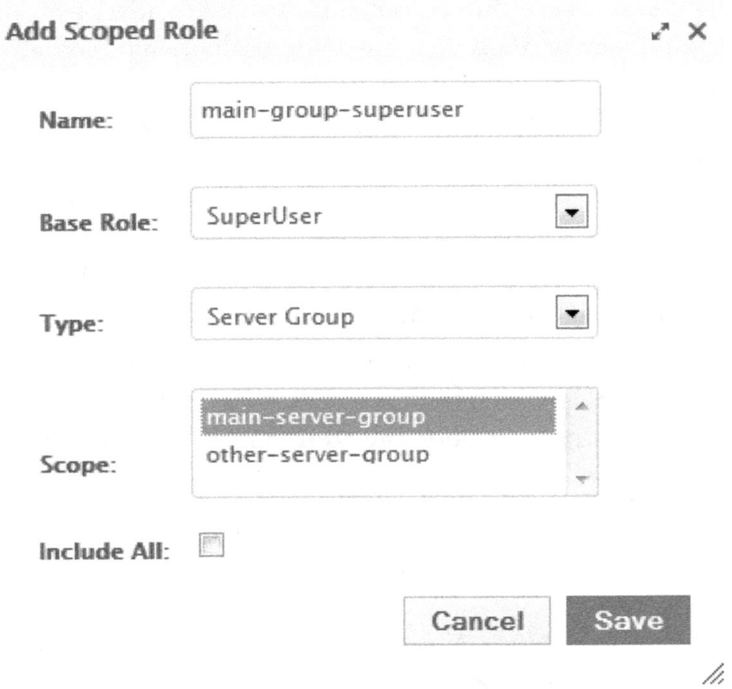

Add Scoped Role ⤢ ✕

Name: main-group-superuser

Base Role: SuperUser ▾

Type: Server Group ▾

Scope:
main-server-group
other-server-group

Include All: ☐

Cancel Save

Enter **main-group-superuser** as name and choose as Base Role SuperUser. The type will be ServerGroup and the Scope of it will be the main-server-group.

Click **Save**. A server reload will be required. Once reloaded, you can either assign an user to the main-group-superuser or if you prefer a quick test of your Server Group Role just choose **Run As** and select the main-group-superuser, like we did in the following picture:

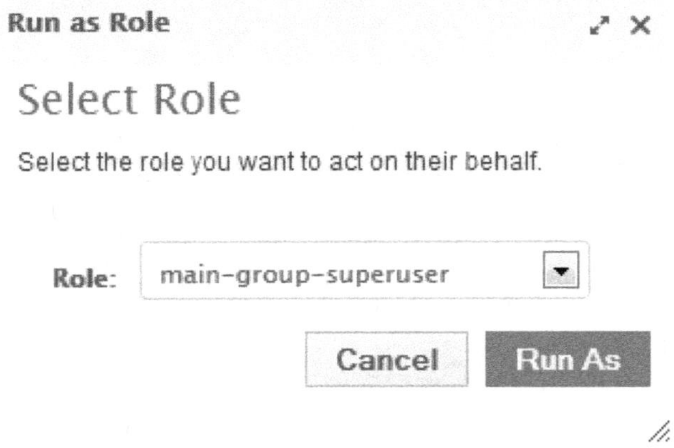

Run as Role ⤢ ✕

Select Role

Select the role you want to act on their behalf.

Role: main-group-superuser ▾

Cancel Run As

Now if you navigate to the **Runtime** tab, for example, and select the **Overview** left option, you can see that you can only manage the **main-server-group** servers, while the other-server-group is not included in the overview panel.

Hosts, groups and server instances

An overview of all hosts, groups and server instances in the domain.

Hosts → Groups ↓	master **Domain: Controller**	★
main-server-group **Profile: full**	server-one Socket Binding: full-sockets Ports: +0	✔
	server-two Socket Binding: full-sockets Ports: +150	✔

Accordingly, if you choose the **Domain** upper tab, you will be able to see just the **main-server-group**. Finally, if you select the profiles tab you can just view profiles that are mapped to the **main-server-group**.

Host-scoped roles

The other available option, that is Host-scoped roles, can restrict access only to a particular host. In the following example, we are running a domain composed of a "**master**" and "**slave**" host. By selecting as scope "master", we will define an Administrator based Role just for that Host:

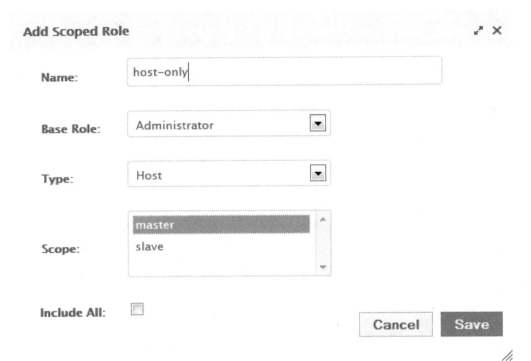

Add Scoped Role

Name: host-only

Base Role: Administrator

Type: Host

Scope:
master
slave

Include All:

Cancel   Save

As you can see from the **Domain** view of your domain, now you can only select the "master" host from your list of hosts, which are part of a domain:

Host Configuration

An overview of all ho

Host:
master

master

Hosts →
Groups ↓

main-server-
up
file: full-ha

JVM Configurations
Interfaces
Host Properties

Configuring Constraints

The highest type of customization that you can apply to your management users is configuring constraints on the single application server resources. Such constraints can tailor which resources are considered "sensitive". It is possible to define two types of constraints:

Sensitivity Constraints are a set of resources that are considered "sensitive". A sensitive resource is generally one that either should be secret, like passwords, or one that will have serious impact on the server, like networking, JVM configuration, or system properties.

Application Resource Constraints are a set of resources, attributes and operations that are usually associated with the deployment of applications and services.

Configuring Sensitivity Constraints

A sensitive resource is generally one that is not shared with every management user such as passwords, network settings or system properties. Resource sensitivity limits which roles are able to read, write or manage a specific resource.

Sensitivity constraint configuration can be reached from the CLI path at **/core-service=management/access=authorization/constraint=sensitivity-classification**

Within the management model, each Sensitivity Constraint is identified as a **classification**. The classifications are then grouped into **types**. Just expand the type element with Tab to discover the available types:

```
[standalone@localhost:9990 /] /core-
service=management/access=authorization/constraint=sensitivity-classification/type=
core             jmx              remoting            undertow
datasources      mail             resource-adapters
jdr              naming           security
```

To configure a sensitivity constraint, you can use the write-attribute operation to set the **configured-requires-read**, **configured-requires-write**, or **configured-requires-addressable** attribute. To make that type of operation sensitive set the value of the attribute to true, otherwise to make it non-sensitive set it to false.

Let's see an example, how to grant a sensitive constraint to your users. For this purpose, we will return to our initial configuration where we defined an user named "wildmaintain" as application server Maintainer. If you log in with that user (or any user running the Maintainer Role) you will see that some resources such as Datasource security settings or Socket bindings are not editable:

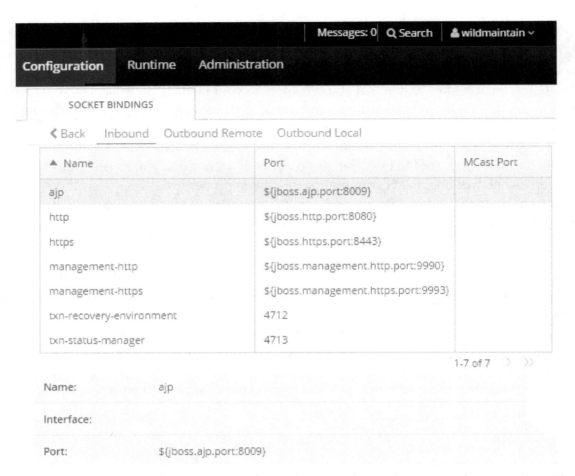

What we are going to do now is specifying that a configured resource, for example socket binding, is not write sensitive so it does not require Administrator or SuperUser privileges in order to write it:

```
/core-service=management/access=authorization/constraint=sensitivity-
classification/type=core/classification=socket-config/:write-attribute(name=configured-
requires-write,value=false)
```

Now move to your server configuration and verify that you are able to edit the sockets bindings for the **Maintainer** role:

☑ Edit

Name: http

Interface:

Port: ${jboss.http.port:8080}   ⌗

Fixed Port?:   false

▶ Multicast

Configuring Application Constraints

Each Application Resource Constraint defines a set of resources, attributes and operations that are usually associated with the deployment of applications and services. When an application resource constraint is enabled management users of the Deployer role are granted access to the resources that it applies to.

Application constraint configuration can be reached from the CLI path at **/core-service=management/access=authorization/constraint=application-classification/.**

Within the management model, each Application Resource Constraint is identified as a classification. The classifications are then grouped into types. Just expand the type element with Tab to discover the available types:

```
[standalone@localhost:9990 /] /core-service=management/access=authorization/cons
traint=application-classification/type=
core              logging            naming              security
datasources       mail               resource-adapters
```

By default, the only Application Resource classification that is enabled is the **core** classification, which includes deployments, deployment overlays, and the deployment operations.

In order to enable an Application Resource, use the write-attribute operation to set the **configured-application** attribute of the classification to **true**. To disable an Application Resource, set this attribute to false.

For example, let's see how to enable editing of the Logging subsystem from a Role which, by default, is not able to do it like the Deployer Role. So just login with an user that is bound to the Deployer role or just choose **Run As Deployer** from the SuperUser profile. If you move to the logging subsystem, you should be able to see that the configuration is not editable:

Periodic Rotating File Handlers

Defines a handler which writes to a file, rotating the log after a time period derived from the in a format understood by java.text.SimpleDateFormat.

Name	Log Level
FILE	ALL

≪ ‹ 1-1 of 1 › ≫

Details

Name:	FILE
Encoding:	
Suffix:	.yyyy-MM-dd

In order to enable the writing of this subsystem you have to set the **configured-application** value to **true** for the **logging type** as follows:

```
/core-service=management/access=authorization/constraint=application-
classification/type=logging/classification=logging-profile/:write-
attribute(name=configured-application,value=true)
```

Now, refresh your console and verify that user is able to Edit the Log configuration options:

ROOT LOGGER	LOG CATEGORIES	HANDLER
Console File Periodic Size	Async Custom	Syslog Handler

Details

☑ Edit

Name: FILE

Encoding:

Suffix: .yyyy-MM-dd

Log Level: ALL

File Relative To: jboss.server.log.dir

Enabling the Secure Socket Layer on WildFly

Having learnt the security basics, we will now see in practice how to enable security on WildFly application server making use of the **Java Secure Socket Extension** (JSSE), which is bundled in the J2SE to leverage the SSL/TLS communication.

The tool that we will use for setting up digital certificates is **keytool**, which is a key and certificate management utility that ships with the Java SE. It enables users to administer their own public/private key pairs and associated certificates for use in self-authentication (where the user authenticates himself/herself to other users or services) or data integrity and authentication services, using digital signatures. It also allows users to cache the public keys (in the form of certificates) of their communicating peers.

The keytool stores the keys and certificates in a file termed a **keystore**, a repository of certificates used for identifying a client or a server. Typically, a keystore contains one client or one server's identity which are protected by using a password.

Depending on the number of certificates required, you can approach secure communication in two ways:

- **One way SSL**: When configuring one way SSL, the server is required to present a certificate to the client in order to verify its identity. To successfully negotiate a SSL connection, the client must acknowledge the server certificate, but the server will accept a connection from any client.
- **Two ways SSL**: If you want a mutual trust between the client and the server, then you can configure your server to request from your clients, as well, a trusted certificate in order to successfully complete the SSL handshake.

In the following section we will show how to create both server and client certificates which are needed for a mutual two-way authentication. You will obviously need just the server side part if you are going to configure one way SSL.

Creating Server and client certificates

Start by generating a public/private key pair for the entity whose alias is "serverkey" and has a "distinguished name" with a common name of "*Server Administrator*", organization of "*Acme*" and two-letter country code of "*GB*".

```
keytool -genkeypair -alias serverkey -keyalg RSA -keysize 2048 -validity 7360 -keystore
server.keystore -keypass mypassword -storepass mypassword -dname "cn=Server
Administrator,o=Acme,C=GB"
```

Now, if you want mutual SSL authentication generate a key pair also for the client, using the alias clientkey and registering a common name for it as well:

```
keytool -genkeypair -alias clientkey -keyalg RSA -keysize 2048 -validity 7360 -keystore
client.keystore -keypass mypassword -storepass mypassword -dname "cn=Desktop
user,o=Acme,C=GB"
```

Next, we will export both the server's and client public key into a certificate named respectively **server.crt** and **client.crt**:

```
keytool -export -alias serverkey -keystore server.keystore -rfc -file server.crt -keypass
mypassword -storepass mypassword
```

```
keytool -export -alias clientkey -keystore client.keystore -rfc -file client.crt -keypass
mypassword -storepass mypassword
```

Now in order to complete successfully the SSL handshake, we need at first to import the client's public key into server's truststore:

```
keytool -import -file server.crt -keystore client.truststore -keypass mypassword -
storepass mypassword
```

The keytool will dump the certificate on your terminal and ask if it is has to be considered trustworthy.

```
Trust this certificate? [no]:  y
```

Answer yes and move on. As final step, also the server certificate needs to be trusted by the client. Therefore, we will import it into the client truststore:

```
keytool -import -file client.crt -keystore server.truststore -keypass mypassword -
storepass mypassword
```

Again, state that you are going to trust the certificate. Well done, you have completed the certificate installation. Now copy the server keystore and truststore files into a folder reachable by the application server. For example its configuration folder:

```
C:\tmp>copy server.keystore C:\wildfly-8.2.0.Final\standalone\configuration
C:\tmp>copy server.truststore C:\wildfly-8.2.0.Final\standalone\configuration
```

Configuring an SSL Realm

Once that you have generated the required certificates, you need to install them on WildFly. This can be done by adding a new **Security Realm**, which contains an identity bound to an SSL key. If you are going to implement a mutual SSL authentication, you will need also to include the truststore information, which is required by the server to authenticate the client.

Based on the keys that we have formerly generated, add this section to your Security Realms:

```xml
<management>
        <security-realms>
            <security-realm name="SSLRealm">
                <server-identities>
                    <ssl>
                        <keystore path="server.keystore"
                                relative-to="jboss.server.config.dir"
                                keystore-password="mypassword" alias="serverkey"/>
                    </ssl>
                </server-identities>
                <authentication>
                    <truststore path="server.truststore"
                                relative-to="jboss.server.config.dir"
                                keystore-password="mypassword"/>
                </authentication>
                . . . . . .
            </security-realm>
            . . . .
</management>
```

In the above server configuration fragment, the first highlighted block deals with keystore configuration for server authentication, while the truststore section needs to be included for mutual SSL authentication.

Having completed the certificates installation, we will see how to use it for securing the two basic application types, that is Web applications and EJB applications.

Securing Web applications

As you might guess, if we are going to tweak the Web server configuration we will need operating on the **Undertow** subsystem. Having our **SSLRealm** already configured, we need just one step to enable secure communication on WildFly, which is adding a new **https-listener** in the undertow subsystem as shown below:

```
<subsystem xmlns="urn:jboss:domain:undertow:1.0">

   . . .

   <server name="default-server">
       <http-listener name="default" socket-binding="http" />
       <https-listener name="default-https" socket-binding="https"
                     security-realm="SSLRealm" />
       <host name="default-host" alias="localhost">
           <location name="/" handler="welcome-content" />
       </host>
   </server>

   . . .

</subsystem>
```

That's all. Start up the application server and verify that the HTTPs listener is started as depicted by the following screenshot:

```
C:\Windows\system32\cmd.exe                                          —  □  X

17:08:54,452 WARN  [org.jboss.metadata.parser.jbossweb.JBossWebMetaDataParser] (
MSC service thread 1-4) <passivation-config/> is no longer supported and will be
 ignored
17:08:54,902 INFO  [org.jboss.as.remoting] (MSC service thread 1-8) JBAS017100:
Listening on 127.0.0.1:9999
17:08:54,925 INFO  [org.wildfly.extension.undertow] (MSC service thread 1-5) JBA
S017519: Undertow HTTP listener default listening on /127.0.0.1:8080
17:08:54,936 INFO  [org.wildfly.extension.undertow] (MSC service thread 1-3) JBA
S017519: Undertow HTTPS listener https listening on /127.0.0.1:8443
17:08:55,277 INFO  [org.jboss.ws.common.management] (MSC service thread 1-4) JBW
S022052: Starting JBoss Web Services - Stack CXF Server 4.2.3.Final
17:08:55,606 INFO  [org.jboss.as.connector.subsystems.datasources] (MSC service
thread 1-1) JBAS010400: Bound data source [java:jboss/datasources/ExampleDS]
17:08:56,264 INFO  [org.infinispan.configuration.cache.EvictionConfigurationBuil
der] (ServerService Thread Pool -- 52) ISPN000152: Passivation configured withou
t an eviction policy being selected. Only manually evicted entities will be pass
ivated.
17:08:56,295 INFO  [org.infinispan.configuration.cache.EvictionConfigurationBuil
der] (ServerService Thread Pool -- 52) ISPN000152: Passivation configured withou
t an eviction policy being selected. Only manually evicted entities will be pass
```

You can verify that your server is running on a secure socket layer by requesting your applications
through the https protocol and using the default port (8443). For example, if you were to deploy
your application named *secure.war*, then in order to access the welcome page of your application
you would issue: https://localhost:8443/secure

Having a quick look with WireShark network tool (http://www.wireshark.org/) reveals that the
data being returned by the server is now encrypted:

Destination	Protocol	Length	Info
127.0.0.1	TCP	348	pcsync-https > 58843 [PSH, ACK] Seq=3433 Ack=1917
127.0.0.1	TCP	66	58843 > pcsync-https [ACK] Seq=1917 Ack=3715 Win=4
127.0.0.1	TCP	428	pcsync-https > 58843 [PSH, ACK] Seq=3715 Ack=1917
127.0.0.1	TCP	66	58843 > pcsync-https [ACK] Seq=1917 Ack=4077 Win=4
127.0.0.1	TCP	140	pcsync-https > 58843 [PSH, ACK] Seq=4077 Ack=1917
127.0.0.1	TCP	66	58843 > pcsync-https [ACK] Seq=1917 Ack=4151 Win=4
127.0.0.1	UDP	74	Source port: 33519 Destination port: 33519

▷ Frame 113: 140 bytes on wire (1120 bits), 140 bytes captured (1120 bits) on interface 0
▷ Ethernet II, Src: 00:00:00_00:00:00 (00:00:00:00:00:00), Dst: 00:00:00_00:00:00 (00:00:00
▷ Internet Protocol Version 4, Src: 127.0.0.1 (127.0.0.1), Dst: 127.0.0.1 (127.0.0.1)
▷ Transmission Control Protocol, Src Port: pcsync-https (8443), Dst Port: 58843 (58843), Se
▽ Data (74 bytes)
     Data: 17030100203bb11eae1fca593ae7a7cf56da92bf3ed5ac92...
     [Length: 74]

How to secure the application server with a CA signed certificate

If you try to connect via https to your site using a self-signed certificate, the browser security sandbox will warn the user about the potential security threat. That's correct as the certificate has not been signed by any recognized CA.

Having your certificate signed requires issuing a **Certificate Signing Request (CSR)** to a CA that will return a signed certificate to be installed on your server. This implies a cost for your organization, which depends on how many certificates you are requesting, the encryption strength and other factors. We will document here all the steps that need to be performed:

1. At, first generate a **Certificate Signing Request (CSR)** using the keystore. This step has been already shown in the earlier section "Creating Server and client certificates":

```
keytool -export -alias serverkey -keystore server.keystore -rfc -file server.crt -keypass
mypassword -storepass mypassword
```

This will create a new certificate request named **server.crt**, bearing the format:

```
-----BEGIN NEW CERTIFICATE REQUEST-----
. . . . . .
-----END NEW CERTIFICATE REQUEST-----
```

2. Now you need to **transmit this certificate to a CA**; request for a trial certificate at Verisign, for example. (http://www.verisign.com)
3. At the end of the enrollment phase, the CA will return a signed certificate that needs to be **imported into your keychain**. Supposing that you have saved your CA certificate in a file named *root.ca*:

```
keytool -import -keystore server.jks -alias testkey1 -storepass mypassword -keypass
mypassword -file root.ca
```

Now your web browser will recognize your new certificate as being signed by a CA, so it won't complain that it cannot validate the certificate.

Encrypting the Management Interfaces channel

The certificates that we have created so far can be used as well for encrypting the communication of management interfaces.

In order to do that, you need to apply an **ssl** element to the Security Realm used by the management interface. The ssl element will contain a reference to the keystore created by the keytool utility. Let's see, how to encrypt the communication channel of the **LdapRealm** described in the "*Securing the Management Interfaces with LDAP*" section:

```
<security-realm name="LdapRealm">
  <server-identities>
    <ssl>
      <keystore path="server.keystore" relative-to="jboss.server.config.dir" keystore-
password="mypassword" alias="serverkey" />
    </ssl>
  </server-identities>
  <authentication>
    <ldap connection="ldap_connection" base-dn="ou=People,dc=jboss,dc=com">
      <username-filter attribute="uid" />
    </ldap>
  </authentication>
</security-realm>
```

We have highlighted the ssl section that has been added to the server-identities element. You need one more step, as the management interfaces need to be bound to the **management-https** socket binding (instead of the default management-http):

```
<management-interfaces>
        <http-interface security-realm="ManagementRealm" http-upgrade-enabled="true">
          <socket-binding http="management-https"/>
        </http-interface>
</management-interfaces>
```

Appendix

The appendix of this book contains some additional information about minor subsystems, which have fewer configuration options available, yet they could be interesting if you are going to work on a specific area of the application server. We will mention them here in the appendix as complimentary section:

The naming subsystem

The Java Naming and Directory Interface (JNDI) is a Java API for a directory service that allows Java software clients to discover and look up data and objects via a name. Like all other Java APIs also, JNDI is independent of the underlying implementation, however it specifies a service provider interface (SPI) that allows directory service implementations to be plugged into the framework. The Enterprise resources (such as datasources and JMS destinations) are stored in the JNDI tree so that they can be consumed by applications that are deployed on the application server. Nevertheless, you can use JNDI to store attributes which will be used by the server/severs a bit like application properties. In this case the advantage of using JNDI instead of basic Properties is that JNDI provides a tree structure for bindings which you don't have in a simple Property file. WildFly ships with a **naming** subsystem that contains the **bindings** element. In order to add some JNDI bindings to the application server just add some name/value attributes in it:

```
<subsystem xmlns="urn:jboss:domain:naming:2.0">
    <bindings>
<simple name="java:/jndi/mykey" value="MyValue"/>
    </bindings>
    <remote-naming/>
</subsystem>
```

284

Please note that JNDI entries need to be bound in a namespace starting with one of [java:global, java:jboss, java:/]"

You can achieve the same goal by using the CLI as follows:

```
/subsystem=naming/binding=java\:\/jndi\/mykey/:add(binding-type=simple,value=MyValue)
```

Naming Alias

Naming alias has been introduced to create a link from a JNDI binding to another. You can think about it as a symbolic link in Unix Systems. This can be useful for example if you are migrating from one application server JNDI binding structure to another and the JNDI bindings are stored in your application code.

In order to achieve naming aliases you can use the name and lookup attribute of the lookup element:

```
<subsystem xmlns="urn:jboss:domain:naming:2.0">
    <bindings>
        <lookup name="java:global/MyOldEJB"
                lookup="java:global/my-ear/my-ejb-module/ExampleEJB"/>
    </bindings>
    <remote-naming/>
</subsystem>
```

Again, you can achieve the same goal using the CLI as follows:

```
/subsystem=naming/binding=java\:global\/MyOldEJB/:add(binding-
type=lookup,lookup=java:global/my-ear/my-ejb-module/ExampleEJB)
```

The batch subsystem

WildFly ships with a subsystem named batch, which is the administration side of **JSR 352**, also known as **Batch API for Java applications**. This JSR specifies a programming model for batch applications and a runtime for scheduling and executing jobs.

Out of the box, the following configuration is included:

```
<subsystem xmlns="urn:jboss:domain:batch:1.0">
    <job-repository>
        <in-memory/>
    </job-repository>
    <thread-pool>
        <max-threads count="10"/>
        <keepalive-time time="30" unit="seconds"/>
    </thread-pool>
</subsystem>
```

In terms of configuration, what is worth to know is that Job executions are stored in a **repository**, which enables querying of current and historical job status. The default location of the job repository is **in-memory**, which means that you can query the repository programmatically using the **Batch API.** On the other hand, if you want to inspect the Job Repository using typical administration tools, then you can opt for using a **JDBC Repository**, which can then be queried using standard SQL commands.

Setting the job repository to use JDBC is just a matter of executing a couple of CLI commands:

```
/subsystem=batch/:write-attribute(name=job-repository-type,value=jdbc)
/subsystem=batch/job-repository=jdbc/:write-attribute(name=jndi-name,value=java:
/MySQLDS)
```

In this example, we are setting the job repository to use the datasource, which is bound to the **java:/MySQLDS** namespace.

Once that you have a JDBC repository, the tables will be automatically created for you once that you start running jobs on the application server. Here is the list of tables created:

```
mysql> show tables;
+---------------------------+
| Tables_in_as7development  |
+---------------------------+
| JOB_EXECUTION             |
| JOB_INSTANCE              |
| PARTITION_EXECUTION       |
| STEP_EXECUTION            |
+---------------------------+
4 rows in set (0.00 sec)
```

You can query for the Jobs, which have been executed by a particular application through the **JOB_INSTANCE** table:

```
mysql> select * from JOB_INSTANCE ;
+---------------+---------+-----------+----------------------+
| JOBINSTANCEID | VERSION | JOBNAME   | APPLICATIONNAME      |
+---------------+---------+-----------+----------------------+
|             1 |    NULL | simpleJob | javaee7-batch-chunk  |
|             2 |    NULL | simpleJob | javaee7-batch-chunk  |
|             3 |    NULL | simpleJob | javaee7-batch-chunk  |
+---------------+---------+-----------+----------------------+
```

On the other hand, if you want some execution details about jobs, then you can query the JOB_EXECUTION table:

```
mysql> select JOBEXECUTIONID, ENDTIME, BATCHSTATUS, EXITSTATUS from JOB_EXECUTION;
+----------------+---------------------+-------------+------------+
| JOBEXECUTIONID | ENDTIME             | BATCHSTATUS | EXITSTATUS |
+----------------+---------------------+-------------+------------+
|              1 | 2014-06-17 15:48:35 | FAILED      | FAILED     |
|              2 | 2014-06-17 15:52:40 | COMPLETED   | COMPLETED  |
|              3 | 2014-06-17 15:58:28 | COMPLETED   | COMPLETED  |
+----------------+---------------------+-------------+------------+
```

The mail subsystem

WildFly mail subsystem is contained in all server configurations and exposes a Mail service bound at the JNDI name "**java:jboss/mail/Default**":

```
<subsystem xmlns="urn:jboss:domain:mail:2.0">
    <mail-session name="default" jndi-name="java:jboss/mail/Default">
        <smtp-server outbound-socket-binding-ref="mail-smtp" />
    </mail-session>
</subsystem>
```

The Mail Session in turn references an smtp host bound at localhost at port 25:

```
<outbound-socket-binding name="mail-smtp">
    <remote-destination host="localhost" port="25"/>
</outbound-socket-binding>
```

In order to configure the connection towards a pop/smtp server we need to set up username and password in the **mail-session** element and, if necessary, enable ssl. The following CLI scripts can be used to connect to **GMail** SMTP server using an example account (adjust user and password accordingly):

```
/subsystem=mail/mail-session=default/server=smtp/:write-attribute(name=username,value=
myuser@gmail.com)

/subsystem=mail/mail-session=default/server=smtp/:write-
attribute(name=password,value=mypassword)

/subsystem=mail/mail-session=default/server=smtp/:write-attribute(name=ssl,value=true)

/subsystem=mail/mail-session=default/:write-attribute(name=from,value=
admin@mydomain.com)
```

Now reload your server configuration; your mail subsystem should look like this:

```
<subsystem xmlns="urn:jboss:domain:mail:2.0">
    <mail-session name="default" jndi-name="java:jboss/mail/Default"
                  from="admin@mydomain.com">
        <smtp-server outbound-socket-binding-ref="mail-smtp" ssl="true"
                     username="myuser@gmail.com" password="mypassword"/>
    </mail-session>
</subsystem>
```

Done with the mail session configuration, we will now set the outbound sockets for your outgoing messages. This translates in setting host and port to GMail's (or your mail provider) defaults:

```
/socket-binding-group=standard-sockets/remote-destination-outbound-socket-binding=mail-
smtp/:write-attribute(name=host,value=smtp.gmail.com)
```

```
/socket-binding-group=standard-sockets/remote-destination-outbound-socket-binding=mail-
smtp/:write-attribute(name=port,value=465)
```

The expected outcome of this action on your configuration will be:

```
<outbound-socket-binding name="mail-smtp">
  <remote-destination host="smtp.gmail.com" port="465"/>
</outbound-socket-binding>
```

> Important notice for Google users: If you see the following error
>
> **javax.mail.AuthenticationFailedException: 535-5.7.1 Username and Password not accepted.**
>
> It means that you need to generate an application specific password instead of your original password. You can generate one at the link "https://accounts.google.com/IssuedAuthSubTokens" and use the generated application specific password in place your original password.

The threads subsystem

The threads subsystem is not included anymore in the default configuration of the application server. The reason for this decision is that an uncontrolled use of general-purpose thread pools (in particular of unbounded thread pools) across various subsystems could lead to an unstable application server state.

At the time of writing, some subsystems (notably the Infinispan and JGroups) still rely upon the threads subsystem, as evident from the following picture:

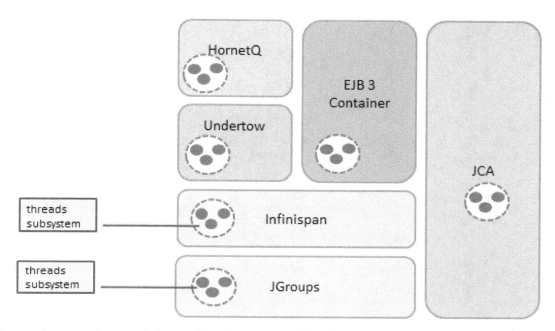

WildFly Thread Pools

In the future releases of the application server, all subsystem will have a specific thread pool configuration; therefore, you are encouraged not to rely on the **org.jboss.as.threads** subsystem at least for new installations. (Otherwise, a migration will be necessary for your configuration). On the other hand, if you are upgrading from an existing JBoss AS 7 configuration, which uses the threads from **org.jboss.as.threads**, you can still enable this subsystem with few simple steps: At first, include the subsystem at the top of your configuration:

```
<extensions>

    . . . .

        <extension module="org.jboss.as.threads"/>
</extensions>
```

Then, include as well the threads subsystem itself (the simple snippet that follows will suffice):

```
<subsystem xmlns="urn:jboss:domain:threads:1.1">
</subsystem>
```

Once included, reload/restart your server and you will notice that the **threads** option will resurrect in the management instruments, as shown by the following picture:

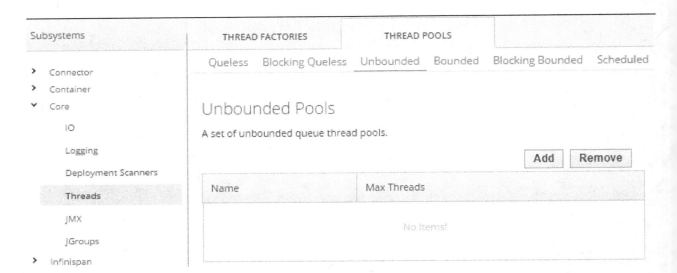

www.ingramcontent.com/pod-product-compliance
Lightning Source LLC
LaVergne TN
LVHW082347060326
832902LV00016B/2699